Financial
Freedom

Financial Freedom

A Positive Strategy for Putting Your Money to Work

James A. Barry, Jr., CFP

Admitted to the Registry of
Financial Planning Practitioners

McGraw-Hill, Inc.

New York St. Louis San Francisco Auckland Bogotá
Caracas Lisbon London Madrid Mexico Milan
Montreal New Delhi Paris San Juan São Paulo
Singapore Sydney Tokyo Toronto

Library of Congress Cataloging-in-Publication Data

Barry, James A., date.
   Financial freedom : a positive strategy for putting your money to
work / James A. Barry, Jr.
      p.   cm.
   "Based on a work with the same title previously published by
Reston/Prentice-Hall in 1982"—T.p. verso.
   Includes index.
   ISBN 0-07-003983-6   —ISBN 0-07-003982-8 (pbk.)
   1. Finance, Personal. 2. Investments. I. Title.
HG179.B337 1993
332.024—dc20   92-28259
                                                            CIP

This book is printed on recycled, acid-free paper containing a minimum of 50% recycled de-inked fiber.

Based on a work with the same title previously published by Reston/
Prentice-Hall in 1982.

1 2 3 4 5 6 7 8 9 0 DOC/DOC 9 8 7 6 5 4 3 2

ISBN 0-07-003983-6 {HC}
ISBN 0-07-003982-8 {PBK}

*The sponsoring editor for this book was Betsy Brown, the developmental editor
and editing supervisor was Barbara B. Toniolo, and the production supervisor
was Donald M. Schmidt. It was set in Baskerville by Carol Woolverton,
Lexington, Mass., in cooperation with Warren Publishing Services.*

Printed and bound by R. R. Donnelley & Sons Company.

Disclaimer

This book contains the author's opinion on the subject. Neither the author nor the publisher is engaged in offering legal,
tax, accounting, investment, or similar professional services.
Some material may be affected by changes in the law or in the
interpretation of laws since the book was written. Laws also
vary from state to state. Therefore, no guarantee can be given
as to the accuracy and completeness of information. In addition, recommendations made by the author as well as strategies outlined in the text may not necessarily be suitable
depending on changes or new interpretations of the law or
depending upon a reader's personal financial situation. For
legal, tax, accounting, investment, or other professional advice, it is suggested that the reader consult a competent practitioner. The author hereby specifically disclaims any liability for
loss incurred as a consequence of any material presented in
this book.

Dedicated to my loving wife and partner,
Rosemarie Barry,
without whom this book
could not have become a reality

Contents

Part 3. Action . . .

Preface

The phrase *financial freedom* must be considered very subjectively. Each of us defines the phrase according to how it applies, individually, to our personal situations. To one person it might mean living comfortably, an annual vacation, and sending the children to college. To someone else it might mean the financial freedom to retire at 40 and travel continuously. To yet another person it may mean luxury cars, charitable giving, and trust funds for the family. This book will, I hope, provide the impetus for you to launch a personal plan to develop your money power.

If your definition of financial freedom includes making your money work for you to achieve short- and long-term goals, then you will find valuable tools within the covers of this book. During the course of this book we'll explore together the methods of putting your money to work for you in order to achieve your goals. We'll start with defining your goals, then we'll explore some of the potential pitfalls, and, finally, we'll look at the various vehicles that will take us down the road to your financial freedom.

I have always believed that when it comes to money matters, there are three kinds of people in this world: *those who make things happen, those who watch things happen, and those who scratch their heads and wonder what the heck happened.* I have little time for the watchers and head scratchers—the opportunities they let pass are the opportunities that you and I can seize and take advantage of. The fact that you are reading this book indicates that you are probably the first type of person—you want to make things happen for yourself and your family. You have realized that most of us can take control of our financial lives.

To help you learn how to gain that control, this book provides a short, introductory course in financial planning—how to put some punch into your money power. This is only the start—the launching pad to your financial freedom. Financial planning aims at control of your income and puts you in charge of your money's growth. I have no magic formula for you to follow since people differ in their approaches to handling money. We each have different emotional compositions. Only you can determine your personal risk/reward profile, or "comfort zone." Some people find high-risk, high-reward investments exhilarating. Others can tolerate only moderate risk if they are to avoid losing sleep at night. Still others believe in prudence and the elimination of as much risk as possible. Remember, you cannot eliminate risk entirely; there is no such thing as a riskless investment. Risk is a part of life, whether you are at home, at work, in your car, or in an airplane.

In this book I point out from time to time what I believe to be the power of positive thinking. It's as simple as looking at a glass partially filled with water and deciding if it is half-empty or half-full. If you see the glass as half-full, I believe that you are a step ahead of the game. There are many instances, documented by physicians and other professionals, of profound healings or improvements in conditions of people terminally or catastrophically ill. One well-known physician whose specialty is cancer has written a book detailing the importance of the power of the mind and a positive attitude in the healing process.

This book is not the ultimate encyclopedia of investments. Again, it is a starting point. It does not try to be all things to all people, nor does it treat all investments as equal, which they clearly are not. Instead, this book contains a sampler of various investments that will allow us to explore how each one and its risk/reward potential might fit into your financial plan. Notice that word *us.* You must enter into a dialogue with me, for it will be up to you to use the information presented here, or at least to consider it and file it away for future reference. Understand too that the information in this book is designed to add to your financial education not to sell you on any particular product. Nothing that you read here should be construed as a recommendation that you, personally, buy a product. That decision must be made in light of your personal circumstances.

Some of the new areas we are taking a look at in this book are portfolio optimization and asset allocation, global investing, living trusts, single premium variable life, single premium whole life, and single premium annuities, both fixed and variable.

You will find a chapter devoted to professionals in the financial field and there will be times when I suggest you seek expert help. You must realize that this is merely a way of pointing out where you can or should use OPB—other people's brains—to help you make money and avoid costly mistakes. There are times when surrounding yourself with professionals might be the least costly alternative for you. But if you want to be your own quarterback, and feel you have the energy, time, and resources (and education) to do so, be my guest. You certainly ought to be able to make some intelligent decisions after reading this book. OPB isn't a new concept, you use it every day of your life. For instance, if you have a root canal you rely upon a professional; if you drive an automobile, someone else built it; if you buy a house, most likely it was built by an architect and a contractor—the list is endless. If you decide you want to be your own planner, fine, but you must be serious about it.

Think of this book as OPB and find in it what is useful to you. By the time you have finished reading it, I hope you will have a clear picture of your current assets, both in terms of dollars and in terms of your knowledge. Understanding those assets will help you to recognize your weaknesses as well as your strengths and how to utilize them properly.

Where do the opportunities lie at this point in history? To gain insight into this question, we need to look at the national economic picture that has taken shape in the past decade. I like to point out that when you are driving an automobile you can't steer by looking in the rear-view mirror. You must pay attention to it, but you must look forward and to your left and right. The same is true with investments—you can't rely solely on the historic figures. The world has changed and you must consider these changes.

Today we live in a world of instant communication—we can communicate from our cars to our homes, to our businesses. You can receive a fax while you are driving down the freeway! But this communication revolution has bombarded us with such a mass of information that it is almost paralyzing. The down side is that it's too much information at one time because most of us have a hard time separating the useful information from the useless information as it pertains to us. The tendency is to do nothing because the average person doesn't like to make changes. Through the information contained here, you can learn how to change things in your life to reach your ultimate goal, financial freedom.

This book provides the information you need to set your goals and develop your own personal strategy—your personal plan of putting your money to work—to gain your financial freedom. You have one of the most important creations, physical or spiritual, that exists—the brain. It is the ultimate computer. I suggest to you that the most powerful hardware you possess is the three and one-half pound brain in your head and that the software you have to operate it is all of your experiences—past, present, future, both good and bad. Keep in mind, though, that the average person only uses *10 percent* of his or her brain! If you can elevate that even another 3 percent, think what you could accomplish! So the first thing you need to work on is change, and you have the power of your brain to work with.

If you do not take charge of your financial life, others will do it for you and not necessarily for your benefit. There are two kinds of income-producing activities: people at work and money at work. Use this book to learn how to make both a part of your game plan.

Acknowledgments

I would like to express my sincerest gratitude to the many individuals with whom I've worked to present the ideas and information contained in this book. I am especially appreciative of:

The professionals at McGraw-Hill who provided editorial assistance, guidance, and direction at every step of the process, particularly Betsy N. Brown, senior business editor, and Barbara B. Toniolo, developmental editor.

Aronda R. Davidson, project coordinator, whose skill and perseverance contributed significantly to the completion of this book in every way.

James M. Barry, CFP, my son and associate, whose heart and wisdom, both in business and out, contributed to the research, direction, and completion of this book.

Sir John Templeton, the *Dean of Global Investing,* and Frank Helsom, CFA, CIC, Vice Chairman of Templeton Investment Counsel, Inc., and their staff, who contributed valuable information and research materials.

Board Certified Tax Lawyer and Certified Public Accountant Robert M. Arlen and Certified Public Accountant Robert Liszewski, who reviewed text and provided informational materials.

Attorney Robert A. Huth, Jr., P.A., Partner and Shareholder of English, McCaughan & O'Bryan, who reviewed text and contributed pertinent information.

William McAree, CLU, President, The McAree Agency, and his daughter, Lisa McAree, CLU and Vice President of The McAree Agency, for their assistance, overview, and specific research information.

Mark A. Stock, CLU, ChFC, and Senior Regional Marketing Director of Nationwide Insurance Company.

Many thanks also to the following folks for their assistance and resource materials, which contributed greatly to the completion of this book:

Thomas Luka, CLU, ChFC, Senior Vice President of Insurance Products and William W. Scott, Jr., President, Massachusetts Financial Services.

Ed Antoian, Senior Portfolio Manager, The Delaware Group.

William Kimbrough, Vice President of Delaware Distributors Inc., and to The Delaware Group.

Philip Edelstein, Regional Vice President of GT Global Financial Services, and to G.T. Global Financial Services.

John Filoon, Senior Vice President of Phoenix Equity Planning Corporation and to The Phoenix Group.

Michael Cemo, President of AIM Distributors, Inc., and to AIM Group of Mutual Funds.

Don Philips and Morningstar, Inc.

Thanks to the following businesses and institutions for their information and cooperation:

College for Financial Planning; the International Association of Financial Planning; American College; Ibbotson and Associates; and the Investment Company Institute.

My associates at The Barry Financial Group who provided review and research information: Joe L. Fernandez, Jr., CLU, Eric Smith, John Loftis, Michele (Midge) Novoth, Roy Cook, Thom Cassidy, CPA, Donald Warren, Attorney, Gerard Olsen.

Thanks to those individuals who provided valuable support services: Betty Radford, Vanessa Inhofer, Camille Romano, Della Ragusa and Ramona Register-Gentry.

Finally, I am very grateful to my clients and friends, who encouraged me once again to address the topic of *financial freedom.* I also want to express my appreciation to my daughters, Irene Barry Leicht and Rosemarie Barry Wood, for their support and encouragement throughout this project.

I am sure that some names have been omitted in error. From those of you whose names I failed to list, I ask forgiveness.

Financial
Freedom

PART 1
Understanding...

1
You and
Your Money

There are three kinds of people . . .
which one are you?

FREEDOM FOCUS

- *Do you understand the money machine?*
- *Why is retirement planning a necessity?*
- *What is the Rule of 72?*
- *How does inflation affect you?*
- *Is your biggest enemy procrastination?*

There are three kinds of people in this world when it comes to handling their money:

1. The first kind *makes* things happen.
2. The second kind *watches* things happen.
3. The third kind scratches their heads and *asks* what happened.

You are probably reading this book because you intend to be the first kind of person and make things happen in your quest for financial freedom. Although you may not say, "I'm going to be a watcher in life," you will make that decision by default if you continue to procrastinate and let the opportunities pass you by. The third kind of person is simply too confused about what's going on to make an attempt to learn about the opportunities and methods available. Decide right now that you are not going to be content to watch others take charge of their lives while you sit on the sidelines. In this book, you'll be guided through the steps necessary for putting your personal plan together and be introduced to the opportunities for fulfilling your quest for *financial freedom.*

Have you ever thought about owning a money machine? Perhaps you've dreamed of winning a lottery and suddenly possessing hundreds, thousands, or even millions of dollars. Would you tell everyone immediately of your good fortune and set up a "wish-list" hotline? Perhaps you've even considered the possibility on paper, writing out exactly what you would do first—disconnect the phone; buy a new house, cars, jewelry; or party for a few days with a group of friends. Maybe you've considered charitable giving or educational and scholarship trust funds for your children, grandchildren, or children of friends. If you are like most people, fighting a losing battle against inflation and taxation, with bills mounting, you would be tempted to take the money and run! A lottery is certainly one example of a money machine—with very limited recipients.

This book is about a money machine that you have personal access to. A money machine you can and should exploit to the fullest, with no fear of reprisals. That money machine is you! Yes, you, yourself—whether you are a man or a woman, whether you are well along in your career or just starting out, whether you are old or young or somewhere in between, whether you are the head of a major company or a worker on an assembly line. This is one of the most important facts you will ever learn about yourself: *You are a money machine!*

You have probably never thought of yourself in quite this way before. But it's true: You are a money machine, regardless of your age or financial situation at this moment. Whether you are a student with your first job, an experienced professional approaching retirement, or someone holding down two jobs to make ends meet, you should recognize that one of your key functions in life is the steady, reliable production of an income.

Consider for a moment how much your money machine has produced as of now and how much of that total you have been able to save or increase through profitable investments. Figure 1-1 shows how much a conservatively paid individual might make over the course of a 36-year

Figure 1-1. The money machine at work. An employee began working at age 24 at an annual salary of $25,000, with a 2 percent yearly increase. Line A reflects annual compensation and Line B reflects cumulative compensation at the ages indicated. The figures are rounded off.

career. The figures assume that this person begins work at age 24, after college graduation, with a starting salary of $25,000 per year. If that individual receives an average salary increase of 2 percent per year, after 36 years his or her total annual compensation would be approximately $51,000. Hold on—total accumulated earnings over the entire 36-year period would be approximately $1,350,851! When you look at it from this point of view, your money machine becomes much more meaningful. But remember, that money machine wears out—we do not live forever; we age, we die, and we can become disabled. Every one of us has something in common as far as the money machine is concerned: Somewhere in the future each of us will cease to produce money.

At this point in your life, you may have established a higher level of earnings for yourself, so your total lifetime income could very well top a million dollars. Think of it! Where is all that money going? Is it slipping through your fingers or sinking into a dark hole labeled "expenses"?

Statistics tell a frightening and sad story about the financial situation of many older Americans. According to one source, a large majority of us rely on social security benefits as our main source of economic survival once we reach age 65—this despite the abundance of retirement plans and investment programs available to us. At the root of this problem is *procrastination,* which few of us manage to overcome. We all want to be financially secure in our senior years; we plan to establish a sound investment program. None of us plans to end up destitute or on the welfare rolls. But how many of you, even at the modest age of 42, have yet to initiate an IRA account? The gap that spans intention and action is often as wide as the Grand Canyon. *Many of us simply do not initiate constructive action soon enough to save ourselves and our families from financial disaster.* The good news is that it doesn't have to be that way.

It can't be said too many times: It's not *what* you make, it's *what you do with the dollars that you make* that counts. If you have time and discipline on your side, and you eliminate the word *procrastination,* you can become wealthy in America.

Financial Planning for Retirement

The need to plan wisely and well for retirement has never been greater than it is today. Take a look at what is happening to you, personally:

- Inflation is taking its bite out of the purchasing power of your dollar.
- Taxes continue to increase at the local, state, and federal levels.
- The social security system is inadequate to meet the needs of an aging nation.
- Problems within our nation's health programs are mounting.

Although this section presents some distressing statistics, please don't become despondent because that merely becomes another form of procrastination. But do let these figures instill in you the determination to *do something* about your financial future. It is never too late to take action. I constantly hear, "I'm too young Jim, I'm only 40 years old and I can't touch that money I put into an IRA program until I'm 59½ years old. Right now I need to buy my teenager a car and we need a new entertainment system at home." On the other hand, a 75-year-old may say, "Long-term? I don't even buy green bananas because they might not ripen by morning!" So each one of us has excuses for doing nothing. There are steps you can take with the help of a competent adviser to separate yourself from the great number of people who, because of fear, ignorance, or other factors, fail to plan for the future. There are more investment opportunities available today than at any other time in your life, your father's life, or your grandfather's life. There is more disposable income available to you, provided you know where it is going.

The great majority of people are followers—they do not like to stand out from the crowd. If a male student attending Berkeley during the 1960s had a crew cut, he was an oddball. But if a male student attended the state university in the 1950s and had shoulder length hair, *he* was an oddball. These people were separate from the crowd. And I suggest to you that a majority of the people who are successful with money march to a different drummer. They are not the followers of the world; they are the doers.

It's not too difficult to be financially successful in life. The difficulty is putting procrastination behind you and taking charge of your financial life. Historically, there have been reasons to procrastinate, to put off your journey to financial freedom. Almost every year since I was born there have been reasons not to get up in the morning! Consider the following, which represent just a few of those reasons:

1934	The Depression
1935	The Civil War in Spain
1937	Recession
1939	War in Europe
1940	France falls
1941	Pearl Harbor
1944	Consumer goods shortage
1946	Dow Jones average tops 200—market "too high"
1948	Berlin blockade
1949	Russia explodes A-bomb
1950	Korean War
1953	Russia explodes H-bomb
1955	Eisenhower illness
1956	Suez crisis
1959	Castro seizes power in Cuba
1961	Berlin Wall erected
1962	Cuban missile crisis
1963	Kennedy assassinated
1966	Vietnam war escalates
1968	USS Pueblo seized
1971	Wage–price freeze
1972	Largest trade deficit in history

1973   Energy crisis

1974   Steepest market drop in four decades

1978   Interest rates rise

1979   Oil prices skyrocket

1982   Worst recession in 40 years

1984   Record federal deficits

1987   Record-setting market decline

1989   Junk bonds debacle

1990   Middle East crisis

1991   Bank and savings and loans fiasco

But it is only when you can put procrastination behind you that you will be able to set goals and take the steps necessary to reach those goals. Many worthwhile investment vehicles and opportunities are discussed in the pages of this book. But first, let's consider the *bad* news. Since 1939 there have been only three years of a deflationary economy. Since 1954 there has never been a single year of deflation. For a year-by-year look at inflation since 1970, refer to Figure 1-2. As you can see, since

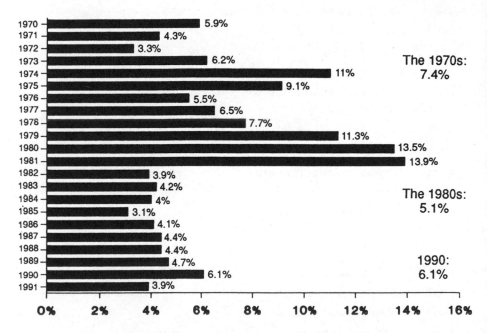

Figure 1-2. Inflation rates since 1970. The 20-year average is 6.42 percent. The 50-year average is 4.5 percent.

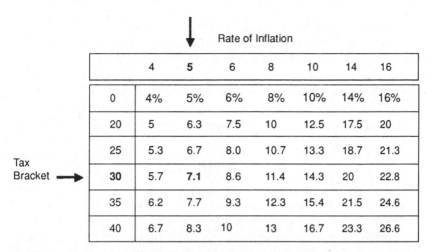

Rate of Inflation

	4	5	6	8	10	14	16
0	4%	5%	6%	8%	10%	14%	16%
20	5	6.3	7.5	10	12.5	17.5	20
25	5.3	6.7	8.0	10.7	13.3	18.7	21.3
30	5.7	7.1	8.6	11.4	14.3	20	22.8
35	6.2	7.7	9.3	12.3	15.4	21.5	24.6
40	6.7	8.3	10	13	16.7	23.3	26.6

Tax Bracket ➡

Figure 1-3. Double jeopardy: Taxes and inflation. Shown here are the investment returns required to maintain the purchasing power of investments under various inflation and tax rates. If your tax bracket is 30 percent and the projected rate of inflation is 5 percent, you will have to earn 7.1 percent on a taxable investment *just to break even.*

1970, we've had inflation rates run the gamut from 3.1 to 13.9 percent. The bottom line is that inflation is not going to go away; it will continue to eat away at the buying power of your dollars. Not only must you consider the problems of inflation, but taxation will also take a bite out of your dollars. Figure 1-3 illustrates just that. For instance, if inflation is at 5 percent and you are in the 30 percent tax bracket, you will need a return of at least 7.1 percent on your investments *just to maintain the purchasing power of your dollars.*

But what if you have needs in addition to maintaining your current standard of living? Then you not only have to worry about maintaining the purchasing power of your dollars, you also have to find a way to make your money grow enough to be able to meet special needs—college tuition, medical needs, retirement planning, long-term care, etc.

Money at Work

There is light at the end of the tunnel. The good news is that under the right working conditions, your money can be put to work with results that will allow you to face inflation, retirement, and special needs with ease. The key to your financial well-being lies in your ability to take advantage of your money and *tax-saving strategies.* You do not want your money to sit on the local beach getting a suntan while you are out working very hard to acquire it. You've got to learn to reverse the sequence of events. Money should constantly—24 hours a day, 7 days a week, fulltime—be working for you as long as the money machine lasts.

Even to long-time members of the financial industry the miracle of compound interest is still fascinating. Table 1-1 demonstrates how long it would take an investment to double at various rates of return compounded annually.

Known as "The Rule of 72," it is a simple formula that will enable you to calculate how long it will take a sum to double at any rate of return. Simply divide the expected rate of return into 72. A 12 percent return, for example, will double your investment in 6 years because 72 divided by 12 equals 6. Because *total return* is referred to throughout this book, it's important for you to understand how total return is defined: Total return always refers to capital gains plus income return after reinvestment of all income dividends and capital gain distributions. Figure 1-4 explains how this works. Keep in mind that any tax consequences are not taken into consideration in the Rule of 72. But under a qualified retirement program, such as an IRA program, we would not consider them because we are deferring those taxes to a later date.

If it is going through your mind right now that there are no investments available today that bring a total return of 12 percent or better,

Table 1-1 The Rule of 72

Total return	Years required to double investment*
1	70
4	18
5	14
6	12
8	9
10	7
12	6
14	5
16	4.6
18	4
20	3.8

*Years rounded off to next highest or lowest in most cases.

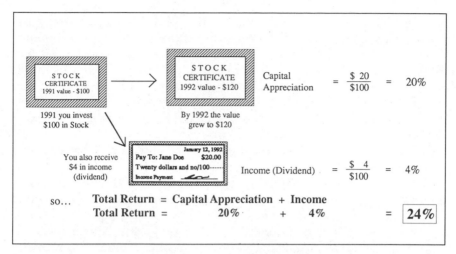

Figure 1-4. Do you understand the concept of total return? It's vital to be able to compute total return on investments if you want to compare the value of one investment versus another investment. (*Source: Ibbotson Associates.*)

you are *wrong.* Such opportunities do exist, and many of them are as accessible to the average investor as they are to very large investors. Some of them also include legal tax-saving strategies or deferral features. Those 12 percent opportunities can be found in some of the major money management companies such as Templeton, AIM Group, Putnam, MFS Group, GT Group, Phoenix Group, Delaware Management, Fidelity, Nationwide, and the list goes on. But remember, the key is that within any of these companies there is the selection process. Each group will offer you a menu of investment options. What you have to do is be informed enough to select the right investments.

It's Not Too Late to Start Planning

If you started to save just 10 percent of your annual earnings on your twenty-fifth birthday, by age 65 you would at the very least be comfortable and secure. And think of the even rosier financial future that would await you if you could multiply those savings through sound investments. Even if you passed your twenty-fifth birthday years ago, it's still not too late for you to realize great and lasting benefits from your money machine.

We all know that some machines perform better than others, of course. Some computers today are so efficient they can process in seconds complex mathematical problems that previously took days to compute. Other computers are merely sophisticated word processors, unable to function in any other manner. You, as a money machine, perform at a certain efficiency level, too. Your skills bring a price in the marketplace, based on supply and demand, that largely depends on how rare they are and how well you have developed them. The marketplace skills that you have to offer society are, in most cases, under your direct control. You can choose to upgrade those skills by taking refresher courses, applying yourself more diligently on the job, learning from more knowledgeable coworkers, and taking similar types of constructive action. But this function, the bringing in of dollars on a regular basis, is just one of the tasks that you must perform as a money machine.

The earning power of those dollars, once they are in your possession, is as much a consideration as the money machine. How do you make those dollars work for you? Do you know how to select investments that will perform specific jobs for you such as see you through your retirement, take care of your loved ones if you should die prematurely, or make a handsome short-term profit? Do you know how to assign tasks to your dollars and see to it that they carry out those tasks? Some portion of your income may have to perform an important job years from now, such as putting your children through college. Can you say with confidence at this point in your life that funds will be on hand to meet that or any other major future needs? It is wise to keep a watchful eye on the future, in order to make sure that the money under your care will be able to perform its assigned tasks whenever necessary.

How you manage your money is a measure of your efficiency as a money machine. In one sense, it is a more important measure than your earning capacity because you may retire at 52 or 60 or you may retire at 65 or 70, but your money will always have to keep working for you. It makes just as much sense to improve your ability to *manage* money as it does to upgrade professional or vocational skills that bring you your income. Yet it is common to see men and women with six-figure incomes selecting stocks, bonds, insurance programs, and other major purchases solely on the basis of advice from a friend or an article in the newspaper. On the other hand, we can also find people whose investment decisions have doubled and tripled their annual salaries. How have they worked such miracles? *They have consciously developed their money-management skills.* And that is what this book is all about. It is designed to give you a working knowledge of the major investment areas so that you can make intelligent, informed decisions on how, when, and where your investment dollar might best perform various types of jobs for you.

Consulting the Pros

Many of you will study this book and other sources and will be able to map out your own road to financial freedom. However, it would be foolish not to recognize that there are also many of you who have much more complex financial situations. For that group, I strongly recommend that you seek the guidance of a financial professional. The financial professional is like an engineer whose primary task is to keep money machines—that is, clients—operating at peak efficiency. You may well need the services of such a person, now or at some point in the future, and you can expect to be asked for certain information that will be used to improve the workings of your money machine. (Often this takes the form of a Data Questionnaire for you to complete, as illustrated in Chapter 3, The Financial Puzzle. There is a blank form included there for you to use.) This information will not only give your financial professional insight into where you are now and where you want to go, but it will also give you a comprehensive overview, for perhaps the first time in your life, of your personal situation. Many people emerge from this data-taking process with a new understanding of their money machine potential and a new resolve to make their money machines more productive. This is not just a gathering of statistics, rather it is also a soul-searching process where you try to get to the root of your investment philosophies and discover what your future needs really are.

It is my intention that by the time you finish this book you will be so knowledgeable in investment matters that you will be able to work closely with all of your advisers in plotting your course toward financial independence. But before you can make wise investment decisions, you must analyze your personal situation. Although each of us is in a unique position, there is an investment program for every individual—married or single, working or retired, young or old, abled or disabled, widow or widower. A portion of your income should be directed right now into an investment program tailored to your needs.

To meet these needs it is imperative that you possess certain knowledge: You must know what your investment options are and what each one is designed to do for you; you must know how to ask meaningful questions of the financial advisers and other professionals you work with—stock brokers, insurance underwriters, mutual fund representatives, trust officers, real estate experts, attorneys, CPAs, etc.; and you must have at least a basic working knowledge of the laws and regulations that affect investment earnings, particularly tax laws. This book explores each of these areas, always with the objective of helping you to achieve your full potential as a money machine. You will discover that a rich diversity of investment opportunities awaits you. Today's sophisticated marketplace has produced a veritable banquet for the man or woman who knows how to make wise investment decisions. And making such decisions is rarely a complicated, mysterious matter. Sir John Templeton put it best, "Common sense is not common today."

Like most other skills worth having, the ability to manage money well must be developed consciously and carefully. But it is an achievable goal, providing you eliminate one word from your vocabulary and your way of thinking right now. The word is *procrastination,* and it has done more to rob people of investment riches than all the marketplace reverses that have taken place in the history of the free enterprise system. You must push procrastination out of your life or you may as well stop reading this book right now, because it will do you no good at all, except perhaps to provide you with some interesting dinner party conversation.

Remember, the financial rewards in our society come to *those who act,* not to those who stand and wait.

2

What Color Is Your Money?

There are at least four distinct types of money that are either produced by your money machine or readily available from outside sources to be channeled through it.

FREEDOM FOCUS

- *Do you know what serious money is?*
- *What role does borrowed money play in your plan?*
- *What is leverage money?*
- *Do you know how to find your idle money?*
- *How do you determine the level of risk you can assume on your way to financial freedom?*

Most of us tend to think of our money in rather nondescript, perhaps abstract, terms. Money is our checking account balance, the total of our savings accounts, or maybe the figures we report on our tax returns. We seldom think of money as a real thing—a box full of bills, or a closet-ful—something we can utilize as a tangible entity.

But now it's time to turn this abstract idea into a concrete image of the money that is available for your use. The first step is to picture your money machine churning out four kinds of bills, printed in different colors. As you will soon discover, there are at least four distinct types of money that are either produced by your money machine or readily available from outside sources to be channeled through it.

Serious Money

The first type, printed in conservative beige, is your *serious money* that you intend to hang on to, come what may. This is your nest egg, your buffer against a rainy day. You are not about to risk losing these dollars, and you always seek safe places to put them. Many people believe that the best place to put their serious money is in a 5 percent savings ac-count. Such accounts, after all, are insured up to $100,000 by the fed-eral government, so there is little likelihood that the funds in them will ever be lost. It is true that they probably won't be lost in a disaster. But what about the disasters that we all have to live with called inflation and taxation? What happens to a sum of money that gains interest at 5 per-cent annually while inflation gallops along at 5, 7, or 9 percent?

Under these conditions, your money actually shrinks in purchasing power as time passes. Unfortunately, inflation doesn't sound any warn-ing bells as it advances on us. Instead, it quietly creeps up even on those of us who thought we were safe. What happens to "safe havens" such as fixed-interest savings accounts in times of inflation? Under present eco-nomic conditions, it is almost impossible to find a truly safe, risk-free place for your serious money. It makes good sense, nonetheless, to place a large portion or all of your serious money into low-risk investments. Later chapters describe some sound, low-risk investment opportunities in detail.

Borrowed Money

Another type of money available to you is *borrowed money*, printed in red to signify debt. Don't let the word *debt* frighten you. Many of us have been taught from childhood to avoid debt: "Neither a borrower nor a lender be." "Lend a dollar, lose a friend." Certainly, borrowing solely for the purpose of buying luxury items, gambling, or putting the borrowed funds to any other unwise use can lead to serious problems. But debt can have another, useful application: To the sensible person working with a well-thought-out financial plan, borrowed money is an extremely valuable investment tool. Judicious use of borrowed money makes sense in certain circumstances, and more than a few people have become very wealthy by this means.

Inflation actually becomes your ally when you borrow money. Suppose, for example, that inflation averages 5 percent a year. This means that if you borrow $100 and you agree to pay it back in a year, the $100 you give back will, in terms of purchasing power, be worth 5 percent less than the $100 you received. You will be paying back the debt with "smaller dollars."

By the same token, whatever you may contemplate purchasing today with borrowed money—a car, a home, or education for your children— is almost sure to increase in price by the time you manage to save up enough to avoid borrowing. The price of housing in this country makes it especially advisable for you to consider using what multimillionaire Bernard Baruch called *OPM*—Other People's Money—to move into a home of your own today.

Leverage Money

And this leads us to the next stream of money flowing through your money machine: your *leverage money*, printed in green to signify rapid growth. This is also borrowed money, but in this case it has a money-making purpose. Leverage money actually allows you to realize a profit *because* you have borrowed money. The purchase of the home we were just talking about is a prime example. Suppose that you buy an $80,000 home with a 20 percent down payment ($16,000). You produce $16,000 to incur a $64,000 debt—the mortgage on the home. As inflation works its inevitable magic on the price of the home (an increase of 5 percent a year would not be unusual), *you and you alone* benefit. The bank that holds your mortgage can never ask you for more than the $64,000 you borrowed, plus whatever interest you agreed to pay. Suppose that at a later date you sell this home at a price 10 percent higher—$88,000. After paying off the $64,000 mortgage, you will have $24,000 left. Deduct your original $16,000 investment from that and you will have $8000 left. This means that you will have realized a 50 percent return on your investment dollar! You may want to review those figures again.

Seem too good to be true? It isn't. Money managers using OPM realize profits like this every day, particularly in real estate transactions. But don't rush out with a down payment on a piece of investment property just yet. An upcoming chapter (Chapter 18) goes into more detail regarding various types of property purchases. In real estate as in all other investment areas, success is usually achieved through tried techniques that have been developed by professionals.

Idle Money

Now turn your attention to the last type of money in your money machine, the yellowing bills that are your *idle money*, money that really isn't doing any work for you at all. Even one dollar of this kind of money is too much to have, but if you're like most people, you have quite a bit of it. Some of your idle money is in the dollars that lie dormant month after month in low-interest-bearing checking accounts.

Another good example is the equity that you can build up through home ownership. The average value of a home in the United States today is over $80,000. If you have lived in your home for a number of years, say 10 or more, you have probably accumulated a substantial amount of equity. Whether you have a large mortgage on it or not, your house will appreciate or depreciate in value, depending upon fluctuations within the national economy, so why not consider increasing the size of your mortgage through refinancing or an equity loan? In some cases, this can be accomplished without raising your monthly payments. Certainly if you own your home outright you should give serious thought to putting a mortgage on it. Why? *So you can turn that intangible equity into hard cash and put it to work for you in some other investment area.* Another incentive for having a mortgage on your home is provided by the Internal Revenue Service, which will allow you to take the interest portion of your yearly mortgage expense as a tax deduction.

Risk Management

It has been said that the difference between rich people and poor people is that rich people know how to use the money they have to acquire more wealth, while poor people tend to cling tightly to the few modest possessions they manage to accumulate. Of course you should never speculate wildly with your assets, however great or small they might be, but you should consider taking *carefully selected, cautious risks* with the aid of an adviser you trust and whose judgment you respect. No fortune has ever been made in this country or any other by a person who followed a policy of total risk avoidance. Think of the great entrepreneurs of this century—Steven Jobs, Ted Turner, or Bill Gage. Some go even further back in history—John D. Rockefeller, Andrew Carnegie, and J. P. Morgan, to name a few. If you read their biographies (and, incidentally, reading the biographies of wealthy, self-made individuals is an excellent idea for those who aspire to financial success themselves), you will discover that they did not turn away from calculated risk. To the contrary, these people and others like them *sought* opportunities to take risks that would enable them to increase their holdings. They recognized that very little progress is made in life by the person who refuses to venture into the competitive arena.

There are two basic principles to follow in the search for financial security:

1. A dream stays a dream until you create a plan to make it come true; then it becomes a reachable goal.

So, how do you determine your goals? In the next chapter we discuss the financial puzzle. Part of that discussion includes a detailed data questionnaire. One has been completed by a fictitious family (Figure 3-1), but there is also a blank questionnaire provided as the appendix to the chapter for your own soul-searching. These questions are designed to help you identify your goals.

2. Don't be unduly afraid of risk. Evaluate the threat it poses to you. Calculate the rewards you stand to reap if you face it, and make your decision accordingly.

Do not let a fear of risk paralyze you into inactivity. The courage to make investment decisions, even when there is some element of risk, is a quality that you must develop on your own. If you succeed in developing it, you will not be sorry, for it will help you to act wisely in a wide variety of situations both in and out of the investment arena. Meeting this challenge is your task.

As we continue through this book you will learn how to create a personal plan that will be your blueprint to financial freedom. It will be a flexible plan, one that contains options for you to pursue as conditions change in the marketplace and as your own needs change. Your dream of financial freedom can and will become a reachable goal.

3
The
Financial Puzzle

Starting right now, you should
begin handling your family finances
exactly as most businesses handle
theirs.

FREEDOM FOCUS

- *Do you know how to take an inventory of your assets and liabilities?*
- *Do you have an income and expense statement for your family?*
- *Have you identified the goals and objectives that will lead to your financial freedom?*

Financial planning *is* a puzzle—but one that you can learn to assemble. In fact, you can and will develop the skills you need to plan your financial future wisely if you apply yourself to the task systematically.

Systematically—this is a key word for you to remember, a key approach for you to use as you examine the financial-planning puzzle. It is easy to be overwhelmed by subjects that we do not understand; a common reaction is to turn away before we have delved very deeply into them. But the financial well-being of you and your family is too important a concern for you to leave to luck. And it need not loom as a profoundly complex challenge. An old adage asks, "How do you eat an elephant?" The answer: "One bite at a time." Similarly, you will want to approach the financial-planning puzzle systematically—one piece at a time.

Organizing the Facts

The first piece of the puzzle is the one labeled "organizing the facts," since you cannot plan for the future until you know your financial standing right now. Like most people, you have probably never taken a really thorough inventory of your assets and liabilities. Yet taking such an inventory is a relatively simple process. As you know, most businesses do this routinely. *Starting right now, you should begin handling your family finances exactly as most businesses handle theirs.* Why? Because your family *is* a business. You and your spouse are the officers, your children are stockholders, and the outside advisers you select to assist you in making decisions vital to your business' growth and development are on the board of directors. The tools that most successful corporations use to assess their financial health can be easily adapted for use by you. Let's start with the most basic of these tools: the balance sheet. Examples of all of the accounting instruments we discuss in this chapter are shown in Figure 3-1. They've been filled out by the fictitious family of John T. Scott. A blank set of forms for your own personal use is included as Appendix 3-1.

The very first section, *Personal Data,* contains the family information such as ages, occupations, family members and their status, as well as a section about your parents. This section is important for at least two reasons:

1. Will you be responsible for the future (or present) needs of your parents?
2. Are you involved in an estate, trust, or future inheritance that you need to plan for?

The next section, *General Information,* identifies other individuals or resources which become important in your planning.

As we continue through the information gathering, refer to the completed data sheet as a resource.

```
┌─────────────────────────────────────────────────────────────────┐
│                         PERSONAL DATA                             │
│                                                                   │
│  1. NAME:  JOHN  T.  SCOTT                                        │
│     Birthdate 10-8-XX   Age 44   Resident State FL   Citizenship USA │
│     Social Security No. XXX-XX-XXXX                               │
│     Health:   Good ✓   Fair____   Do you smoke?  Yes____  No ✓    │
│     Address: 101 PLEASANT DRIVE, DODGE POINT, FLORIDA             │
│                               Telephone no. (914) 999-8888        │
│     Other address (Northern etc.):_____ │
│                               Telephone no. (   )                 │
│                                                                   │
│     Approximate dates when you are at your other address:_____ │
│                                                                   │
│     Name of employer UNITED SOFTWARE CORP   Occupation PROGRAMMER │
│     Employer's address 1120 EXECUTIVE DRIVE, DODGE POINT, FL      │
│                                                                   │
│     Employer's telephone no. (914) 888-9999                      │
│     Circle one: (Married)   Single   Divorced   Widower/Widow    │
│     Prior marriages: Yes____  No ✓                               │
│                                                                   │
│  2. How long have you been married (to present spouse)? 19 Years │
│     Any pre-nuptial agreement? N/A   If yes please explain_____ │
│     _____ │
│     _____ │
│                                                                   │
│  3. SPOUSE'S NAME:  MARY  M.  SCOTT                              │
│     Birthdate 7-4-XX   Age 41   Resident State FL   Citizenship USA │
│     Social Security No. XXX-XX-XXXX                               │
│     Health:   Good ✓   Fair____   Do you smoke?  Yes____  No ✓    │
│                                                                   │
│     Telephone no. (   ) SAME           Occupation BANK TELLER    │
│     Name of employer FIRST NATIONAL BANK                         │
│     Employer's address 100 MAIN STREET, DODGE POINT, FLORIDA     │
│                                                                   │
│     Employer's telephone no. (914) 777-8888                      │
│                                                                   │
│     Prior marriages: Yes____  No ✓                               │
│                                                                   │
│                                 1                                 │
└─────────────────────────────────────────────────────────────────┘
```

Figure 3-1. Example of the Personal Financial Planning Inventory (Appendix 3-1). It is filled in for the fictitious John T. Scott family. (Continued on the next 11 pages.)

FAMILY DATA

CHILDREN'S NAMES 4. (ELDEST FIRST)	DATE OF BIRTH	CIRCLE	%SUPPORT	MARRIED YES-NO	OCCUPATION
THOMAS C.	7-1-XX ⑰	(Son) Dau	100	NO	STUDENT
JENNIFER R.	4-4-XX ⑭	Son (Dau)	100	NO	STUDENT
		Son - Dau			
		Son - Dau			
		Son - Dau			
		Son - Dau			

5. GRANDCHILDREN'S NAMES		CIRCLE	%SUPPORT	MARRIED YES-NO	STATUS
		Son - Dau			
		Son - Dau			
		Son - Dau			
		Son - Dau			
		Son - Dau			
		Son - Dau			

6. OTHER DEPENDENTS OR RELATIVES YOU ARE NOW SUPPORTING.

(Please include any special schooling or medical bills being paid.)

Name:_____How Much Annually $_____

Name:_____How Much Annually $_____

Name:_____How Much Annually $_____

Please give us any additional information you feel would be helpful in planning for any of the above

(i.e. children, grandchildren or others with special needs).

JENNIFER IS IN SPECIAL EDUCATION CLASSES - MILD LEARNING DISABILITY.
THOMAS WILL GRADUATE FROM HIGH SCHOOL THIS SPRING. HE HAS
RECEIVED A SCHOLARSHIP OF $8,000 PER YEAR AT A STATE UNIVERSITY.

2

Figure 3-1. *(Continued)*

PARENTS

	Living Yes-No	Age	Health	State of Residence

7. CLIENT:

Father _GORDON SCOTT_ _NO - DIED OF HEART ATTACK AT AGE 65_

Mother _BARBARA SCOTT_ _YES_ _70_ _FAIR_ _FL_

Are they or will they ever be dependent on you for support? _MOTHER MAY NEED HELP._

How much support? _POSSIBLE $500 A MONTH TO SUPPLEMENT SOCIAL SECURITY FOR NURSING HOME CARE SOME DAY._

8. SPOUSE:

Father _ANDREW CARSON_ _YES_ _63_ _GOOD_ _NY (ATTORNEY)_

Mother _KAREN CARSON_ _YES_ _64_ _GOOD_ _NY_

Are they or will they ever be dependent on you for support? _NO_

How much support? _____

9. Do you or your spouse anticipate any inheritance(s)?

Client:: $ _NO_ When _____ From _____

Spouse: $ _250,000_ When _EVENTUALLY_ From _MOTHER AND FATHER_

GENERAL INFORMATION

10. NAME & ADDRESS OF YOUR ATTORNEY:

DONALD V. YOUNG
213 EXECUTIVE DR., DODGE POINT, FL

Phone: (_914_) _777-6666_

11. NAME & ADDRESS OF YOUR ACCOUNTANT:

JAMES A. STEVENS
824 DOLLAR ST., DODGE POINT, FL

Phone: (_914_) _666-5555_

3

Figure 3-1. *(Continued)*

---

12. **NAME & ADDRESS OF YOUR TRUST OFFICER:** NONE

Phone: (_____) _____

13. **NAME & ADDRESS OF OTHER BANK OFFICER:** NONE

Phone: (_____) _____

14. **NAME & ADDRESS OF LIFE INSURANCE AGENT:**
    CONSTANCE PAINE — PRUDENTIAL LIFE
    1002 ORANGE DRIVE, DODGE POINT, FL
    Phone: (914) 555-4444

15. **NAME & ADDRESS OF PROPERTY AND CASUALTY AGENT:**
    GORDAN JOHNS — ALLSTATE INSURANCE
    2111 ORANGE DRIVE, DODGE POINT, FL
    Phone: (914) 444-3333

16. **NAME & ADDRESS OF YOUR SECURITIES BROKER:**
    ROLAND DANCE — SMITH, SCOTT & Co.
    900 MAIN STREET, DODGE POINT, FL
    Phone: (914) 333-2222

17. **NAME & ADDRESS OF OTHER FINANCIAL CONSULTANT:**
    NONE

Phone: (_____) _____

18. **DO YOU HAVE A WILL?**   YES ✓   NO _____
    If yes in which state was it executed? FLORIDA - 1985

19. **DOES YOUR SPOUSE HAVE A WILL?**   YES ✓   NO _____
    If yes in which state was it executed? FLORIDA - 1985

20. **HAVE GUARDIANS BEEN NAMED FOR YOUR MINOR CHILDREN?**   YES _____   NO ✓
    If yes, Who? Name:_____
    Address:_____

4

Figure 3-1. *(Continued)*

21. HAVE YOU OR YOUR SPOUSE CREATED A LIVING TRUST OR TESTAMENTARY TRUST?

YES_____ NO__✓__ TYPE:_____

Please describe briefly:_____

22. HAVE YOU OR YOUR SPOUSE EVER MADE A GIFT UNDER THE UNIFORM GIFTS TO MINORS ACT?

YES_____ NO__✓__

If yes, in which state?_____

Who is the custodian?_____

Who are the recipients?_____

Are there any other types of gifts you or your spouse have made?

YES_____ NO_____TYPE:_____

_____

23. DO YOU OR YOUR SPOUSE HAVE A FAMILY DURABLE POWER OF ATTORNEY?

YES_____ NO__✓__

24. DO YOU OR YOUR SPOUSE HAVE ANY BUSINESS BUY/SELL AGREEMENTS?   YES_____ NO__✓__

25. DO YOU OR YOUR SPOUSE HAVE ANY INSTALLMENT SALES AGREEMENTS?

YES__✓__ NO_____

Briefly explain any "YES" answers to questions 24 or 25.

25) RECEIVING $1,000 PER MONTH FROM SALE OF
COMPUTER CONSULTING BUSINESS 4 YEARS AGO.
4 YEARS TO GO. PRINCIPAL BALANCE $37,000.

_____

_____

_____

5

Figure 3-1. *(Continued)*

INVENTORY OF ASSETS

ITEM	CLIENT	SPOUSE	JOINT
Checking accounts			2,000
Savings accounts			8,000
Money market funds			-0-
(Banks, CMAs etc.)			-0-
			-0-
Treasury bills			10,000
Certificates of deposits			9-23-XX
Maturity date:			
Life insurance (Face Amt.)	75,000 WHOLE LIFE	25,000 WHOLE LIFE	
(See supplement)	42,000 GROUP TERM		

STOCKS (NAME)	DATE PURCHASED	NO. OF SHARES	PRICE PAID
UNITED SOFTWARE CORP.	6-1-84	200	$12.50 SHARE
AMERICAN COMPUTER Co.	9-15-90	100	7.25 SHARE
AT&T (INHERITED)	7-20-73	100	?

BONDS			
NEW YORK CITY REVENUE			
10 1/2 % - 7/1/2010			10,000

MUTUAL FUNDS

Growth			
Income LANDMARK HI YIELD	1,225 SHARES		5,512.50
Balanced U.S. TOTAL RETURN	251 SHARES		2,259.00
Others			

6

Figure 3-1. *(Continued)*

ITEM	CLIENT	SPOUSE	JOINT
Annuities (List amount (See supplemental information))			
Single Premium Fixed	21,660		
Single Premium Variable			
Limited Partnerships			
Oil & Gas			
Real estate			
Other			
Personal Real Estate			
Principal Residence			90,000
Second Residence			
Rental			
Investment Real Estate			
Rental Residential	50,000 (NO MORTGAGE)		
Rental Commercial			
Other			
Personal Assets			
Household furnishings			7,500
Automobiles			15,000
Jewelry/furs		3,500	
Gold/silver/metals			
Art			
Recreational Vehicles			
Boats	5,000		
Collections (art, coins, etc.)			
Hobby Equipment			
Other			
Retirement Plans			
IRA- FIRST NAT'L BANK- CD's	8,200	4,500	
IRA Rollover			
Keogh			
401K- GUARANTEED INTEREST ACCOUNT		2,100	
403-B			
Pension Plan (Vested amt.)			
Profit Sharing (Vested amt.)	42,500		
Other Types of Assets			

Figure 3-1. *(Continued)*

OUTSTANDING OBLIGATIONS

Retail Charge Accounts	Name	Amount
	VISA	2,100.00
	GENERAL DEPT. STORE	270.00

Short-Term Loans		
Personal Notes		
Family Loans		
Securities Margin Loans		
Bank Loans	AUTOMOBILE	7,500
Income Tax Liability		
Federal		
State		
Property Taxes		
Investment Liabilities		
Mortgages	RESIDENCE	57,000
Liability Judgment		
Family Member Support Obligation(s)		
Child Support		
Alimony		
Other (specify)		

Are there any other liabilities your estate might be called upon to pay?

NO

Do you foresee any future liabilities (business expansion, new home, etc.)?

NO

8

Figure 3-1. *(Continued)*

ANNUAL INCOME

	CLIENT	SPOUSE
Salary	$ 32,000	$ 24,000
Bonus	2,500	
Self Employment Income - Net		
Fees/Commissions		
Social Security		
Pension		
Rental Income	3,600	
Dividends	800	800
Interest (Taxable)	300	300
Interest (Tax Free)		
Trust Income		
Other – *INSTALLMENT SALE*	12,000	
Total Income	51,200	25,100

Annual Living Expenses (Not including income tax expenses)

	CLIENT	SPOUSE
	$ 52,500	$
Federal Income Taxes Paid Last Year	$ 11,000	Don't Know

Please provide additional information if appropriate:

_____

_____

_____

_____

_____

_____

9

Figure 3-1. *(Continued)*

FAMILY HOUSEHOLD EXPENSES

MONTHLY		ANNUALLY
$370	Auto, Gas, Insurance, Oil, Repairs, Taxes, Tires	$4,440
70	Boats, Horses, Airplanes	840
300	Birthdays, Christmas, Wedding gifts	3,600
100	Cleaners, Laundry, Hair Dresser	1,200
300	Clothes	3,600
150	Contributions, Donations, Tithes	1,800
	Country Club Dues, Golf, Tennis-related expenses	
175	Entertaining and Dining out	2,100
700	Food, Cigarettes, Beverages	8,400
675	Home Mortgage, Rent, Insurance and Taxes	8,100
150	Home Repairs, Yard and Pool Maintenance	1,800
	Housekeeper Salary (Include SS taxes)	
125	Medical, Dental, Drugs (Not reimbursed)	1,500
	Music, Dancing, Spa	
40	Newspapers, Books, Magazines, Stamps	480
300	New Household Purchases	3,600
350	Private School and/or College expenses	4,200
50	Sporting Events and related expenses	600
100	Utilities, Gas, Oil, Water, Garbage, Telephone	1,200
300	Other – MISCELLANEOUS	3,600
120	Other – LIFE INSURANCE	1,440
$4,375	**TOTAL ESTIMATED EXPENSES:**	$52,500

Please provide additional information if appropriate:

_____

_____

_____

_____

_____

_____

10

Figure 3-1. *(Continued)*

SUPPLEMENTAL INFORMATION

INSURANCE

Company	Type	Insured	Face Amount	Beneficiary	Premium	Date Purchased
PRUDENTIAL	WHOLE LIFE	JOHN	75,000	MARY	1,100	10-1-87
PRUDENTIAL	WHOLE LIFE	MARY	25,000	JOHN	300	10-1-87
SUN LIFE	GROUP TERM	JOHN	42,000	MARY	—	—

ANNUITIES   Contribution   OWNER/ANNUITANT-JOHN Date Purchased
                                                         BENEFICIARY- MARY

JOHNSTOWN INS. Co. (SPDA)   20,000   11-5-XX

A Salary Continuation Plan at work?   Yes_____ No ___✔___
Do you own disability income insurance?   Yes_✔___ No _____

Company	Type	Face Amount	Annual Premium
PAUL REVERE	DISABILITY	1,500 PER MONTH	1,500

Long-Term Health Care?   Yes_____ No ___✔___   WOULD LIKE TO DISCUSS
                                                        POLICY FOR JOHN'S MOM.

Company	Type	Face Amount	Annual Premium

11

Figure 3-1. *(Continued)*

PERSONAL INVESTMENT GOALS

Are you planning any major expenditure greater than 10% of your investment assets during the
next twelve (12) months?   Yes ✓ No____
NEW CAR IN 6 MONTHS FOR MARY - $12,000. WILL FINANCE $8,000 AFTER TRADE-IN.

Are you planning to provide for your children's or grandchildren's higher education?   Yes ✓ No____
If yes, what percent do you plan to provide? ___80___ (1% - 100%)

When was your property and casualty Insurance last renewed? OCT 199X

Please share with us your financial goals, objectives and concerns including any estate, tax or investment
questions.

LONG TERM GROWTH FOR RETIREMENT.
ADEQUATE RETURN TO OFFSET INFLATION.
START FUND FOR SPECIAL NEEDS OF DAUGHTER.
INVEST AT LEAST $1,000 PER MONTH FOR RETIREMENT.

12

Figure 3-1. *(Continued)*

Constructing Your Balance Sheet

To create a balance sheet for your family business, use the *Inventory of Assets* in Appendix 3-1. List everything your immediate family owns, including things that are not completely paid for yet, and each item's current market value. In addition to the obvious entries, such as your home, automobiles, investment holdings, and savings accounts, be sure to include such possessions as jewelry, stamp collections, rare coins, and other items of value. Think carefully before closing out this form. Ask other members of the family to review this list before you consider it complete. Remember that even such items as a teenager's vintage baseball card collection or your antique furniture should be included if it could bring a reasonable price in the marketplace. Naturally, many of the dollar amounts that you attach to your possessions will have to be estimates that are based on your knowledge of existing market conditions. If you need outside help to determine the worth of special items, such as a collection, you can ask a dealer to give you an estimate. Many such estimates are given free or for a nominal charge.

Now move on to *Outstanding Obligations* (liabilities), which is also included in the appendix. You will need to list every debt that you are carrying, from major commitments such as your mortgage, to small payments made monthly to department stores. Again, have others in your family look over this list to make sure that no obligation, however small, has been omitted.

Once this part of the balance sheet has been completed and tallied, you will have two totals: the sum of your assets and the sum of your outstanding obligations (liabilities). To determine your net worth, simply subtract your liabilities from your assets. Now you know where you stand financially.

In order to track your financial progress (or lack of it), you should prepare a balance sheet for your family business once a month for 6 months. After that, you can follow the example of most of the nation's businesses and prepare it quarterly. Set up a routine for the production of these balance sheets and stick to it! If you are in the habit of paying your bills on a particular day each month, you could also earmark that day for preparation of your balance sheet. Don't let anything deter you from drawing up the sheet on that day. Establishing this routine will serve two purposes: it will enable you to compare your financial situation of one month with that of succeeding and preceding months, and, perhaps more significantly, it will introduce discipline to the handling of your family business' finances. *To realize your greatest potential as a money manager, and to reap the greatest benefits for your family business, you must take a businesslike, disciplined approach to your financial affairs for the rest of your life.*

The Expense Statement

Another tracking tool that you will have to produce with some regularity, especially in the early stages of your analysis, is an expense statement. In the business world, every manager knows that the first test of a company's potential profitability lies in its ability to keep expenses under control. Income must obviously exceed expenses if a corporation is to operate in the black. Yet we all are painfully aware of the tendency of expenses to rise until they have equalled, and in some cases outstripped, income. The expense statement aims at counteracting this tendency by making you aware of your controllable expenses and how well you are controlling them.

To construct this statement, make a list of all of the expenses your family regularly incurs, differentiating between those that are necessary and those that are discretionary. You will find the *Family Household Expenses* section of Appendix 3-1 useful for this. Estimate the maximum amounts of money that you think you should be spending in each of the discretionary areas every month, and then keep track of your actual expenses for 2 or 3 months. At the end of this record-keeping period, you may find that a conscious effort to economize is required of members of your family in certain areas. At the very least, you will have identified the areas that are acting as drains on your income, and you won't have to bear the frustration of wondering every month where all your money has gone.

As you can see, the expense statement also serves as a budget, for it allows you to see what portion of your income is going where. As a general guideline, a middle-income family of four with no major medical expenses and no children in college would expect to have their expenditures approximate the following:

- About 25 percent of gross income goes to food.
- From 28 to 31 percent goes to housing.
- About 19 percent is consumed by tax, insurance, and social security deductions.
- About 8 percent goes to clothing.
- About 5 percent is spent on medical care.
- About 2 percent is spent on personal care.

The Income Statement

A companion of your expense statement should be an income statement. This document, the *Annual Income* section of the appendix, should list every source of income that your family business has and the amount of gross income it brings to you monthly. The income statement should also include projections of expected increases or decreases in income. If you have been employed by a single firm for a number of years, for instance, you will probably be able to predict with reasonable accuracy the amount of your annual bonuses and raises. These projections enable you to see how well your income will stand up against your expenses in the near future.

By combining the expense statement with the income statement, you will have a statement just like the one used by most major U.S. corporations to analyze their potential profitability. What you are developing for yourself with these instruments is a *reporting system* that will allow you to see, in actual dollar amounts, how well your personal business is faring over time.

Setting Your Goals

These analyses will bring you to the starting point of financial planning since they will tell you where you have been and where you stand at present. You will, at last, be ready to face an exhilarating challenge: setting realistic goals for yourself. Remember as you formulate these goals—and you should write them down in specific terms—that they are not cast in concrete. Goals can and should change, depending upon, among other things, your time of life, fluctuations within the economy, and specific demands that may be placed upon your resources. Suppose that one of your primary goals is to achieve financial independence for yourself and your spouse by the time you turn 65. This general goal must be expressed in more specific terms if it is to mean anything. You must state, for instance, that, assuming inflation averages 5 percent a year between now and your retirement, you will need x number of dollars per year to live comfortably after you stop working. And this figure, in turn, will give you an indication of the amount of capital you will have to accumulate between now and your retirement to assure that your combined investment and retirement stipend incomes will be able to support you.

Suppose that another of your major goals is to put your children through college. To make this goal more meaningful, you would have to project the future cost of a 4-year education at the college or colleges your children will probably attend. (A college expense projection appears in Chapter 7.) This figure, combined with a calculation of the number of years that remain before each of your children becomes a college freshman, will help you to determine exactly how much you will have to set aside by what dates.

Goal setting is another piece of the financial planning puzzle. You should share the challenges and satisfactions of this process with all the members of your family business as you complete the *Personal Investment Goals* section of the appendix. If your family is to function as a truly cohesive unit, progressing steadily toward a group of well-defined goals, then all the members of that unit should contribute to the setting of those goals, and all members (except those too young to understand) should have detailed knowledge of how the goals are to be realized.

To keep your family involved in the financial planning process, your business should hold monthly or quarterly meetings at which goals are re-evaluated and strategies revised, if necessary. You should hold the first of these meetings as soon as you've finished reading this book. With other members of your family business, you should fill out the *Personal Financial Planning Inventory* (Appendix 3-1), which we have been discussing. This is very similar to the data sheet that clients of my financial planning practice fill out as a first order of business. You and your family should also discuss the following questions.

Goals

Personal Goals

How do you want to use your personal wealth?_____

_____

What will assure your personal happiness, self-satisfaction, and success?_____

_____

Financial Goals

What are your immediate financial goals? _____

_____

What are your goals for 5, 10, 15 years from now? _____

_____

How will you meet these goals? _____

_____

What is the relative importance to you of income, safety, and growth?_____
_____

Retirement Goals
Do you have a will? _____

When will you retire and why?_____
_____

What will your needs be? _____
_____

How are you going to ensure retirement security?_____
_____

Estate Goals
How important is it for you to leave an estate? _____
_____

To whom do you want to leave it? _____
_____

How much do you want to leave? _____
_____

How much control should your heirs have? _____
_____

What do you want your estate to accomplish?_____
_____

Should you have a Living Trust? _____
_____

Do you have or need a Durable Power of Attorney?_____
_____

Assets and Liabilities
What are your major expenditures today and what will they be in the future? _____
_____

How can you improve your cash flow? _____

_____

How does current spending affect your ability to reach your goals?

_____

_____

What is your net worth? _____

_____

How liquid are you? _____

_____

Should you be more or less liquid? _____

_____

How much can you save and invest per year? _____

_____

Compensation
Should you consider deferred compensation? _____

_____

Should you change the beneficiaries or ownership of your insurance or retirement plans? _____

_____

Should you participate in your company's savings plan, thrift plan, money purchase plan, or similar program?_____

_____

How would a job change or unemployment affect your goals?____

_____

Investments
What annual returns must your investments produce to allow you to reach your goals? _____

_____

What returns have your investments produced in the past? _____

_____

Are you taking too much or not enough risk?_____

How are taxes affecting your investment return? _____

Should you consider tax deferral?_____

How can you improve your investment results? _____

Taxes
How can you reduce the federal, state, or local taxes you pay?____

What taxes do you pay on your current investment program? ____

How will taxes affect your estate? _____

Are there deductions/exemptions that you are not taking? _____

Are you able to keep abreast of changes in tax law?_____

Should you use income averaging?_____

How will retirement affect your tax bracket?_____

Estate
What are your estate goals? _____

How should your estate be distributed? _____

How can you minimize estate erosion?_____

Do you have an up-to-date will? _____

Does your will allow you to meet your estate goals? _____

What opportunities are available to you to increase your estate through your business or employment? _____

How will your business be affected by your death?_____

If you are a principal in a business, do you and your associates have a buy/sell agreement?_____

Insurance
Do you have life insurance? If so, why? If not, why not?_____

Do you have disability insurance? _____

How can you reduce the cost of your insurance program? _____

Is your home adequately insured (to 80 percent of market value)?_____

What part would insurance play in your business if you were to die? _____

If the answers to some of these questions didn't come easily, don't despair. As we consider the remaining pieces of the financial-planning puzzle, areas that may seem complicated or mysterious to you now will become understandable, and it is through that understanding that you will be able to use this information to set in motion your plan for financial freedom.

Some Helpful Tools

If I were to ask you what tools you work with, how would you respond? Maybe a doctor would include the use of drugs and hypodermics; perhaps a contractor would name blueprints, laborers, and nails; a photographer might say cameras, lights, and models. True. All these tools are among those involved in their respective professions. But let's dig a little deeper. The real basic tools for each of us are education, experience, knowledge, talent, ability, ambition, discipline, etc. These are the tools we all work with every day of our lives. One thing is certain—you can't do a job properly without the right tools for that job.

The same is true in designing your financial plan. In order to construct your financial plan to reach your goals, you must have knowledge of certain basic tools. Do you know what inflation is? Do you understand the prime rate? What is the CPI? What is the relationship between inflation and unemployment? And what's all the fuss about the Dow Jones Industrial Average?

The best tool you can have for this task is a basic understanding of some of the terms that are used daily in the financial arena. I'm going to help you with this by examining some of those "tools" and providing you with basic explanations (Appendix 3-2, Tools of the Trade). Don't forget that this book also includes a glossary at the end. You should become familiar with it and use it as a resource.

So, before you move on, take a few minutes to review the terms and topics contained in Appendix 3-2 because these are the terms that you will hear repeatedly when discussing investing and the financial arena. Understanding what they mean in terms of the economy and, more personally, in terms of your own planning, is very important when you are charting your financial future.

APPENDIX 3-1
Personal Financial Planning Inventory

PERSONAL DATA

1. NAME:_____

Birthdate_____ Age _____ Resident State_____ Citizenship_____

Social Security No._____

Health: Good_____ Fair_____   Do you smoke?   Yes_____   No_____

Address:_____

_____ Telephone no.   (_____)_____

Other address (Northern etc.):_____

_____ Telephone no.   (_____)_____

Approximate dates when you are at your other address:_____

Name of employer_____Occupation_____

Employer's address_____

_____

Employer's telephone no.   (_____)_____

Circle one: Married   Single   Divorced   Widower/Widow

Prior marriages: Yes_____   No_____

2. How long have you been married (to present spouse)?   _____Years

Any pre-nuptial agreement?_____ If yes please explain_____

_____

_____

3. SPOUSE'S NAME:_____

Birthdate_____ Age_____ Resident State_____ Citizenship_____

Social Security No._____

Health: Good_____ Fair_____   Do you smoke?   Yes_____   No_____

Telephone no.   (_____)_____   Occupation_____

Name of employer_____

Employer's address_____

_____

Employer's telephone no.   (_____)_____

Prior marriages: Yes_____   No_____

1

FAMILY DATA

CHILDREN'S NAMES 4. (ELDEST FIRST)	DATE OF BIRTH	CIRCLE	%SUPPORT	MARRIED YES-NO	OCCUPATION
_____	_____	Son - Dau	_____	_____	_____
_____	_____	Son - Dau	_____	_____	_____
_____	_____	Son - Dau	_____	_____	_____
_____	_____	Son - Dau	_____	_____	_____
_____	_____	Son - Dau	_____	_____	_____
_____	_____	Son - Dau	_____	_____	_____

5. GRANDCHILDREN'S NAMES		CIRCLE	%SUPPORT	MARRIED YES-NO	STATUS
_____	_____	Son - Dau	_____	_____	_____
_____	_____	Son - Dau	_____	_____	_____
_____	_____	Son - Dau	_____	_____	_____
_____	_____	Son - Dau	_____	_____	_____
_____	_____	Son - Dau	_____	_____	_____
_____	_____	Son - Dau	_____	_____	_____

6. **OTHER DEPENDENTS OR RELATIVES YOU ARE NOW SUPPORTING.**

(Please include any special schooling or medical bills being paid.)

Name:_____How Much Annually $_____

Name:_____How Much Annually $_____

Name:_____How Much Annually $_____

Please give us any additional information you feel would be helpful in planning for any of the above (i.e. children, grandchildren or others with special needs).

_____

_____

_____

PARENTS

	Living Yes-No	Age	Health	State of Residence

7. CLIENT:

Father_____   _____   _____   _____   _____

Mother_____   _____   _____   _____   _____

Are they or will they ever be dependent on you for support?_____

How much support?_____

_____

8. SPOUSE:

Father_____   _____   _____   _____   _____

Mother_____   _____   _____   _____   _____

Are they or will they ever be dependent on you for support?_____

How much support?_____

_____

9. Do you or your spouse anticipate any inheritance(s)?

Client:: $_____ When _____ From _____

Spouse: $_____ When _____ From _____

GENERAL INFORMATION

10. NAME & ADDRESS OF YOUR ATTORNEY:

_____

_____

Phone: (_____) _____

11. NAME & ADDRESS OF YOUR ACCOUNTANT:

_____

_____

Phone: (_____) _____

3

12. **NAME & ADDRESS OF YOUR TRUST OFFICER:**
   _____
   _____

   Phone: (_____) _____

13. **NAME & ADDRESS OF OTHER BANK OFFICER:**
   _____
   _____

   Phone: (_____) _____

14. **NAME & ADDRESS OF LIFE INSURANCE AGENT:**
   _____
   _____

   Phone: (_____) _____

15. **NAME & ADDRESS OF PROPERTY AND CASUALTY AGENT:**
   _____
   _____

   Phone: (_____) _____

16. **NAME & ADDRESS OF YOUR SECURITIES BROKER:**
   _____
   _____

   Phone: (_____) _____

17. **NAME & ADDRESS OF OTHER FINANCIAL CONSULTANT:**
   _____
   _____

   Phone: (_____) _____

18: **DO YOU HAVE A WILL?**   YES_____ NO_____
   If yes in which state was it executed?_____

19. **DOES YOUR SPOUSE HAVE A WILL?**   YES_____ NO_____
   If yes in which state was it executed?_____

20. **HAVE GUARDIANS BEEN NAMED FOR YOUR MINOR CHILDREN?**   YES_____ NO _____
   If yes, Who? Name:_____
                Address:_____

4

21. **HAVE YOU OR YOUR SPOUSE CREATED A LIVING TRUST OR TESTAMENTARY TRUST?**

    YES_____ NO_____   TYPE:_____

    Please describe briefly:_____

22. **HAVE YOU OR YOUR SPOUSE EVER MADE A GIFT UNDER THE UNIFORM GIFTS TO MINORS ACT?**

    YES_____ NO_____

    If yes, in which state?_____

    Who is the custodian?_____

    Who are the recipients?_____

    Are there any other types of gifts you or your spouse have made?

    YES_____ NO_____TYPE:_____

    _____

23. **DO YOU OR YOUR SPOUSE HAVE A FAMILY DURABLE POWER OF ATTORNEY?**

    YES_____ NO_____

24. **DO YOU OR YOUR SPOUSE HAVE ANY BUSINESS BUY/SELL AGREEMENTS?   YES_____ NO_____**

25. **DO YOU OR YOUR SPOUSE HAVE ANY INSTALLMENT SALES AGREEMENTS?**

    YES_____ NO_____

Briefly explain any "YES" answers to questions 24 or 25.

_____

_____

_____

_____

_____

_____

5

INVENTORY OF ASSETS

ITEM	CLIENT	SPOUSE	JOINT
Checking accounts	_____	_____	_____
Savings accounts	_____	_____	_____
Money market funds	_____	_____	_____
(Banks, CMAs etc.)	_____	_____	_____
Treasury bills	_____	_____	_____
Certificates of deposits	_____	_____	_____
Maturity date:	_____	_____	_____
Life insurance (Face Amt.)	_____	_____	_____
(See supplement)	_____	_____	_____

STOCKS (NAME)	DATE PURCHASED	NO. OF SHARES	PRICE PAID
_____	_____	_____	_____
_____	_____	_____	_____
_____	_____	_____	_____
_____	_____	_____	_____
_____	_____	_____	_____
_____	_____	_____	_____

BONDS

_____	_____	_____	_____
_____	_____	_____	_____
_____	_____	_____	_____
_____	_____	_____	_____
_____	_____	_____	_____
_____	_____	_____	_____

MUTUAL FUNDS

Growth	_____	_____	_____
	_____	_____	_____
Income	_____	_____	_____
	_____	_____	_____
Balanced	_____	_____	_____
	_____	_____	_____
Others	_____	_____	_____

6

ITEM	CLIENT	SPOUSE	JOINT
Annuities (List amount - See supplemental information)			
Single Premium Fixed			
Single Premium Variable			
Limited Partnerships			
Oil & Gas			
Real estate			
Other			
Personal Real Estate			
Principal Residence			
Second Residence			
Rental			
Investment Real Estate			
Rental Residential			
Rental Commercial			
Other			
Personal Assets			
Household furnishings			
Automobiles			
Jewelry/furs			
Gold/silver/metals			
Art			
Recreational Vehicles			
Boats			
Collections (art, coins, etc.)			
Hobby Equipment			
Other			
Retirement Plans			
IRA			
IRA Rollover			
Keogh			
401K			
403-B			
Pension Plan (Vested amt.)			
Profit Sharing (Vested amt.)			
Other Types of Assets			

7

OUTSTANDING OBLIGATIONS

Retail Charge Accounts	**Name**	**Amount**
Short-Term Loans		
Personal Notes		
Family Loans		
Securities Margin Loans		
Bank Loans		
Income Tax Liability		
Federal		
State		
Property Taxes		
Investment Liabilities		
Mortgages		
Liability Judgment		
Family Member Support Obligation(s)		
Child Support		
Alimony		
Other (specify)		

Are there any other liabilities your estate might be called upon to pay?

Do you foresee any future liabilities (business expansion, new home, etc.)?

ANNUAL INCOME

	CLIENT	SPOUSE
	$	$
Salary		
Bonus		
Self Employment Income - Net		
Fees/Commissions		
Social Security		
Pension		
Rental Income		
Dividends		
Interest (Taxable)		
Interest (Tax Free)		
Trust Income		
Other		
Total Income		

Annual Living Expenses (Not including income tax expenses)

	CLIENT	SPOUSE
	$	$
Federal Income Taxes Paid Last Year	$	

Please provide additional Information if appropriate:

_____

_____

_____

_____

_____

_____

FAMILY HOUSEHOLD EXPENSES

MONTHLY   **ANNUALLY**

MONTHLY		ANNUALLY
_____	Auto, Gas, Insurance, Oil, Repairs, Taxes, Tires	_____
_____	Boats, Horses, Airplanes	_____
_____	Birthdays, Christmas, Wedding gifts	_____
_____	Cleaners, Laundry, Hair Dresser	_____
_____	Clothes	_____
_____	Contributions, Donations, Tithes	_____
_____	Country Club Dues, Golf, Tennis-related expenses	_____
_____	Entertaining and Dining out	_____
_____	Food, Cigarettes, Beverages	_____
_____	Home Mortgage, Rent, Insurance and Taxes	_____
_____	Home Repairs, Yard and Pool Maintenance	_____
_____	Housekeeper Salary (Include SS taxes)	_____
_____	Medical, Dental, Drugs (Not reimbursed)	_____
_____	Music, Dancing, Spa	_____
_____	Newspapers, Books, Magazines, Stamps	_____
_____	New Household Purchases	_____
_____	Private School and/or College expenses	_____
_____	Sporting Events and related expenses	_____
_____	Utilities, Gas, Oil, Water, Garbage, Telephone	_____
_____	Other	_____
_____	Other	_____

_____   **TOTAL ESTIMATED EXPENSES:**   _____

Please provide additional information if appropriate:

_____

_____

_____

_____

_____

_____

10

SUPPLEMENTAL INFORMATION

INSURANCE

Company	Type	Insured	Face Amount	Beneficiary	Premium	Date Purchased

ANNUITIES

	Contribution	Date Purchased

A Salary Continuation Plan at work?   Yes_____ No _____

Do you own disability income insurance?   Yes_____ No _____

Company	Type	Face Amount	Annual Premium

Long-Term Health Care?   Yes_____ No _____

Company	Type	Face Amount	Annual Premium

11

PERSONAL INVESTMENT GOALS

Are you planning any major expenditure greater than 10% of your investment assets during the next twelve (12) months?   Yes_____ No_____

Are you planning to provide for your children's or grandchildren's higher education?   Yes_____ No_____
If yes, what percent do you plan to provide? _____ (1% - 100%)

When was your property and casualty Insurance last renewed?_____

Please share with us your financial goals, objectives and concerns including any estate, tax or investment questions.

_____

_____

_____

_____

_____

12

APPENDIX 3-2
Tools of the Trade

Averages and Indexes

Market indexes and averages track the performance of groups of securities. National and regional stock exchanges all have their own indexes. The difference between averages and indexes lies primarily within the number of components used. An average is based on a small number of securities; an index uses a broader sampling.

You are constantly being bombarded with performance reports by television, radio, newspapers, and magazines. On trains, subways, or buses, people will ask strangers about the Dow, Futures Index, or price of gold. In fact, one story goes that the average businessperson will spend considerable time and effort pricing and selecting the right tie for a suit, yet will drop several thousand dollars on a stock based on a "hot tip" from someone who goes to the same health club!

So let's take a closer look at some of the more familiar ones. Stock indexes and averages are used in technical analysis. Technical analysis refers to the study of all factors related to the actual *supply and demand* of stocks. Stock charts and various technical indicators are the technical analyst's tools. In contrast, fundamental analysis is the study of all relevant factors (economic data, company fundamentals, industry conditions, etc.) that can influence the future course of corporate earnings and dividends and, thus, stock prices. The technician looks at who's buying, whether the price is up, and what the investor sentiment is, whereas the fundamentalist analyzes company management, the financial statements, the market, and the product. The technical approach has most frequently been helpful for determining the timing of a transaction, either a purchase or a sale. (However, long-term investors find that it has proved less than satisfactory for their purposes.)

Dow Jones Industrial Average (DJIA). The DJIA or Dow is the most commonly quoted average as well as the longest running stock average in the world. At 30 stocks, it is a relatively small average, but those 30 stocks are the most widely recognized of the "blue chips." *Blue chips* is a term used to describe what are considered to be high-quality stocks from stable, long-established companies. If the market closed "up" 20 points, then those 30 stocks averaged a rise of 20 points for the trading session. Similarly, if it closed "down" 20 points, those same stocks averaged a fall of 20 points. (A point equals one dollar as it refers to the stock market index.) Incidentally, a prolonged surge in the DJIA upward indicates a Bull Market; a sustained surge downward indicates a *Bear Market.*

The DJIA first appeared in 1896, 14 years after Charles Dow and Edward Jones formed a company whose purpose was to produce unbiased, honest news stories about business. In 1928 the DJIA became the 30-stock index it remains today. (Don't be misled by that; occasionally one stock is replaced by another, but the DJIA is still composed of 30 individual stocks.) Some of the stocks represented include: IBM, General Electric, General Motors, Disney, Texaco, etc. (For a look at the stocks which actually make up the Dow, see Table 3-1.) All of these stocks pay a regular dividend (although the DJIA is quoted without considering the dividend) and rarely run into financial problems.

In 1928, the Dow Jones Average rose above 200 points for the first time. It had almost doubled before the crash of 1929, and did not go over 200 again until 1950. In the next 26 years (1928–1954) it would rise only 100 points. After 60 years the DJIA finally made its first 500-point move (1986), and then, October 19, 1987, it dropped 500 points in one day. (That drop was called a financial accident, a disaster, and numerous other names—but to this day, we still don't know all the reasons why it happened, even after the results of the special commission investigation, the Brady Report.) If you look at the DJIA for the period 1965 to 1990, and adjust for inflation, you will find that it is worth only three-quarters of its 1965 value. But keep in mind that the 30 stocks of the Dow (which are each assigned a "weight") represent only 1.3 percent of all listed New York Stock Exchange (NYSE) securities.

Although not as popular as the DJIA, there are a few other Dow Jones averages to be familiar with. They include the *Dow Jones Transportation*

Table 3-1. Stocks of the Dow Jones Industrial Averages

Alcoa	Exxon	Minn. Mining
Allied-Signal	General Electric	Philip Morris
American Express	General Motors	Procter & Gamble
AT&T	Goodyear	Sears Roebuck
Bethlehem Steel	IBM	Texaco
Boeing	Intl. Paper	Union Carbide
Caterpillar Inc.	J.P. Morgan	United Tech.
Chevron Corp.	Kodak	Walt Disney Co.
Coca-Cola	McDonald's	Westinghouse
Du Pont	Merck	Woolworth

SOURCE: *The Wall Street Journal,* May 3, 1991. Effective with trading Monday, May 6, 1991, Caterpillar, Disney, and J.P. Morgan were added to the Dow and Navistar, Primerica, and USX Corp. were removed.

Average, consisting of 20 common stocks including airlines, trucking companies, and railroads; the *Dow Jones Utility Average*, consisting of 15 major utility companies throughout the United States (which have performed consistently and excellently over the past three decades); and the *Dow Jones Composite Average*, representing the 65 stocks included in the industrial, transportation, and utility averages.

Standard & Poor's 500 Index (S&P 500).   This index includes over 500 stocks from the 83 industrial groups, which are broken down into four indexes: Industrial, Transportation, Financial, and Public Utilities. These are normally smaller capitalized stocks. The primary difference between the Standard & Poor's 500 Index and the DJIA (other than sheer numbers) is that the S&P 500 Index is based on the total market value of all shares of the common stocks of companies it represents in the index and the DJIA is simply a weighted average of the prices of its 30 stocks based on a very complicated formula. Total market value of the S&P 500 is around $2.0 trillion. The S&P 500 is used as one of the leading economic indicators, representing stock market activity, by the U.S. Commerce Department. The S&P 500 should not be confused with the less familiar S&P 400. The S&P 400 is comprised of smaller companies.

New York Stock Exchange (NYSE) Index.   The NYSE was founded in 1792 to provide a facility for the orderly trading of selected securities. The NYSE publishes a composite index of *all* its listed stocks. Membership is limited to 1366 members. A member is an individual (not a firm) who owns a seat on the exchange. The NYSE Composite Stock Index was initiated in 1966 and provides a comprehensive measure of market trends on the NYSE.

The NYSE categorizes its index into four groups: Industrial, Transportation, Utilities, and Finance. About 80 percent of the total market value of the NYSE is represented by the S&P 500. The largest equity marketplace in the United States, the NYSE is responsible for 80 percent of all volume traded domestically. All transactions in listed securities take place on the floor of the exchange between competing buyers and sellers.

National Association of Securities Dealers Automated Quotation System (NASDAQ).   NASDAQ is recognized as the automated version of the old Over-the-Counter (OTC) market, which was the first marketplace for securities trading in the United States. It is a communications system designed to make quotes on OTC securities (generally securities not listed on exchanges) available to members and nonmembers. Rather than showing actual trades, it reflects only the bid and ask for the security. It is the second largest securities marketplace in the United

States and the third largest in the world (following the New York Stock Exchange and the Tokyo Exchange), comprised of 5300 domestic and foreign securities representing over 4500 companies. Its trading volume increased 1600 percent during the 1980s.

NASDAQ employs sophisticated computerized systems to monitor securities transactions. These systems were designed with the capacity to handle the more than 300 million-share standard trading days which are anticipated in the future.

One outstanding feature of the NASDAQ is the market link established with the London Stock Exchange—the first such intercontinental link of major world markets. The advanced computerized systems, the intercontinental link, and the free play of economic forces determining the number of market makers in any NASDAQ security all contribute to its accelerated growth.

NASDAQ differs from the NYSE and the AMEX primarily in its method of trading. In the OTC/NASDAQ markets there are no specialists trading securities so market makers compete in a free marketplace which is less stringent and formalized than the NYSE and the AMEX.

National Market System (NMS).   Created in 1982, it combines the standard features of NASDAQ with reports of actual transaction prices. Presently there are a large number of issues trading as NASDAQ NMS with additional issues continually being added. Apple Computer, MCI Communications, American Greetings and Adolph Coors represent the type of prominence of many of the companies included in the NASDAQ National Market. The Federal Reserve Board has stated that all securities included in the NASDAQ NMS are marginable—such a statement is an indication of the strength of the National Market.

Value Line Composite Index.   With about 1700 common stocks, it represents 97 industry groups. Its composition changes slightly from time to time. Some people consider it the best indication of the movement of equity portfolios held by the average investor. When market watchers want an unbiased reflection of the performance of the broad equity marketplace, they turn to the Value Line Composite.

The Value Line Composite Index is produced by Value Line, Inc., which was founded by the late Arnold Berhard during the Depression. Even though it has underperformed the S&P 500 and the DJIA, most still feel that it is the most accurate reflection of the average investor's portfolio.

American Stock Exchange (AMEX).   This is the second largest stock exchange in the United States. In addition to stock, it handles transactions in bonds and options. Until 1958 it was known as the New York Curb Exchange.

Business Cycle

A business cycle (which describes the expansion or contraction of the economy as a whole) has four phases: expansion, peak, recession, and trough. Expansion represents a period of growth; peak refers to the highest point of the growth phase; recession is a slowdown of growth; and the trough phase is the lowest point of the cycle. These cycles create price changes which ultimately lead to inflation or deflation. The root causes of inflation and deflation lie in the change of total money spent in relation to the amount of goods and services offered for sale.

Consumer Price Index (CPI)

CPI is a consumer-oriented measurement of inflation. A group of over 300 goods and services, which are considered to affect the majority of consumers in the United States, is tracked with the changes in their prices being recorded. Data is collected from such places as grocery stores, department stores, gas stations, and other places of business. Certain items have a higher value than others, such as rent, transportation, and food and beverages.

Don't necessarily believe what the federal government says the CPI is in any given year because, like inflation, CPI is a very personal, subjective measurement. Specifically, try to convince the parents of three college-age children that inflation is only averaging 5 percent a year when their kids' tuition went up 18%. The retired man living in Arizona on a fixed income would disagree that inflation is averaging in the single digit range when the cost of the medication he must take daily to control his blood pressure has risen 220 percent during the past 10 years.

Increases in CPI and inflation are two very important reasons why you need to make your money grow. Where you are economically, your medical needs, and your family situation will determine how you are affected by increases in CPI and inflation. It is especially important to those individuals who are part of the "sandwich generation." These are the couples—generally in their fifties—that have the dual responsibilities of children with college expenses and parents who require custodial or nursing home care. Those couples sandwiched between providing for the financial needs of the older and the younger generation are the "sandwich generation."

Disposable Personal Income

Simply stated, personal income is all of your income from all sources before the deduction of any personal income taxes (as well as some other taxes) and with no adjustments for inflation. The U.S. Department of Commerce tracks our per capita personal income each year. It provides national and regional studies. Don't be misled by references to disposable personal income as defined by the federal government—it does not take into account inflation, taxes, clothing, food, or shelter. Most of us consider our disposable personal income as that which we have left *after* all those considerations.

Federal Reserve System (the Fed)

The Federal Reserve System, established by an Act of Congress in 1913, is the nation's central bank. The act divided the country into twelve Federal Reserve districts with the responsibility for coordinating the activities of the district banks resting with the Fed's Board of Governors in Washington, D.C. This board is appointed by the president with confirmation by the Senate. It was designed to operate independently of the current political powers by appointing its members to lengthy and staggered terms of service. Whether or not this independence has been achieved is debatable. Additionally, most of us aren't aware that the Fed operates as a for-profit organization with the profits being given back to the federal government.

By law, the Fed works to control the money supply in order to moderate or prevent the severity of inflation and depression. The Fed has four of its own tools to control or influence the money supply:

1. Open market operations—buying and selling government securities (Treasury bills, notes, and bonds)—are used to implement monetary policy in order to add cash to or take it away from the money supply. This is the method most frequently used. It is the most effective and flexible method, and the easiest to reverse.

2. The Fed can change the amount of reserves commercial banks are required to hold against their deposits. Even a small change will create a massive change. If a bank has to hold (reserve) more of its deposits, then it has less to lend. Conversely, if that reserve requirement is reduced, then it has more to lend.

3. The discount rate—the rate of interest the Fed charges a commercial bank to borrow—can be changed. An increase in the rate tightens money while a decrease eases the money supply. This tool is used infrequently by the Fed. Its use usually indicates a shift or reversal in monetary policy.

4. The Fed can raise or lower margin requirements. A margin requirement is the minimum percent of total value investors must deposit to purchase or sell securities in a margin account. The initial margin requirement for stocks (not all stocks qualify) has been raised twelve

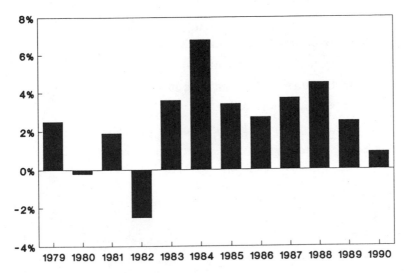

Figure 3-2. Growth of the real gross domestic product (GDP). Note the changes in percentages from year to year. (*Source: U.S. Department of Commerce.*)

times and lowered ten times by the Fed. But this is its least effective tool for controlling credit because it only affects the stock market. The first three tools affect the entire banking system.

Gross Domestic Product (GDP)

The United States GDP (formerly known as GNP—Gross National Product) measures the value of the output of all the goods and services produced by the United States in a 1-year period. The GDP is the largest individual measure of economic activity in the United States and, as such, indicates the economic health of our country. Refer to Figure 3-2 for an illustration of the changes in the growth of real GDP. The U.S. Department of Commerce releases these figures quarterly and seasonally adjusts them to an average annual rate. *Real GDP* means that the monetary figures have been adjusted for inflation.

Index of Leading Economic Indicators

Every investor's dream is to own a crystal ball. We all want to know what will happen to the economy in the future. The U.S. Department of Commerce is trying to help. It produces the Index of Leading (as in direction) Economic Indicators, designed to forecast economic trends, which is a fairly accurate predictor of the economic health of the country when looked at over the long-run, not just a month-at-a-glance. The Index of Leading Economic Indicators includes:

Average workweek for industrial workers

New claims for state unemployment insurance

New orders for consumer goods

Companies receiving slower deliveries from vendors

Net new business formations

Industry orders for new equipment

New building permits

Net changes in inventories

Crude materials prices

Changes in consumer and business credit outstanding

Stock prices (500 common stock issues)

Money supply (M_2)

Individual components are subject to revision if they distort certain data or the whole picture. At best you can hope that they are right, but remember that these figures are just a barometer—no one has the ability to accurately forecast the future.

Inflation

Probably the term we are most familiar with, even from childhood, is *inflation* (frequently illustrated by the Consumer Price Index or CPI rate). That's understandable because the United States has a long history of inflation, with available records dating back to the 1800s. During the period 1900 to 1980, the average annual rate of inflation was 2.5%; but since 1970 the rate has been 6.25%. Price increases since 1950 are greater than the total level of price increases in the preceding 100 years.

Inflation is the rate of increase of prices over a period of time; if an item costs more today than it did last year, obviously you can buy less of that item for the same price. In 1969 a gallon of premium gasoline cost 24 cents, today that same gallon of gasoline costs $1.24. Inflation is the exact opposite of deflation—*deflation is a decline in the price level that causes the purchasing power of money to rise.* In 1940, if your mother's mission was to put as much bread on the table as possible with one dollar, she could come home from the store with at least 10 loaves of bread. Today she would be lucky to buy 1 loaf of bread with that same dollar—that is inflation. Inflation is a very individual measurement. For example, the taxes on the home that I live in rose 28% during one recent year, yet taxes on a comparable home on the west coast of Florida rose only 9% during that same period. Now, who would you guess thought the rate of inflation was higher?

Ironically, since 1960, the higher the rate of inflation, the lower the level of unemployment, thereby providing what might be the only good news about inflation. When wages (or the levels of employment) go up, price increases inevitably follow. Experts agree that the most watched indicator for renewed inflation is labor expense—those expenses make up two-thirds of the Gross Domestic Product. When labor costs rise, then the price of the product will almost always increase. Just look at the rate of inflation over the last two decades along with the unemployment (average annual) rate for the period 1971 through 1991, as shown in Table 3-2.

Table 3-2. Comparison of Consumer Price Index (CPI), Unemployment, and Prime Rate, 1971–1991

Year	CPI change* (in percents)	Unemployment rate (annual average, in percents)**	Prime rate[†] (in percents)
1991	3.90	7.1	6.50
1990	6.11	6.1	10.00
1989	4.65	5.3	10.50
1988	4.42	5.5	10.50
1987	4.43	6.2	8.75
1986	1.10	7.0	7.50
1985	3.80	7.2	9.50
1984	3.95	7.5	11.06
1983	3.79	9.6	11.00
1982	3.83	9.7	11.50
1981	8.92	7.6	15.75
1980	12.52	7.1	20.35
1979	13.29	5.8	15.30
1978	9.02	6.1	11.55
1977	6.70	7.1	7.75
1976	4.86	7.7	6.35
1975	6.94	8.5	7.26
1974	12.34	5.6	10.50
1973	8.71	4.9	9.75
1972	3.41	5.6	5.79
1971	3.27	5.9	5.25

*SOURCE: U.S. Department of Commerce.
**SOURCE: U.S. Department of Labor, Bureau of Labor Statistics.
†Average bank rate at year's end.

Money Supply

Money is the "unit of value" by which goods and services are measured and the "medium of exchange" through which business is transacted. The Fed uses its tools to try to control the supply of money and credit so the amount of each remains correctly proportioned to effect maximum conditions which, hopefully, will create a stable, growing economy. If the money supply expands too rapidly in relationship to the economy's production of goods and services, it could lead to inflation. But if the money supply doesn't keep pace with the economy's productions, prices will fall and production might slow down, leading to unemployment. If unchecked, a depression will result.

There are two types of money: currency—which includes paper money and (sometimes) coins—and deposits—which include demand deposits on interest- and noninterest-bearing checking accounts as well as deposits which are less accessible, such as savings accounts, mutual funds, money market accounts, etc.

All money is not equal. Liquidity or accessibility provides an important basis on which several categories of money have been developed for representing and measuring money supply. For reference, these categories are called M_1, M_2, M_3, and L. Table 3-3 defines the various types of money supplies.

Prime Rate

Prime rate is a financial standard quoted in newspapers and magazines and broadcast over radio and television. Many financial analysts precede their statements with "If the prime rate . . . ." So what is it? Simply, *the prime rate is the interest rate banks charge their most creditworthy customers— those whose ability to repay the loan presents the least risk.* If you read that the prime rate is at 7 percent, that is the best indicator you can get of where interest rates are at that time. But the prime rate is the rate quoted for the pure use of money; the rate you end up with may have to take other details into consideration, such as your past history, risk involved, etc. It is affected by the costs of a bank's borrowing from the Federal Reserve, Treasury bills, commercial paper, and money market fund interest levels.

Most banks across the nation stay in sync with the general prime rate quoted and money is then loaned to small or less well established businesses at about 2 percent above prime rate. Under some circumstances, a bank will loan money at a rate lower than the prime to its best customers. Viewed in this light, the prime rate becomes an indicator of the rate at which a bank can easily lend money and still profit. Recently some of

Table 3-3. The M Categories for Measuring the Money Supply

M_1

1. Currency (including coin) in the hands of the public
2. Travelers checks
3. Demand deposits (balance in checking accounts)
4. Balances in NOW and Super NOW accounts
5. Balances in accounts with Automatic Transfer Service (ATS)
6. Balances in credit union share draft accounts

M_2

1. All the categories of M_1
2. Savings and small time deposits (less than $200,000) at depository institutions
3. Overnight repurchase agreements with maturities longer than one day at commercial banks and savings and loan associations
4. Certain Eurodollar deposits
5. Shares in money market mutual funds held primarily by households and small businesses

M_3

1. All of the categories of M_1 and M_2
2. Large time deposits ($100,000 or more) at depository institutions
3. Repurchase agreements with maturities longer than one day at commercial banks and savings and loan associations
4. Shares in money market mutual funds which are used by large financial institutions and corporations

L

M_3 plus other liquid assets such as term Eurodollars held by nonbank U.S. residents, bankers' acceptances, commercial paper, Treasury bills, and other liquid government securities and U.S. savings bonds.

SOURCE: For M categories, "What's All This About the M's?" Federal Reserve Bank of New York, July 1983.

the major mutual funds have also begun to benefit from the interest levels of the prime rate by offering funds which invest in the loans made by banks at the prime rate.

At one point in our history the prime rate was very predictable. For 14 years, from 1933 to 1947, the prime rate stayed at a record low of 1.5 percent. Then it began a roller coaster ride with tremendous swings up and back down. Over the next 31 years, the prime rate changed 143 times, followed by 112 changes in just the next 6 years (1978–1984). In 1991 we experienced 6 changes.

The changes in prime rate have a tremendous emotional effect on the informed person. Consider the business person who is borrowing at 9 percent to build a new plant. Suddenly the rate jumps to 15 percent and then swings down to 11 percent. How do you plan? When do you build? When do you buy inventory and when do you borrow? So the typical business person might be less interested in knowing when we have a high prime, as in seeing a steady prime rate maintained.

In April 1980, the prime rate hit a mind-boggling 20 percent, but barely 3 months later dropped to 11 percent—only to climb to a record high of 21.5 percent in December of that same year! When the prime rate dropped to under 9 percent it was paralleled by an inflation rate below 5 percent. Given the close relationship between the prime rate and inflation, if inflation goes higher, you might expect that the prime rate will also climb.

Summary

This is not an all-inclusive list of "tools." There are numerous other indicators, such as what is going on internally in our country—political instability, failed industry, the state of the national debt, and on and on. You also have to look outside our country to see what is going on worldwide, economically and politically.

The important point is that you do have tools available to you, so be aware of them and use them to your advantage.

4

The Role of the Adviser

When talking to a financial professional, there are no dumb questions.

FREEDOM FOCUS

- *Which professionals should you consider in your selection process?*
- *What are the questions you should ask?*
- *How do you investigate these professionals?*

Choose Carefully

If you are a sports fan, you are undoubtedly familiar with the critical decision making all coaches face once a year. They have to pick the right players for their teams if they want a winning season. You may never have thought of yourself in this light before, but you are a coach too. The team you have to put together will consist of your financial advisers and it will last season after season if you pick your players wisely the first time. But your team cannot afford to play games because they are dealing with your financial future.

Too many people unwisely trust luck to lead them to competent financial advisers, and, once they have found some likely candidates, they fail to ask any questions except, "How much do you charge?" This pattern can be attributed to at least two factors.

1. Because the various aspects of financial planning are somewhat complex, most people are eager to find someone who seems capable of handling this job, and so they may latch onto the insurance agent who calls out of the blue or the stock broker who answers the phone in the local branch of a brokerage firm.

2. The value we place on higher education leads us to assume that anyone with a degree must be competent.

You should question the competence and dedication of anyone being considered for your financial planning team. Wouldn't it be wonderful if there existed an informational and statistical index to assist you in selecting your financial professionals? It's an excellent idea, because it would help us to tell the professionals who are truly worthy of our trust from those who are just barely qualified to be in business. Unfortunately, it is left up to the individual to perform the necessary research. The professional that you select should understand your goals and objectives, your willingness to take risks with your money, your financial strengths and weaknesses. This person must have the same information with regard to your spouse and any of your children who are old enough to take personal charge of assets they might inherit from you. In short, this professional must know all about the corporation that is your personal financial situation and what it is about your family business that makes it different from all others.

In considering your draft choices, look for people who have the time and inclination to treat you as an individual and who express a willingness to work as team members rather than solo performers. Beware of the financial professional who is so busy that he or she scarcely has time to talk to you for 5 minutes on the phone; who doesn't ask you about the plans, goals, and dreams that make you different from other clients; who claims to have expertise in areas that fall outside his or her specialty; and who seems less than enthusiastic at your suggestion that he or she establish contact with others on your financial planning team. Such people are working more in their own interests than in yours.

Financial planning is a very personal business. It's not just putting together a balance sheet or statement of net worth—that's mechanical. The real challenge is to find a person who is also sensitive to your needs and desires. The professional should recognize that while you may look exactly like the last client visited, you have needs inherent to your personal situation. When you visit a professional with whom you are considering embarking on a long-term relationship, you should walk away from that meeting feeling like this person knows you as an individual—not just as client number 181.

For example, I recently met with a client who was widowed at age 59 after 40 years of marriage. Her husband ran two major businesses and she managed the household and the care of the family. As a result, she had not been involved in business or investment decisions. The husband took charge of those aspects. Unexpectedly she became the head of their "family corporation" after spending 40 years of marriage never having made an investment decision. Does that present a whole set of its own problems? The answer is, "Yes!" If I, as the professional, don't take all these facts into consideration, then I am short-changing my client. I make it a part of my evaluation to try to put myself into my client's shoes and be aware of the emotions that might be relative to the financial planning process of that particular individual.

Another meeting involved a respected surgeon, his wife, myself, and two attorneys. The attorneys were discussing trust arrangements for this family. As all the related terminology was being tossed about, I looked at the wife. Though she was nodding agreement I detected panic. I literally said, "Time out, guys," and stopped the meeting. I asked the wife if she really understood what the attorneys were trying to explain. She looked at me with relief and said that she did not understand the technical terms and explanations. At that point we all began to communicate—to speak in terms that we all could understand rather than in professional jargon. After the attorneys left, the doctor and his wife both expressed their appreciation for the new degree of comfort they felt about the arrangements being made on their behalf. Knowledge, education, and background are extremely important—but all things being equal, select the professional who communicates an understanding of you as a distinct individual. Where do you begin?

Ask Questions

In the absence of an index of competence, you must devise some method of rating the professionals yourself. I know of only one method, and that is *asking questions*. You should go into your first meeting with your financial planner, stock broker, insurance agent, or any other financial adviser prepared to ask *everything* you need to know in order to evaluate his or her ability to serve you well.

What is a good question? *Any* question that you want to have answered, including the very basic ones that you're afraid will sound stu-

pid, is a good question. There are *no* dumb questions. The only dumb
question is the one you will not ask—maybe because you fear being em-
barrassed or maybe because you are intimidated by the professional. In
fact, these are often the best questions to ask because they will bring you
the fundamental information that will give you some insight into the
specialties of various types of advisers. If you don't know the difference
between term and whole life insurance, ask about it. If you've never *really* understood what selling a stock short is all about, ask for an explanation. Ask the potential members of your financial planning team
everything up to and including their shirt sizes, if this information will
help you decide whether to entrust the important task of handling your
money to them.

Some specific questions you should ask any of these professionals
should include questions about their background, education, and experience:

How long has the practitioner been working with clients in the total
financial planning process?

What type of clientele does the practitioner serve? (Some practices are
limited to specific groups or types.)

Will he or she provide references and a sample financial plan?

How is the practitioner compensated and should you expect additional charges for periodic reviews and revisions?

Does his or her area of expertise include investments, insurance
and/or tax strategies, and retirement planning?

Will the planner provide specific or generic investment advice and will
it be in the form of a written plan with strategies to meet specific
goals?

Does the planner have a close working relationship with other professionals such as accountants or attorneys (very important)?

Will the person you are talking to be the person with whom you will
be working, or only be coordinating the efforts of those developing
your plan?

What special licenses and registrations does he or she have? For instance, is he or she registered with the state (if required) as an investment adviser? Is he or she registered by the Securities and Exchange
Commission or the National Association of Securities Dealers?

Another area that can't be stressed too much is *disclosure, disclosure,
disclosure.* An investment firm or individual should have a printed disclo-

sure statement of the operation and principals. This statement will provide some background on each of the principals, history of the corporation, methods of operation, and the fees that they charge. If professionals in this field cannot provide you with such a statement, be very cautious in further dealings with them.

Since selecting the right advisers is one of the most important steps you will take in your march toward financial independence, it is important to look at the types of financial advisers you are likely to need and the guidelines you should use in determining their probable ability to serve you well.

The Professionals

Attorneys

Many people view attorneys as all-knowing individuals whose advice and counsel should be sought on a wide variety of matters, from drawing up wills to evaluating "hot tips" on the stock market and tax incentive programs. Because lawyers attend college for 6 to 8 years, they are often thought to be broadly educated men and women who are well equipped to give expert advice on questions that fall outside their area of specialization. It is not my intention to downgrade attorneys in any way, but something needs to be said about choosing attorneys for financial counsel.

First, you must determine what service you can expect, keeping in mind that an attorney *must* have the time and ability to gain extensive knowledge of your personal situation, in all its aspects, so that he or she is well equipped to counsel you on the matters that you present.

Most attorneys today are specialists, owing to the complexities of the law in all areas of society. It is advisable to avoid anyone claiming he or she can handle any and all matters you might want to discuss. In any case, your major concern will be the attorney's experience in financial matters. This is not to say that you should avoid a law firm that handles a number of different specialties and refers cases from one in-house attorney to another. This type of firm, in fact, is becoming more and more popular because of its built-in versatility. In any case, your major concern will be the attorney's experience in financial matters.

Which of your financial concerns are appropriate to bring to your attorney? Obviously, only an attorney is qualified to draw up legal documents, so any financial transaction that requires legally binding documentation should be handled by an attorney. And this means "handled" in the most complete sense of the word. Your attorney should be willing to take personal charge of every matter that you bring to him or her, regardless of its "routine" nature or modest dimensions. He or she should understand the part that each transaction plays in your overall plan, and he or she should give evidence of this understanding through his or her ability to ask intelligent questions.

Specific documents lawyers normally draw up include (but are not limited to):

Wills and living wills

Power of attorney

Durable power of attorney

Pre-nuptial agreements

Trust agreements

Buy–sell agreements between business partners

Real estate transactions

Beware of the attorney who turns out stereotyped legal "boiler-plate," which in this age of the word processor is very popular in some law firms. You should be offended if your attorney sends you a "standard" letter or draws up a "standard" contract for you, since such treatment indicates that your attorney may not be willing to put time and effort into writing legal instruments tailored precisely to your needs and wishes.

Should you consult your attorney on the advisability of making an investment? No. Not unless he or she is a registered investment adviser with the Securities and Exchange Commission and with the state, where appropriate. Most attorneys will not put themselves in a position of passing judgment on an investment unless this is their field of expertise or they are actively involved in the investment. This does not mean, of course, that you should not consult him or her on the legal aspects of any investment you might be considering. But asking your attorney to advise you on the money-making potential of an investment opportunity is not fair, because the attorney usually has no special training in evaluating and selecting such vehicles. One mark of good lawyers is their unwillingness to dabble professionally in fields outside their area of competence. Value your attorney for the sound professional services he or she renders, and respect your attorney for acknowledging that he or she, like each of us, has limitations. Your attorney will be more useful to you in the long run if you both recognize that these limitations do exist.

Make sure that the attorney you select is willing to be a team player. He or she should have no reservations about sitting down periodically with your other advisers to exchange ideas and discuss your overall game plan.

You should also find out whether your attorney has a close, mutually rewarding relationship with a financial institution. If he or she is a board member of a bank or has any other close tie with a financial institution, he or she may see the channeling of funds to that institution as one of his or her most important functions. In some cases, for example, a bank will direct a depositor to a particular attorney for the purpose of drawing up a will and that attorney, in turn, will recommend that the bank be named executor or personal representative under the will. This type of "sweetheart" arrangement is neither illegal nor unethical, but you should be aware of its existence before you decide to retain an attorney. (The key is disclosure. Without that you cannot make valid decisions.)

If you absolutely don't know where to start, begin with the Martindale-Hubbell Law Directory, available in most public libraries, which provides a geographical list of attorneys in the United States, along with their educational background. An excellent reference is your state's Bar Association. They will provide you with the names of attorneys with expertise in the areas in which you are interested.

Accountants

There is a common misconception that an accountant is someone you only consult at tax time. In most cases, in February or March, we bring to the accountant our shoe-box full of receipts for the preceding year to plan our taxes. The year has already ended—is that tax planning? No it isn't. Are you in need of a CPA or a bookkeeper at that point? Tax planning cannot take place after the year is over. Since your accountant is the member of your team responsible for calculating your taxes, he or she, too, should have an accurate, running overview of your entire financial situation. To give him or her such a comprehensive overview, you should be in touch *quarterly* so that he or she can run a pro-forma on your income—an analysis aimed at predicting your tax obligation. If there *is* one time of year to be more concerned about seeking your accountant out, that time would be January 1. Why? Because the beginning of the year is the best time to discuss whether you will need sound tax planning to reduce your income tax obligation during the year ahead.

Even if your income is not yet in the six-figure category, do not ignore the potential benefits of tax incentive programs and proper accounting advice. As your wage-earning year begins, you and your accountant should explore all options that are available to reduce your tax obligation.

Remember that there must be sound economics behind any tax incentive program that you enter. Historically, a great number of us have made many of our investment decisions by the "tax-tail that wags the dog." We should take the opposite approach: Investment decisions should be made on the merits of the investment—on making money, whether it be from real estate, mutual funds, annuity programs, etc. If you have a tax savings at the same time, great, but don't lose sight of making money. I like to remind people that "nothing of nothing is nothing." Does the principal invested grow? Is inflation likely to continue to grow? Important questions to ask about potential investments as tax-shelters are: Is the program designed to make a profit? If so, is it likely to make one? If the answer to either question is no, you could be penalized by the IRS, which in recent years has cracked down on programs that serve solely as tax shelters.

Unlike attorneys, many accountants are generalists rather than specialists, although some certified public accountants do specialize in certain areas. In this profession, too, you will find large firms consisting of specialists doing business together. Many accountants' primary expertise lies in record keeping, bookkeeping, and preparing of income tax returns. Most of them are also competent to advise you on trust-planning vehicles, the tax advantages connected with these vehicles, and structuring a business. Some specialize in bringing companies public and raising funds for expansion purposes.

If you do not want to retain an accountant to keep your financial records year-round, you can ask for tips on how to keep these records in good order yourself. Then, when your accountant prepares your income tax return, he or she will have all the information needed to do an accurate and thorough job.

Fees charged by accountants or CPAs vary widely, depending upon the services you wish to have performed and the complexity of your case. Some fees paid to attorneys, accountants, financial planners, and other advisers are tax deductible. Accountants and all other financial professionals discussed in this chapter should offer one meeting free of charge, at which your needs can be explored and you can become acquainted with your potential adviser. Since financial planning calls for long-term associations, you should retain only those individuals with whom you feel confident and comfortable. If mutual good feelings do not develop at the outset, you should probably try someone else. All fee and billing information should be made clear to you during your first meeting with a potential financial adviser.

In the case of an accountant, you can expect a small fee to be quoted for a simple service, such as the preparation of an uncomplicated tax return. If your tax return is lengthy and complex, however, and if you have to consult your accountant once per quarter, for a record review and a pro-forma, your annual fee might exceed $1000.

Stock Brokers

Your primary concern in selecting a stock broker is to find one who does not simply take orders. Unfortunately, this field has become an extremely broad one open to many individuals with only the most basic of qualifications and, many times, a lack of experience in real financial planning. Keep in mind that there are generally only two occasions when this type of broker makes money—when he or she buys stocks and when he or she sells stocks. You do not want to trust your financial planning to a broker of this calibre. Like all your financial advisers, your stock broker should know you personally. He or she should know how much you know about the market and why you are inquiring about a particular stock. Above all, he or she should know your tolerance, both financial and temperamental, for taking risks.

Good stock brokers earn their keep in many ways. As brokerage houses have diversified to deal in real estate, oil and gas ventures, insurance, annuities, commodities, gold and silver, and even rare coins, as well as the traditional stocks and bonds, many brokers have added to their personal credentials by becoming Certified Financial Planners, being Admitted to the Registry of Financial Planning Practitioners (see Financial Planner section in this chapter), Chartered Life Underwriters, or Chartered Financial Consultants (see Life Insurance Underwriters section in this chapter).

Your stock broker can help you make money by searching out investments suited to meet particular objectives, and he or she can help you save money by warning you to stay away from ventures that may, on their surface, look attractive. Because brokers are immersed in the investment world, they receive information that may never reach an outsider. Brokers use this in-house information (also called due diligence) to advise their clients on the pros and cons of various investments.

It is important to find a broker who has had substantial experience. There are a lot of stock brokers who have never experienced a bear market—a declining market that lasts over a drawn-out period of time, for example the 18-month period during 1973 and 1974. If they've only experienced bull markets—an increasing market where people make money—and not ever been embattled on the down side, they may lack the balance that comes from experiencing both markets. It's a kind of "market maturity" that comes from learning how to participate in the market defensively as well as offensively. These people will not panic, will not be afraid to talk to you, and will recognize that there are also opportunities that present themselves during a bear market. Ideally, your stock broker should also be a Certified Financial Planner (CFP) (see Financial Planner section in this chapter). This credential will become increasingly useful in the 1990s, which promises to be an economically complex decade. When opening an account with a stock brokerage house, try to identify the most experienced professional in the office through the office manager, other financial professionals in the community, or your friends who do business with the office. You might also spend a day or two in the office, watching the ticker tape and observing who seems to be the busiest, most productive broker of the group.

One type of account that I recommend you to stay away from is the full discretionary account. This is an account that gives the authority to the broker to buy and sell at any time without any discussion or approval from you. *Do not do that.* I have heard tales where accounts of many tens of thousands of dollars (and sometimes hundreds of thousands) were lost due to indiscriminate buying and selling from this type of account. Buyer beware! Also be sure that whatever brokerage firm you do business with has proper insurance coverage. Additionally, be cautious of accounts held in street names—where all the stocks and bonds bought are held in the name of the firm. Unless that firm is of a substantial nature, and you've done all your homework as to its insurance coverages, these types of accounts open the doors to the possibility of many problems, such as an unscrupulous broker trading or selling your stock and pocketing the profit.

Professional Money Managers

Not everyone needs the services of a professional money manager for his or her stocks, bonds, and money market instruments. A money manager is the person who is responsible for the daily management of the monies, whether they be in mutual funds or an advisory account, etc. As you would expect, a money manager is generally responsible for the management of very large sums of money. The certified financial planner is more of a quarterback. He or she puts all the pieces together—cash flow, tax needs, trust needs—and coordinates the various pieces to make sure the program is successful. However, if you plan to enter a serious long-term investment program involving a percentage of your serious money—that is, money you do not want to subject to high risk, you might want to hire a professional money manager. If you do hire a professional money manager, make sure he or she is registered as an investment adviser with the Securities and Exchange Commission. During the initial interview, ask the questions we discussed earlier in the chapter. Ask whether he or she receives commissions on the sale or purchase of securities. Such commissions are not illegal, but since they might affect the advice you are given, you have a right to know about them. Again, three of the most important considerations are disclosure, disclosure, disclosure.

Outside of integrity, it is most important to know about the performance of a professional money manager. You should therefore ask for a complete report of a potential money manager's performance on several different accounts during the past few years. You should know what the objectives of these accounts are—growth, for example, or income—and how well the money manager has guided each account toward its goal. The money manager should also give you information that will enable you to compare his or her performance with standard economic barometers such as the Dow Jones Industrial Average and Standard and Poor's Stock Index. This will enable you to put his or her performance into an overall economic perspective.

For a minute let's compare the professional money manager who manages portfolios for individual clients to the professional money manager who manages mutual fund portfolios. The big difference? Managers of the mutual funds have their performances printed as public record in newspapers across the nation *every day*. Obviously this is not the same with managers of private portfolios. How do you substantiate this money manager? If you are looking at records, make sure they are records which have been audited by independent CPAs not associated with the manager's firm. It is sometimes difficult to substantiate their records, but with the guidelines we've established thus far, you should be able to eliminate many of the questions.

Select a professional money manager who asks you questions. Such questions are a sign of the money manager's interest in finding the investment opportunities that will fit your financial situation. Of course, this adviser must be fully informed of your personal and financial goals, your family situation, your risk tolerance level, your financial "comfort zones"—those investment areas in which you feel at ease.

You should be ready to ask questions, too. A professional money manager worthy of your business will be happy to take as much time as is needed to answer them, and to provide you with a list of satisfied clients. Ask what type of accounts he or she manages—are they corporate or individual? Is he or she a long-term or short-term manager? Does he or she use technical input versus fundamental (see Appendix 3-2, Tools of the Trade)?

Fees charged by professional money managers normally start at about one half of 1 percent a year of the assets that are being managed, and run as high as 3 percent, depending upon the size of the portfolio and the attention it requires.

Life Insurance Underwriters

Probably no financial area is less understood by the general public than insurance, particularly life insurance. Your first step in obtaining insurance should be to understand the purpose or benefits of the insurance in question.

Here are some key questions to ask about a prospective life insurance underwriter:

Is he or she an independent agent or does he or she represent a single life insurance company?

Does he or she concentrate his or her efforts on selling permanent, cash value life insurance (policies with built-in "savings account" features), emphasize term life insurance protection (death benefits only), universal life (interest sensitive), or is he or she willing to explore your needs and desires before making a recommendation?

If he or she represents a single company, is this person willing to shop among other companies for the particular life insurance product that you want if his or her company doesn't sell it or might not be competitive in that area?

Above all, your life insurance underwriter should be willing and able to see your needs in a "big picture" framework. This type of underwriter will devote more than token effort to finding out what your current needs are and what your future needs are likely to be.

The premier designations among life insurance underwriters are Chartered Life Underwriter (CLU) and Chartered Financial Consultant (ChFC). To earn either of these titles, an underwriter must pass a series of very difficult examinations. A CLU, then, is usually a competent professional. Another way to investigate the professionalism and versatility of an underwriter is to ask whether he or she is licensed with the National Association of Securities Dealers (NASD). This license enables him or her to sell other products, such as variable annuities and mutual funds, and it will give you some insight into the professional's view of the scope of his or her work. An underwriter with NASD credentials will be able to offer you access to many more investment opportunities than one who deals solely in life insurance.

All too often, the Chartered Property Casualty Underwriter (CPCU) is overlooked whenever financial planning teams are assembled. Do not let this happen in your case. Few individuals will provide more valuable service to you than your property and casualty home and automobile agent. Only those who have demonstrated comprehensive professional knowledge through study and testing beyond that required for state certification are entitled to write CPCU after their names. This designation is awarded by the American Institute for Property and Liability Underwriters to those who take a series of comprehensive courses and examinations.

Life underwriters normally make their livings by commissions and there is nothing wrong with that, provided the product is right. The important question is this: Does your potential life insurance underwriter stress the investment merits of the program he or she wants to sell you over the death protection benefits? Remember that life insurance is designed, first and foremost, to protect your most precious capability—your earning power—against your premature death.

You must deal with a life insurance underwriter who understands your entire situation—your needs, your income capabilities, your investment philosophies and in the future.

Life insurance is the only product I know of that instantly creates a million dollar (or whatever amount you purchase) estate at the stroke of a pen and you pay for it as you go. Any other investment program is normally contingent on your having the time to live to its completion. Is there any guarantee on life? Clearly no. But consider for a moment just how challenging this is: If inflation averages a modest 5 percent a year for the next 15 years, and if you now need $25,000 annually to meet your obligations, 15 years from now you will need about $50,000 a year to buy exactly the same goods and services. You will therefore have to double the amount of money you earn just to keep pace with inflation.

Obviously, most whole life insurance policies will be of little or no use in meeting the inflation challenge. But there is a bigger picture to look at here—taking care of those you might leave behind, including business partners.

A truly professional life insurance underwriter will give you an honest accounting of the important differences that exist between policies. He or she will not insist that you consider only whole life because of its "investment value," but will encourage you to look into other types of financial programs in addition to insurance, for he or she will know that a sound mix of investments is necessary for you to reach your goals. Many underwriters also carry Certified Financial Planner (CFP) credentials (see Financial Planner section in this chapter). In recent years, in fact, the life insurance industry has turned its attention more and more to the delivery of comprehensive financial planning services, a trend that is likely to continue during the 1990s.

Bank Trust Officers

The bank trust officer, or some other representative of a bank trust department, is often useful to persons seeking confidential, trustworthy assistance in a financial management program. The institution can generally be relied upon to provide competent, professional services for as long as you or your heirs wish the services to be performed. That is important because if you, for example, appoint a daughter as a trust officer and you have a son-in-law or other children who could try to influence actions as they relate to the trust, it is possible that problems could arise. A bank trust officer can provide independent administration.

When dealing with a trust department, you will receive accurate monthly or quarterly computer printouts detailing all relevant financial data. You can give the bank varying degrees of responsibility for your funds, ranging from total control to the simple task of carrying out specific instructions.

Historically, these types of associations with banks offer low returns on investments, a consequence of the pronounced conservatism of most banking institutions. However, during the last decade (characterized by the savings and loans crisis) banks were not so conservative. They became more aggressive in their loaning pattern and in underwriting real estate. You can steer clear of these problems by combining the accounting services of a bank trust department with the professional services of a money management firm. Under this arrangement, the bank simply acts in a custodial capacity, keeping track of transactions, issuing checks, and carrying out similar functions. The money management firm makes all the strategic investment decisions.

Similarly, you can appoint a financially astute friend or business associate to administer your living trust or trust created under your will that cannot, for tax or other reasons, be handled by your spouse. The individual can be made a cotrustee with the bank (with the authority to "fire" the bank if he or she sees fit), or he or she can be made sole trustee with the power to select a bank. A word of caution: Some states do not allow you to act as your own trustee, be sure to check with your adviser. It makes sense to name a second trustee in your will or trust agreement, too, in case the individual who is your first choice dies or becomes disabled.

Few people are aware of the many moderately priced services that are available at their local banks. A bank can be the executor (also known as personal representative) of your will, for example. Or it can serve as your children's guardian in the event of the death of both parents. Or if you are in business, the bank can be asked to act as trustee in a buy–sell agreement between you and your associates.

A bank trust department can give you a wide range of investment, estate planning, and income tax planning ideas. Whatever your time of life or your financial situation, you should find out about available services from a local bank trust officer—even if you think that you are not yet ready to take advantage of those services or that you will never want them. If only for the sake of obtaining information, ask this officer what his or her department can do for you, how it will carry out its duties, how much these services will cost, and how the bank could interrelate with other members of your financial planning team.

You should also become acquainted with your everyday banking facilities (loans, mortgages) and other bank officials besides the trust officer. A loan officer, for instance, can provide sound business advice at no cost and may approve additional funds for you to put into your company, if you are looking for financial assistance. If you have never visited your bank and talked with one of the vice presidents about the institution's services, you should make such a trip a high-priority item on your calendar.

Financial Planners

The financial planner is the quarterback on your asset management team. This person will, among other services, perform an in-depth analysis of your financial situation, coordinate the activities of everyone else on your team, create a balanced investment program, and, in some cases, implement that program by buying and selling investments for you. Before you select someone to fill this vital role, remember that the profession of financial planning is a relatively new one. It has been in existence as a recognized discipline distinct from others in the financial arena since 1969. Many people lay claim to the title of financial planner, but few are really able to perform all the functions that the job entails.

Anyone you are considering retaining as your financial planner should give you concrete evidence of his or her competence and ability to relate to you as an individual. Again, you can learn a great deal about them by the questions they ask. Does he or she want to know about your hopes and plans? Does he or she ask about your financial background, where you are now, and where you want to go? Does he or she probe your comfort zones and your ability to face risk? Is he or she as interested in your spouse's strengths and weaknesses as in yours? Does he or she understand that planning must be done with the big picture of your family corporation in mind, and not just with an eye for short-term profit? Do you enjoy talking to and dealing with him or her? Do you intuitively trust this person?

One way to investigate the technical competence of a financial planner is to ask whether he or she has had training through the College for Financial Planning. The College for Financial Planning offers a six-course curriculum that leads to the designation Certified Financial Planner and qualifies one for testing administered by the International Board of Standards and Practices for Certified Financial Planners, Inc. (IBCFP).

This Certified Financial Planner curriculum consists of six comprehensive courses:

Fundamentals of Financial Planning

Insurance Planning

Investment Planning

Income Tax Planning

Retirement Planning and Employee Benefits

Estate Planning

The Registry of Financial Planning Practitioners is recognized within the industry as the only program which identifies individuals who have met professional financial planning standards and who practice financial planning as their primary vocation. The professional standards include educational, practice, experiential, and knowledge requirements. Requirements are stringent and applicants must be members in good standing with the IAFP.

Another indication of a financial planner's probable ability to serve you well is involvement at the grassroots level with others in his or her field. If he or she is active in the local chapter of the International Association of Financial Planning, he or she is most likely keeping abreast of current developments in the financial field by sharing ideas at meetings and reading professional publications.

You can obtain a list of qualified financial planners who work in or near your city by contacting either of these organizations at the following addresses:

International Association of Financial Planning, Inc.
Two Concourse Parkway, Suite 800
Atlanta, GA 30328

College for Financial Planning
4695 South Monaco Street
Denver, CO 80237-3403

You may also request, free of charge from the IAFP, the *Directory of the Registry of Financial Planning Practitioners*, the *Consumer Guide to Financial Independence*, and the *Financial Planning Consumer Bill of Rights*.

The fees that financial planners charge to create investment blueprints for clients vary considerably. The fee that you will be charged for particular services from any planner should be agreed upon during your first, no-charge meeting. At this time, you should also be told exactly what you can expect to receive for this fee.

Before you decide to retain a financial planner, you should ask for two or three professional references, such as attorneys, trust officers, or CPAs in the community who can vouch for the planner's character and competence. In addition, the planner should give you a disclosure statement with details of his or her background and the backgrounds of key staff members. The statement should also tell you how long the firm has been in business and how its fees are set. The company's principals and top-ranking employees (or the corporation itself) should in most cases be registered as investment advisers with the Securities and Exchange Commission, as well as the state in which they practice.

If additional fees might be charged in the future for services you do not now require, you should be informed of the probable amount and frequency of such fees. It is advisable to obtain a letter of intent from a financial planning firm before signing a contract. Even if you do sign a contract, you should be able to cancel it with no penalty within a specified time period, usually 3 to 5 days.

Select your financial planner carefully, because his or her expertise (or lack of it) in all phases of investments will have a far-reaching effect upon your life.

Keep in mind that all these designations generally require that the holder of the designation acquire continuing education credits. Ask the professionals you are meeting with if they participate in those requirements. It is one of the ways they stay current in the industry.

The American Marketplace: An Ever-Changing Challenge

Remember that no matter how competent and successful your financial planner is, *you* are always the chief operating officer of your family corporation. As such, you should never stop informing yourself on conditions in the marketplace and the constant stream of new investment vehicles that makes the American financial arena a place of unparalleled excitement and opportunity.

Again, when choosing your financial advisers, don't let the matter of their fees become the tail that wags the dog. Remember that your primary purpose is to obtain expert, individualized advice that will help you progress toward your goals. *Advisers who fill this bill will save you many times the amount of their annual fees in reduced taxes or will bring you many times those fees in profits realized from good investments.*

In Review

In review, you should look for appropriate education, licenses, and professional designations which may include:

Certified Financial Planner

Chartered Financial Consultant

Chartered Life Underwriter

Certified Public Accountant

Member of the Bar Association

Member, International Association for Financial Planning

Member, Registry of Financial Planning Practitioners

Membership in appropriate professional associations

Registered Representative with the Securities and Exchange Commission

Registered as an adviser with State or the NASD

Ask questions about background, education, experience, qualifications, professional affiliations and references, and methods of compensation. Meet with more than one professional before you make a decision. Check them out through the Chamber of Commerce and the Better Business Bureau.

You must be comfortable with the selection you make. Hopefully, you will be entering a long-term relationship with this person to plot a course to achieve your financial goals.

It is not my wish to create the impression that you need to hire a team of professionals that could, in fact, reduce the rates of returns on your investments because of all their fees. You might very well be able to do much of the planning yourself. What you need, in my opinion, is one person who is able to understand you, your strengths and weaknesses, your goals and objectives and guide you through this maze. And don't be passive in your financial planning. Be an active participant because you and your family members are the designers. Who knows you better than you and your family members.

There is tremendous knowledge available to you through the public and college libraries, financial planning and investing seminars, and community education. The media are doing a much better job of offering education to listeners and readers.

The key, however, is that the earlier you start, the better off you will be. You may decide to start with an IRA or a mutual fund for as little as $50. Or you may say, "I want to develop a plan now, while I'm relatively young and put it into action." If you can do that to your satisfaction, fine. If you are frightened or confused by all the terms and possibilities, select an adviser to assist you. Remember, it's not what you make, it's what you do with the money you make that counts.

5

The Personal Investment Pyramid

When properly constructed, this pyramid puts your investments into a balanced relationship and dramatically increases your ability to fight inflation and taxation. It provides you with a proper perspective for diversification.

FREEDOM FOCUS

- *How do you construct your personal investment pyramid?*
- *How do you find your comfort zone?*
- *What is the role of liquidity in your personal investment pyramid?*

What comes to mind when you think of a pyramid? King Tut, perhaps? The sphinx? Pyramid power? If you said "pyramid power," we're on the same wavelength, but I'd like to fine-tune your thinking past the plastic pyramids that will supposedly provide you with mystical powers. The kind of pyramid we are concerned with here packs the sort of power that can make a real difference in your life. When properly constructed, this pyramid puts your investments into a balanced relationship and dramatically increases your ability to wage the lifelong battle we all must join against inflation and taxation. So let's take a close look at it. The time you spend studying this pyramid will be worth more to you than any trip you might take to the Sahara to snap pictures of the Egyptian pyramids.

The pyramid's construction reflects the risk/reward characteristics of various types of investments. The pyramid is flanked by "bad news, good news" arrows. The bad news about investments situated *high* on the pyramid is that they carry a fairly great risk of loss of capital. The good news is that, if things go right, these investments will bring very large returns. The bad news about investments placed *low* on the pyramid is that the interest rates and dividends they pay usually fail to keep pace with inflation, especially when you take into consideration taxation. (The two evils of inflation and taxation eat away the purchasing power of your principal.) The good news is that it is unlikely you will ever lose your capital in one lump sum.

Put in somewhat different terms, what the pyramid illustrates is that there is no such thing as a riskless investment. Remember, every single investment that we own has a risk/reward ratio attached to it. You can relate that risk/reward to your personal life. Look at a skydiver and a couch potato—which one would you consider is the greatest risk taker? Most of us would select the skydiver. On the other hand, a couch potato could have a heart attack due to lack of exercise. What you must do as you look at any potential investment is identify the reward and see if you are willing to accept the risk associated with achieving the reward of that investment. Those investments located low on the investment pyramid guarantee (as much as possible) your principal, but time and inflation gradually erode the purchasing power of that principal. The higher you go up the pyramid, the less assurance you have that your principal will survive economic reverses, but the greater the potential will be for a large reward.

The pyramid reflects very individual value judgments. Where one or another type of investment should be placed is a highly subjective decision that is based on such factors as a person's willingness to take risks and his or her knowledge of particular investment vehicles. The pyramid that I have created in Figure 5-1 is for illustrative purposes only. This is a very personal thing and you might create one that is quite different, but still valid. Also, the pyramid constructed here is by no means all-inclusive. It contains what I think are good representative investment opportunities situated at various points on the risk/reward scale, but many additions could certainly be made. We have investment opportunities today that we didn't have a few years ago, such as collateralized

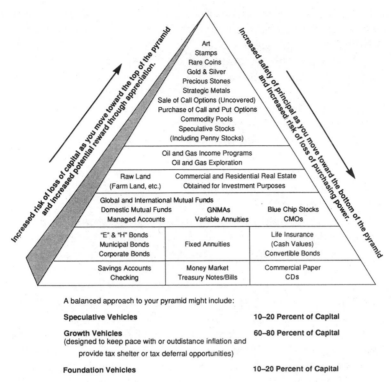

A balanced approach to your pyramid might include:

Speculative Vehicles   **10–20 Percent of Capital**

Growth Vehicles   **60–80 Percent of Capital**
(designed to keep pace with or outdistance inflation and
    provide tax shelter or tax deferral opportunities)

Foundation Vehicles   **10–20 Percent of Capital**

Figure 5-1. Example of a filled-in personal investment pyramid. Investment vehicles are distributed according to the example given below the pyramid.

mortgage obligations (CMOs), zero coupon bonds (tax-free and taxable), government security funds, junk bonds, etc.

When you build your own pyramid, you might want to add color to it to make it even more graphic. Very speculative investments, for instance, might be colored in red; middle-range investments might be toned down to orange; and your bottom rows might carry blue or green colors.

At or near the base of the pyramid we find vehicles that have traditionally been considered "safe," such as passbook savings accounts, bonds, and fixed annuities. These areas are generally thought to be secure investments in which your principal will remain protected forever, barring a worldwide depression that triggers the wholesale collapse of all the major economies. Right? Not quite. We have been shaken to our very foundations by upsets to what we have traditionally considered safe—the banking industry, savings and loan industry, and the life insurance companies. Also, while it is true that options at the bottom of the pyramid offer a high degree of safety, they do nothing to protect your principal against inflation, whose effect is greatest at the bottom of the investment pyramid.

Consider for a moment what can happen to $1000 that sits in a 7 percent certificate of deposit during a year when inflation is running at 5 percent. (This is for illustrative purposes only, please substitute the rate of CDs and the rate of inflation that apply to your frame of reference.) Your end-of-year statement will report that your money has earned $70 in interest. There is certainly more to the story than that, but the rest of it is never reported. If it were, here is how one such report might read:

> Dear Depositor:
>   First Federal is pleased to report to you that your $1000 certificate of deposit has earned $70 during the past calendar year. Unfortunately, the inflation rate has been 5 percent, which means that the purchasing power of your principal has been reduced by $50. As you can see, this has resulted in a net gain to you of $20. We look forward to serving you in the year ahead.

At that point, you would probably start looking for somewhere else to put your money, and with good reason. But the story isn't finished yet. That $70 in interest is fully taxable unless it is under a qualified program. If you and your spouse filing jointly are in a 30+ percent tax bracket, the federal government will claim 30 percent of that $70, or $21. That means you are now left with only $49 in spendable income from your $1000 "safe" investment, which has shrunk before your eyes to $950 and will continue to shrink for as long as inflation is with us.

What do you think of the safety of such a vehicle now? Are you beginning to recognize that there are no totally safe investment areas left? Are you beginning to see that to keep a step ahead of inflation and the tax collector, you will have to venture out of these areas at the bottom of the pyramid and move toward investments that carry greater risk and greater reward? And are these thoughts making you somewhat uncomfortable? If your answers to all the above questions are "yes," you are to be congratulated. The uneasiness that you are experiencing means that you are coming of age as an investor—a process that never occurs without some discomfort.

Investments and Your "Comfort Zone"

The "comfort zone" is an investment area that for some reason—longstanding habit, perhaps, or automatic acceptance of your parents' investment philosophy—offers the investor a sense of security. But we have just established that there is no real safety in these "guaranteed principal" vehicles. It is time, then, to take the first step toward introducing constructive change into your personal investment pyramid, and to recognize that if you are to be a successful investor you must evaluate each investment you hold in terms of its *total return* to you, not merely in terms of interest, dividends, or capital appreciation. Total return is the most important factor for you to consider as an investor (see Figure 1-4 to review how *total return* is computed).

This cannot be stated too often or too strongly: *We are in uncharted economic waters today. We have never before faced the worldwide political scenario that we face today: Berlin Wall down; changes in the former Soviet states; inflation rates up, down, sideways; interest rates up, down, sideways; etc.* These things mean more to you and me than an endless stream of disturbing headlines to be read over our morning coffee. They mean trouble, and big trouble, in our pocketbooks, both today and in the future. For the first time in our history as a nation, we are facing problems that are not likely to go away through negotiations, military action, or plain old good luck. We're in a whole new ballgame internationally, and you, as a person wise enough to want to begin building for the future of your personal family corporation right now, need to understand that the kind of financial planning that worked for our parents is not going to work for us. We're facing new problems and we must come up with new solutions. New solutions *are* available, but in order to take advantage of them, you have to be willing to take some degree of risk with a portion of your investment dollar. In other words, it is time to venture out of your comfort zone—not altogether, of course, but to an extent appropriate to your personal circumstances.

To give you some idea of the necessity of taking certain calculated risks, consider Table 5-1, which indicates the returns your investments

Table 5-1. Investment Pyramid Rates of Return Required to Beat Inflation

Income tax bracket	Inflation rate (in percentages)					
	3	5	7	8	10	12
15%	3.53%	5.88%	8.24%	9.41%	11.76%	14.12%
28	4.17	6.94	9.72	11.11	13.89	16.67
31	4.35	7.25	10.14	11.59	14.49	17.39

NOTE: Above figures based on joint return tax rates. Alternate minimum taxes (AMT) may require a higher pretax investment return to reach break-even.

will have to generate under various rates of inflation if you are simply to break even.

Spreading Your Risk

How much of your investment dollar should you put into high-risk, high-reward areas in order to meet the challenge of keeping pace with and, preferably, outdistancing inflation? This judgment has to be made by you and the other adults in your family in consultation with your financial adviser. One rule of thumb is to put no more than 10 to 20 percent of your money into the high-risk, high-reward areas at or near the top of the pyramid.

If you are still actively pursuing your career and are years away from retirement, you can afford to venture into comparatively high-risk areas because, if the money you put into a speculative investment disappears forever, you can earn it back. The loss will be a shock and a disappointment, of course, but it won't spell irreversible financial disaster for you. Still, even if you have the best of recovery potential, you should probably hold your high-risk investments to no more than 20 percent of your total portfolio.

If, on the other hand, you are close to or are in your retirement years, you must be more conservative about risk-taking because you have no way of replacing the dollars that might be lost to speculation. In this case, 5 to 10 percent of your investment dollars could be directed to the high-risk areas.

In either case, the bulk of your money should be placed into vehicles positioned around the center of the pyramid where you will face moderate risk and reap moderate rewards. It is advisable to keep 10–20 percent of your investment dollars in vehicles at the bottom of the pyramid. As you know, inflation will take its toll in this area, but at least your principal will not be lost in one fell swoop. A financial adviser who knows your emotional make-up and that of others in your family, your financial obligations, and your ability to replace lost wealth can help you to allocate appropriate portions of your investment dollar to each area of the pyramid as you progress toward and into retirement.

The pyramid is more than a graphic representation of the distribution of your investment monies. It is also useful in generating cash flow statements for your family corporation. These statements are important because they give you estimates of how much cash flow your investments are likely to produce for you during the year, and thus enable you to do some tax planning in advance. Remember, it is only through advance planning that you can hope to enter sensible investment programs that might have tax savings attached to them.

Liquidity

Because vehicles at the bottom of the pyramid tend to be liquid and those at the top to be nonliquid, by arranging your current portfolio in the framework of a pyramid you will be able to determine the extent of your liquidity at the present time. While you certainly would not want every one of your investments to be liquid, it would be prudent to make sure that at least most of them are. Think of the position of a surviving spouse who inherits an estate that is almost entirely nonliquid. It is not at all unusual for most of a businessperson's wealth to be tied to the stock of his or her company, which is most often a privately held concern. This type of stock cannot be traded on the open market, and, in fact, might lose a considerable amount of its ability to attract private purchasers when the original owner—very often a moving force in the business—dies. That stock may be worth $100,000 or $200,000 *on paper,* but what is its real value to your heirs, who may know little or nothing about the business that has issued it and who need to raise cash *immediately* to pay estate taxes.

To repeat: Think in terms of keeping enough of your holdings liquid to get your loved ones through the financial difficulty that your death or a major illness could cause and meeting the other short-term needs that could arise, such as a medical emergency, replacing or repairing a damaged vehicle, a down payment on real estate, or college tuition.

Rearranging Your Investment Pyramid

At this point, it would be useful to construct two investment pyramids, one showing your present investment distribution and one showing a more potentially profitable mix of vehicles. You can construct the first one yourself by simply penciling your current investments onto the blank pyramid shown in Figure 5-2. If you have any doubts about where a particular investment might fall on the pyramid, ask yourself if its main feature is safety of capital or growth potential. Place investments that preserve capital (or try to) near the bottom of your pyramid and place those that involve greater risk and greater potential reward toward the middle or top.

You will notice that this pyramid has a scale running alongside it. This

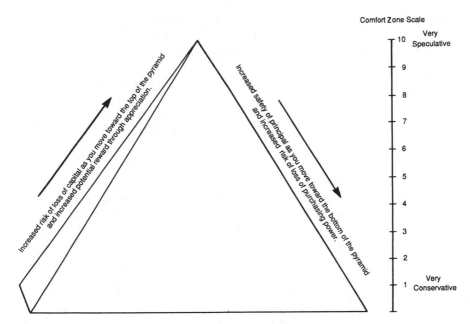

Figure 5-2. Blank personal investment pyramid. Use it to depict how *your* investment vehicles are distributed. The scale on the right will help you determine your comfort zone.

will help you classify your comfort zone. If your investments tend to bunch near the bottom of the pyramid, you are a conservative investor who avoids risk. Middle-range and higher numbers indicate greater willingness to take calculated risks in exchange for greater potential returns.

If you find your pyramid is bottom-heavy, your objective should be to redirect some of your money to higher positions on the pyramid. But that is more easily said than done because it involves an *emotional* as well as a financial adjustment in your life. Human beings by and large hate change. Most of us avoid it, particularly if we have to take a fundamentally new approach to the way we do things. But sometimes we have to change in order to survive. It is very difficult to change, but you must embrace change and see it as an opportunity rather than something to be frightened of.

If you decide that your comfort zone needs to be pushed up the scale a few notches, you should proceed deliberately and cautiously. You should also consult a qualified financial professional, particularly in view of the dangers that face amateur investors who dabble in new, high-risk ventures. There are many sound vehicles in the marketplace that offer investors a chance to reap substantial rewards, but there are also incompetent and unscrupulous promoters. Buyer beware—do your homework, your due diligence, and know your product before buying it!

Move through the levels of the pyramid itself and examine the possible options (which are discussed later in this book) for placing your investment dollars. Some of these options are undoubtedly known to you, but you probably have not been exposed to them in the detail required to make independent investment decisions. Others might come as complete surprises to you.

As we begin to explore some of these options, let's turn our attention to Chapter 6, A World of Opportunity. Here you'll see that investment opportunities abound world-wide.

6

A World of Opportunity

The phenomena of the changing
global landscape are creating a
multitude of investment
opportunities.

FREEDOM FOCUS

- *Do you know where the majority of investment opportunities are?*
- *Are you familiar with the "major players" in the global arena?*
- *How will global investing benefit you?*
- *What is the best way to invest globally?*

Imagine for a moment that we are in an average American home and we are going to take a tour around the world without venturing outside. First, look in the living or family room at the Italian leather sofa and the VCR, TV, and stereo, all from Japan or Korea. In the bathroom, we find a German-made electric razor and Swiss-made watch. In the kitchen, we have English china and crystal, French cookware, and American appliances. In the garage is the family car (assembled in America) and the

Swedish import with its tires from France. And we've only visited the garage and three rooms. Get the picture? (With a Japanese camera!)

This is not an isolated example. This phenomenon repeats itself millions of times each day in every major industrialized nation on Earth. But there is more!

Many products that are staples of our American lifestyle are made by non-U.S. companies. By purchasing them you are contributing to the profits of these companies. Why not take double advantage of your present household purchases? You will readily recognize some of the following products, shown with their country of origin:

Tetley Tea (England)

Sony Walkman (Japan)

One-A-Day vitamins (Germany)

Sharp TV (Japan)

L'Oreal Preference (France)

Lean Cuisine dinners (Switzerland)

Multinational corporations are multiplying and many foreign companies now have manufacturing plants based in the United States. And the United States is doing the same. Witness an American fast food chain in China. Scores of American firms now sell more of their products outside U.S. borders than within.

According to one source, the United States accounts for only one-third of the world's investment opportunities. But it's not because we are offering less. Indeed, excellent opportunities are still abundant and well worth pursuing. Rather, it's because many areas of the world are growing more rapidly than the United States.

Do you miss out on that much if you limit your investment portfolio to U.S. stocks? Absolutely! For example, the 21 largest *banks* in the world; the 10 largest *appliance* companies; 9 of the 10 largest *financial services* companies; 8 of the 10 largest *insurance* companies; 8 of the 10 largest *utility* companies; 8 of the 10 largest *machinery* companies; 8 of the 10 largest *chemical* companies; 7 of the 10 largest *electronics* companies; and 7 of the 10 largest *automobile* companies are foreign owned (see Table 6-1).

Moreover, the stock markets of other nations often far outperform ours here at home. Only twice during the past 11 years has the U.S. stock market been among the five best performers in the world. Does it make sense to ignore the other 70 percent of the world's capitalization? To do so would be to ignore some of the world's most outstanding op-

Table 6-1. Some of the Largest Foreign Employers in the United States

Home office	Foreign parent	United States subsidiary	United States employment
Mulheim, Germany	Tangelmann	Great Atlantic & Pacific Tea Co.	74,000
London	Hanson	Hanson Industries	50,000
Vevey, Switzerland	Nestle	Nestlé Enterprises Alcon Laboratories Carnation	48,027
Tokyo	Honda Motor	American Honda Motor	46,238
Zurich	ABB ASEA Brown Boveri	ASEA Brown Boveri	40,000
London	British Petroleum	BP America	37,000
The Hague	Royal Dutch/ Shell Group	Shell Oil	32,434
Munich	Siemens	Siemens	31,000
Tokyo	Bridgestone	Bridgestone/Firestone	28,000
Tokyo	Sony	Sony Corp. of America	20,000
Toyota City, Japan	Toyota Motor	Toyota Motor Sales, USA Toyota Motor Manufacturing	8,070*

*Does not include 2800 employees of New United Motor Manufacturing, a joint venture between Toyota and General Motors.

DATA: *Business Week* survey.

portunities for growth. World market dominance is constantly changing (see Table 6-2).

How Does Globalization Affect You?

It means that we can no longer think of ourselves just as Americans or French, or Asian. We must begin to think of ourselves as global citizens. We are all part of a larger picture—the world. Table 6-3 provides even more insight into just how "global" we are.

Table 6-2. Top-Performing Stock Markets*

Year	First	Second	Third	Fourth	Fifth
1981	Sweden +39	Denmark +25	Sing./Mal. +18	Japan +16	Spain +12
1982	Sweden +24	U.S.A. +22	Neth. +17	Belgium +10	Germany +10
1983	Norway +82	Denmark +69	Australia +56	Sweden +50	Neth. +38
1984	Hong Kong +47	Spain +42	Japan +17	Belgium +13	Neth. +12
1985	Austria +177	Germany +137	Italy +134	Switz. +108	France +83
1986	Spain +123	Italy +109	Japan +100	Belgium +81	France +79
1987	Japan +43	Spain +38	U.K. +35	Canada +15	Denmark +14
1988	Belgium +55	Denmark +54	Sweden +49	Norway +43	France +39
1989	Austria +105	Germany +47	Norway +46	Denmark +45	Singapore +42
1990	U.K. +10	Hong Kong +9	Austria +7	Norway +1	Denmark 0
1991	Hong Kong +50	Austria +36	U.S.A. +31	Sing./Mal. +25	NZ +21

*Figures preceded by a plus indicate that the market ended the year up by the percentage indicated. For example, in 1981, Sweden had the world's top performing stock market, closing at 39 percent above the previous year.

SOURCE: Morgan Stanley Capital International. Past performance is, of course, no guarantee of future results.

Free enterprise is spreading rapidly around the globe. In the 1990s, Western Europe swept away trade barriers in favor of a single marketplace with the vast consumer potential of 320 million human beings. Eastern Europe, with markets once thought unassailable by the West, saw the fall of communism overnight. Now those markets pose enormous possibilities and the final steps have already been made. Along the Pacific Rim and in pockets of the Americas, developing nations are seeing their economies (and stock markets) growing at rates surpassing those of the United States and other major industrialized countries. Vast political and economic shifts are taking place in what used to be

Table 6-3. Familiar U.S. Brand Names Not Produced by U.S. Companies

Products	Companies	Products	Companies
Airwick deodorant	Ciba-Geigy	Lean Cuisine frozen foods	Nestlé
Alpo dogfood	Grand Metropolitan	Lifebuoy soap	Unilever
Aquafresh toothpaste	Beecham	Lucky Strike cigarettes	BAT
Baskin Robbins ice cream	Allied Lyons	Mighty Dog dogfood	Nestlé
Birds Eye frozen foods	Unilever	Panasonic electronics	Matsushita
Burger King foods	Grand Metropolitan	Princes Hotels	Lonrho
Carnation foods	Nestlé	Purina Dog Chow dogfood	British Pet
Close-up toothpaste	Unilever	Q-Tips swabs	Unilever
Dannon yogurt	BSN	Ragu spaghetti sauce	Unilever
Dewars scotch	Guinness	Sunkist sodas	Cadbury Schweppes
Doubleday books	Bertelsmann Lyons	Tetley tea	Allied Lyons
French's mustard	Reckitt & Coleman Forte	Travelodge motels	Trusthouse Forte
Frigidaire refrigerators	Electrolux	TV Guide magazine	Newscorp
Glidden paint	Imperial Chemical	Valium medication	Hoffman-LaRoche
Imperial margarine	Unilever	Vaseline lotion	Unilever

the Soviet Union, with many nations offering economic assistance to assure these changes.

In plain English, all of these phenomena are part of the changing global landscape—changes that create both opportunity and uncertainty. Today's global climate is more conducive to business, and to investment, than at any other time in the world's history.

Who Are the Players?

Although it would be impossible to cover every country and its future prospects for your investment dollars, we will take a look at some of the major players.

The Pacific Region (Japan, Hong Kong, Korea, Taiwan, Thailand, Singapore, Malaysia, and Australia) represents 38 percent of the world's stock market capital. It has experienced outstanding economic growth during the past 5 years. Japan is the most economically mature of these. Because its search for affordable production of goods has caused a spill-over of Japanese investment into neighboring countries, it has fostered their development as economically independent and prosperous nations.

The newly industrialized countries (NICs) of Hong Kong, Korea, Thailand, Singapore, Malaysia, and Taiwan offer some of the cheapest world labor forces and richest untapped natural resources. The result is some of the world's fastest growing sources of low cost manufacturing. These countries present an inviting economic climate for the manufacture and assembly of consumer electronics products.

The Pacific Region offers yet another country with the potential for strong economic growth—China. The industrialization of China will create opportunities in such areas as electricity, construction materials, public transportation, and fundamental telecommunications. These low technology and essential industries are now the foundation of a natural growth progression occurring in the NICs of Southeast Asia.

Japan, although a part of the Pacific Region, is the world's largest and most dynamic stock market and merits an individual review in spite of its recent substantial reversal. With 9 of the world's 15 largest publicly held companies, the Japanese are truly international business community leaders. Japan's dedication to building a strong economy during the postwar period has established it as a dominant force in the world's financial markets. With such tremendous growth, it is not surprising to learn that Japan is currently the world's largest provider of capital—indeed, 13 of the world's 15 largest banks are Japanese. Today its domestic economy is emerging as the driving force behind productivity.

European stock markets make up the world's third largest source of equity capital. Europe's impressive manufacturing capacity, diverse industrial base, quality labor pools, and many leading multinational blue chip corporations make it a remarkable environment for growth. Again and again European markets have proven that they represent tremendous investment potential. In 8 of the past 10 years, the number one performing stock market has been European (see Table 6-4).

By the end of 1992, the 12 countries of the European Economic Com-

Table 6-4. European Stock Market Returns
Ten Years Ended June 30, 1990

Belgium	26.6%	Norway	15.5%
Sweden	22.0%	Denmark	18.5%
Spain	19.6%	West Germany	18.8%
Austria	20.0%	Netherlands	23.6%
France	22.2%	United Kingdom	19.4%
Italy	14.7%	Switzerland	15.4%

SOURCE: Morgan Stanley Capital International. Figures represent average annualized returns.

munity (Belgium, Denmark, France, Greece, Ireland, Italy, Luxembourg, The Netherlands, Portugal, Spain, United Kingdom, and Germany) will be joined into a single market that rivals the United States and Japan for size, output, and purchasing power. Plans call for the removal of trade barriers, ensuring the free flow of people, goods, services, and capital across national borders. Recently, the United States reached a trade agreement on free trade zones with Canada and Mexico which may mean phenomenal opportunities for the investor. Eastern Europe is undergoing massive economic reforms and with this economic deregulation and the elimination of internal trade barriers, many European companies are now investing in and competing for exposure to the whole European market. Companies currently restricted to manufacturing and distributing within their own national boundaries will soon be able to locate facilities anywhere in Europe, taking advantage of the free flow of money, workers, goods, and services across borders without tariffs or restriction. They further benefit as these deregulatory acts lead to efficiency. As economics teaches, efficiency stimulates growth. The result will likely be competitive markets, corporate growth, and higher profits.

What Is Global Investing?

Global investing is simply taking advantage of quality growth opportunities outside the United States. Formerly, most of those opportunities existed here in the United States—the United States accounted for two-thirds of world stock market capitalization. That's no longer true. Yes, there still are excellent opportunities here, but today they account for less than a third of the world equity market.

Increasing your investment returns, expanding investment opportunity, and reducing portfolio risk are three compelling reasons for global investing. Among the nations providing the most potential for growth today are those which are industrializing, have the cheapest labor and the richest natural resources, yet remain undervalued.

European markets have proven again and again that they represent tremendous investment potential. Over the past 10 years, the European market index has consistently produced greater total returns than the S&P 500 Index in the United States [Source: Morgan Stanley Capital International (GT Semi annual report)].

How Can You Invest?

No discussion of global investing would be complete without citing Sir John Templeton, who has led the way in global investing for 50 years. He cites three approaches to international investing.

1. *The universal search for value.* This is the approach of the active and informed international investor seeking to reap high investment returns by discovering value among a wide range of opportunities.

2. *International hedging.* A method which uses foreign securities, currency and option contracts, and other such instruments to reduce or offset inventory price, interest rate, and exchange rate business or portfolio risks.

3. *Search for the world market portfolio.* This is the approach of the investor who builds a portfolio of securities, mutual funds, and foreign currency contracts in an attempt to duplicate the performance of world capital markets.

Each of these types of investor has a specific objective and a set of criteria to measure investment possibilities. But the word that characterizes the Templeton approach most precisely is *adaptability*.

But there are a number of barriers for the individual investor to overcome. These include lack of information; different accounting and reporting standards; variable transaction costs, withholding, and other taxes; liquidity problems; foreign currency risks; political or sovereignty risks; delivery and settlement delays; and foreign investor restriction. These obstacles make it nearly impossible for the average individual to participate independently in a global market.

Another important area of global investing is in the currencies of certain countries. I have a client who was one of nine children. Born in one country, he became a citizen of another at the urging of his father. The reason was very simple. He was the son who would continue to run the family's multi-million dollar business when his father died, and it was his father's wish that he avoid military service and perhaps avoid a premature death. The son has millions invested in foreign currencies in Germany, Spain, Mexico, the United States, and France, and is building a new plant in Moscow, of which the family will own 85 percent. Does he understand the relationship between a ruble and a dollar, a Deutsche mark and a franc? You bet he does. He has, out of design and necessity, become a global investor.

But does the average American citizen even know the names of the currencies of other countries? (See Table 6-5.) Will you know when an Austrian market will outperform a German market? Do you know the restrictions on nonresidents as investors? There are many questions which must be answered before you invest here. Resources must be identified, information gathered, and analyses made which take into account the political and the economic status of each area you consider. Does it make sense for the average investor to take on this task? No! Most of us don't have the talent or ability required to accomplish this, and those of us who do are too involved in careers doing the things that we know best. But there is a way for any individual to take part in this global opportunity.

What's the Best Way to Invest?

To me, the answer is obvious—mutual funds. (See Chapter 10 for a discussion of mutual fund basics.) There are hundreds of global and international mutual funds—Templeton, G.T. Global, Massachusetts Financial Services, Fidelity, etc. How do you select the right mutual fund? Visit your financial planning professional, read about the companies that interest you, call them and ask for prospectuses on the funds

Table 6-5. Major Countries and Their Currencies

Country	Currency	Country	Currency
Australia	Australian dollar	Japan	Yen
Great Britain	Pound	Mexico	Peso
Canada	Canadian dollar	Netherlands	Guilder
Denmark	Krone	New Zealand	N.Z. dollar
France	Franc	Norway	Krone
Germany	Mark	Singapore	Singapore dollar
Hong Kong	Hong Kong dollar	Sweden	Krone
Italy	Lira	Switzerland	Swiss Franc

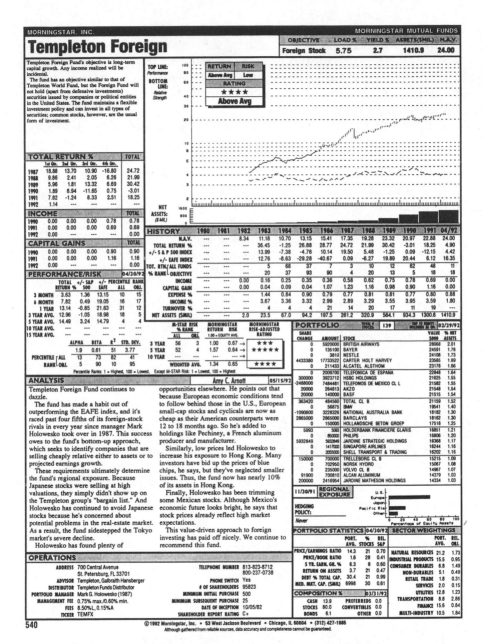

Figure 6-1. Morningstar's report on the Templeton Foreign mutual fund. It provides a huge amount of information to aid a prospective buyer in choosing a fund. (*Source: Morningstar Mutual Funds. Reprinted by permission, Morningstar, Inc., 53 West Jackson Boulevard, Chicago, Ill. 60604.*)

you are considering. (When we use the terms *international* or *global*, we are using them as interchangeable terms, but in actuality, *global* refers to a fund in which the fund managers invest in a variety of countries, as well as their own country; *international* refers to a fund in which the fund managers invest in countries other than their own.)

Once you've decided to invest in mutual funds, and you wish to personally investigate the funds available to you, there are several resources which analyze the individual funds and their performance. Such reports may be useful to you in narrowing the range of funds from which you may choose to invest. One of the best services is Morningstar, Inc. As you can see in Figure 6-1, Morningstar provides a statement of the fund's objective, a brief analysis of the fund's history and management, income information, capital gains, performance data, portfolio holdings, and a breakdown of percentage of holdings within the top five countries, as well as the percentage of stocks, cash, and bonds that compose the fund.

But be intelligent. As John Templeton says, "The very first point in any investment program is don't take the risk of having all of your assets in any one corporation or industry or nation. . . . Diversify." In other words, never own a single stock or a single industry in today's environment because that is not proper diversification. The chances of securing your financial freedom without diversification are practically nil.

If you were born in a relatively small country such as Switzerland or Japan, your mind set might never permit you to invest your money in one single country. Why? Because of the geographic boundaries, the lack of diverse investment opportunities within your own country, and the fact that you are to a large extent an importer and would already be accustomed to dealing with countries other than your own. If you travel 400 miles in any direction in Switzerland, you're likely to end up in one of five different countries, each with its own language and currency system. The thinking of Americans would be almost the opposite. They are more prone to "buy American" and are used to being self-sufficient in terms of goods, services, and investment opportunities. Because of its size, the United States offers an abundance of investment resources. A single language is spoken; a single currency system is used. But we must update the software in our personal computers—our brains—to become international or global investors. In doing so, we gain the advantage of additional diversification and tap into the other two-thirds of our world's investment opportunities.

Let me leave you to look at Table 6-6. It provides a short list of some global/international funds, their performance, and how to contact them.

Table 6-6. Global/International Mutual Funds

Fund with address/phone	Performance (total return)		
	1 Year	5 Years	10 Years
EuroPacific Growth 333 S. Hope Street Los Angeles, CA 90071 1-800-421-0180	13.98%	13.86%	—%
Ivy International One Park Pond Road Hingham, MA 02043 1-800-235-3322	9.86	15.30	—
Scudder International 175 Federal Street Boston, MA 02110 1-800-225-2470	11.78	9.16	16.26
New Perspective 333 S. Hope Street Los Angeles, CA 90071 1-800-421-0180	22.64	13.63	17.11
Templeton Growth **Templeton Foreign** 700 Central Avenue St. Petersburg, FL 33701 1-800-237-0738	31.33 18.25	13.27 17.88	15.83 —
SoGen International 50 Rockefeller Plaza, 3rd Floor New York, NY 10020 1-800-334-2143	17.95	12.12	17.37

SOURCE: 1992 Morningstar, Inc.
NOTE: Figures as of year-end 1991.

PART 2
Planning...

7

Higher Education—
Higher Costs

*Some economists predict that by the
year 2008 a bachelor's degree could
cost almost $176,000 at a private
university and $82,400 at a public
university.*

FREEDOM FOCUS

- *Where do bonds, annuities, and mutual funds fit into your plan?*
- *What are the financial aid and scholarship options?*
- *How do you get started?*

High school graduation day—it's finally here. Some of you will greet
this news with a great deal of excitement and anticipation, but some of
you will face it with anxiety and perhaps regret. Why? It's not because
your child doesn't deserve the joy of the occasion. Rather, it's because
you haven't prepared to meet the expenses of your child's college education. Recent studies say that the children of tomorrow will have to be
better educated than their parents in order to achieve the same, not
better, lifestyle the parents enjoyed.

109

Cheri graduated third in the county and received national merit recognition. She also received queries from several recognized colleges which hoped she would select them to continue her education. However, because of cutbacks in scholarship money and financial aid, no one could offer her a full, 4-year scholarship, which is what she had hoped for. With another child already in college and one 3 years behind Cheri, the family did not have the funds available to send Cheri to one of those preferred colleges.

Raymond was captain of the basketball team, a standout forward, and an academic All American. He was accepted by the school of his choice—in another state. Raymond and his two younger brothers come from a single-parent home. His mother had always thought that his athletic ability would pay for all his college expenses. She was wrong.

Alexandra's parents were as thrilled as Alexandra when she read the acceptance letter from her father's alma mater. Alexandra was captain of the debating team and hoped to be a lawyer. But she did not receive any scholarship money and her parents were devastated when they realized that the bonds they had bought 15 years ago, specifically to pay for college, would not cover even 2 years of today's tuition.

You see, the cost of those 4 years away at school are more than most of their parents paid for their homes. Financial aid, which used to be a given, has come under close scrutiny and is not as readily available. Many of the tax benefits to parents of college bound children have been eliminated. More and more, parents are finding that they don't have the resources to pay for a college education, with the costs of tuition, books, room and board all spiraling. Even those parents who thought they could handle the cost of college out of their current incomes realize that they were wrong. There simply was no way to predict that the cost of a college education would increase as dramatically as it has over the past two decades. And there is more bad news: There are no indications that this trend will reverse itself. Some economists predict that by the year 2008 a bachelor's degree could cost almost $176,000 at a private university and $82,400 at a public university.

The biggest single problem in saving for college tuition, retirement, a new home, or whatever your goal is inflation—the loss of purchasing power of your dollars. We have never had a year of deflation since 1954. In Table 7-1, you can estimate the rate of increase in the cost of tuition (or inflation)—will it be 3 percent or 8 percent? Somewhere in between, or perhaps even higher? Assume you select the 4 percent figure and your child is 5 years away from entering college. In 5 years, at a 4 percent projected cost of living increase, you will need $1.22 to replace each of the dollars you have today. In Table 7-2, you can see another way of measuring that rate of inflation. In 5 years from now at 4 percent annual inflation, the value of today's dollar will be only 82 cents.

Table 7-1. Future Cost of Living Increases

	Average annual rate of inflation (or increases in tuition)					
Years	3%	4%	5%	6%	7%	8%
1	$1.03	$1.04	$1.05	$1.06	$1.07	$1.08
2	1.06	1.08	1.10	1.12	1.14	1.17
3	1.09	1.12	1.16	1.19	1.23	1.26
4	1.13	1.17	1.22	1.26	1.31	1.36
5	1.16	1.22	1.28	1.34	1.40	1.47
6	1.19	1.27	1.34	1.42	1.50	1.59
7	1.23	1.32	1.41	1.50	1.61	1.71
8	1.27	1.37	1.48	1.59	1.72	1.85
9	1.30	1.42	1.55	1.69	1.84	2.00
10	1.34	1.48	1.63	1.79	1.97	2.16
15	1.56	1.80	2.08	2.40	2.76	3.17
20	1.81	2.19	2.65	3.21	3.87	4.66
25	2.09	2.67	3.39	4.29	5.43	6.85
30	2.43	3.24	4.32	5.74	7.61	10.06

NOTE: Inflation figures used compounding. All figures rounded to nearest one-hundredth.

Table 7-2. How Much Will Today's Dollar Be Worth at a Later Date?

	Average annual rate of inflation					
Years	3%	4%	5%	6%	7%	8%
5	$0.86	$0.82	$0.78	$0.75	$0.71	$0.68
6	.84	.79	.75	.70	.67	.63
7	.81	.76	.71	.67	.62	.58
8	.79	.73	.68	.63	.58	.54
9	.77	.70	.64	.59	.54	.50
10	.74	.68	.61	.56	.51	.46
15	.64	.56	.48	.42	.36	.32
20	.55	.46	.38	.31	.26	.21
25	.48	.38	.30	.23	.18	.15
30	.41	.31	.23	.17	.13	.10

Meeting College Expenses

Planning ahead and investing regularly are the surest ways to meet your financial goals. College is expensive, but prudent financial management can bring it within reach of most family budgets. Table 7-3 shows how much you'd have to invest each month to meet the projected cost of public and private college, assuming your money compounds at a rate of 8 percent. Of course, your child or grandchild may be able to get some help from loans and scholarships and could also contribute earnings from a summer job. But Table 7-3 is a good way to estimate how much you should be putting aside.

If one of your goals is to pay for college for a child or grandchild, you can and must take control now. Remember, even if you can't afford the

Table 7-3. The Cost of College

Years until child begins college	Projected 4-year cost*		Required monthly investment	
	Public	Private	Public	Private
1	$ 27,973	$ 59,200	$2,243	$4,755
2	29,598	62,752	1,141	2,420
3	31,374	66,517	774	1,641
4	33,257	70,508	590	1,251
5	35,252	74,739	480	1,017
6	37,367	79,223	406	861
7	39,609	83,976	353	749
8	41,986	89,015	314	665
9	44,505	94,356	283	599
10	47,175	100,017	258	547
11	50,006	106,018	237	503
12	53,006	112,379	220	467
13	56,187	119,112	206	436
14	59,558	126,269	193	410
15	63,131	133,846	182	387
16	66,919	141,876	173	366
17	70,934	150,389	164	348
18	75,190	159,412	157	332

*Four-year costs including tuition, fees, room and board, books and transportation, based on the College Annual Survey of Colleges. Projected costs assume a 6 percent annual increase.

bottom line today—and think how much worse it will be by the time your child is college age—the important thing is to get started, *to get off dead center.* You can move toward your goal at a pace that's comfortable for you. Any amount invested regularly will keep you on the road to achieving your goal.

How do you decide what your strategy will be? You must consider several things. What is the age of your child? What is your tax bracket? How much are you likely to need? Will inflation affect your strategy?

What Is the Answer?

Some people are married to the idea of bonds, especially zero coupon bonds, and consider them a nice, conservative investment. They love zero coupon bonds because you buy them at a tremendous discount and they mature at the face amount when the child is ready for college, maybe 18 years later. But a bond is a bond—it is still fixed in nature and may not be appreciating at a rate to keep pace with inflation. Even if it is a tax-free bond, it is still a debt instrument and debt instruments, long-term, are affected tremendously by inflation, losing buying power. Although bonds can be a part of your strategy, they should not represent your total investment. If you are investing in bonds, first make sure that they are at least A rated or better to reduce credit risk. What you have to remember is that if long-term interest rates drop, the value of your bonds will rise and you can then sell them for a nice profit. *But . . .* if interest rates climb, then the value of your bonds will drop; however, if you hold them to maturity you will collect all the money you paid for them. If you have to sell before the maturity date and the market value of your bond is down, then you will get less than you paid. I'm not against bonds, but I do have reservations about investing in them solely to meet future expenses.

Because of the concern over growing college costs, a variety of bonds have been issued to meet the specific needs of parents. A particularly interesting one is the College Savings Bond (baccalaureate bond) which has appeared in at least 15 states in the last decade. Basically, these are municipal bonds which are federal and state tax free. Some of those states pay an added bonus if the child attends a public or private school within the state. In state universities and colleges in at least four states (and growing) a guaranteed tuition plan allows you to pay the state a lump sum to buy four years of future tuition at a discount. As of this writing there are still some tax wrinkles to be ironed out. Keep in mind that each state has its own restrictions governing these bond programs.

United States Savings Bonds will pay tax-free interest to those using

them for college education—but the parents' joint incomes must be
$60,000 or less, or $40,000 or less for single parents. The interest exclusion fades beyond that point and disappears altogether once the combined incomes reach $90,000, or $55,000 for single parents.

Annuities offer a variety of payout options, and can certainly benefit a
college savings program. If you choose this option, do so with your tax
situation in mind along with the information you will find in Chapter
11, The Annuity Advantage. If you are using a typical annuity program
for college education funds, any withdrawals prior to your reaching age
59½ could be subject to taxes plus penalties for early withdrawals, unless you receive substantially equal payments over a 5-year period. This
might not be the ideal vehicle for funding future college costs because
of certain restrictions and penalties for early withdrawal.

If time is on your side, meaning your child or children are very young
and you have the time to invest for the long term, I favor the use of
mutual funds as a means of meeting future college costs. Although it
may sound radical, such a time frame would allow you to invest a part of
your money in aggressive growth funds for even greater potential financial reward. Mutual funds offer diversity and flexibility; moreover, they
can be purchased by anyone and offer investing by lump sum, dollar-
cost averaging, or intermittent investments. (These methods are discussed more fully in Chapter 10, The Magic of Mutual Funds.)
Dollar-cost averaging with mutual funds (see Table 7-4) can work espe-

Table 7-4. Dollar Cost Averaging*

	Investment amount	Share price	Shares purchased
January	$100	$10.00	10
April	100	12.50	8
July	100	5.00	20
October	100	10.00	10
	Average price per share: ($37.50 divided by 4)	**$9.38**	
	YOUR average cost per share: ($400 divided by 48)	**$8.33**	
	Your savings per share:	**$1.05**	

*Dollar-cost averaging can lower your average price per share, as demonstrated here.
It doesn't guarantee a profit and won't protect you against loss in a declining market, but
the key is to stick to the program even through periods of declining prices. Invest an
amount you can afford and probably won't need to withdraw. You should consider your
dollar-cost averaging program a long-term commitment.

cially well because it allows you to invest relatively small dollar amounts and still receive professional management, extensive diversification, and low investment costs.

In planning, don't overlook the importance of life insurance on the parents or legal guardians of students. In the event of premature death, proceeds from an insurance policy could guarantee the funds for college tuition.

Other Possibilities

Although there is not as much financial aid available today as in previous years, dig deep for information. Contact the financial aid officers of the colleges you are considering and ask for assistance in obtaining information. There are informational brochures available. One is the guide, *Don't Miss Out*, available from Octameron Associates, P.O. Box 3437, Alexandria, VA 22302. Your child's high school guidance counselor will also be able to put you in touch with aid information.

If you are applying for almost all federal financial aid, you will need to submit to a financial needs test to determine the eligibility of your children.

If you are at the point where you need a loan, check with your banking institution. There are some federally subsidized low interest Perkins Loans available. The PLUS loan, Parent Loans for Undergraduate Students, is another possibility with repayment beginning within 60 days after you take it out. Again, check with your participating bank or commercial lender. Your state's education department may offer subsidized student loans to residents.

Of course, scholarships are available in a broad variety of forms, some based solely on academics and some based on other qualifications such as need, ethnic background, or artistic, musical, and athletic abilities. Many civic and community organizations offer scholarships—making a few phone calls and filling out a few applications could result in some extra funding for college.

The key to saving for college costs is discipline: Determine your future need, how much time you have to reach your goal, and initiate a program. Your program might include bonds, mutual funds, and prepaying tuition. Whatever the program, staying with it is the key. Remember, how do you eat an elephant? One bite at a time.

8

Insurance—
The Critical
Safeguard

*The best kind of insurance you can
have is the kind you have on your
life the day you die.*

FREEDOM FOCUS

- *How much insurance do you need?*
- *What are the three basic kinds of coverage?*
- *How do you check out an insurance company?*
- *Can you protect your estate through insurance?*

We've all heard of Murphy's Law—if something can go wrong it will. But
when you step back and analyze most of these scenarios, the things that
go wrong do so because of a failure to plan. But we can take some of the
sting out of misfortune through planning: by anticipating unwanted
events and building compensation for family members and business associates into our financial plans. That compensation goes under the
name *insurance,* and its uses today are many and varied.

Life Insurance—
A Building Block

Take a moment and turn to the investment pyramid shown in Chapter 5. Look once again at the blocks your pyramid should be built upon: savings sufficient to meet an emergency, investments that can quickly be converted to cash (such as money market funds and savings accounts), and a sound life insurance program. Note that items at the bottom of the pyramid have several characteristics in common. They are all highly liquid, which means that you or your heirs could have access to the dollars they represent quickly and easily should a need for those dollars arise. The items at the foot of the pyramid are also low-risk repositories for your money, in the sense that (with the exception of bonds) your principal stands virtually no chance of eroding because of adverse marketplace conditions. (It will, however, erode in terms of purchasing power as inflation takes its toll on the value of the dollar. But this is a drawback you have to accept for the 10 to 20 percent of your portfolio that anchors your financial pyramid. The profitability of your middle- and top-of-the-pyramid investments should more than offset this loss.)

If you are not alone in the world, you need a sound life insurance program that will help your heirs to cope financially in the event of your premature death. The primary purpose of life insurance is to *create an instant estate* for your family should you, their chief money machine, prove unable to build that estate gradually over a long lifetime. Of all the financial vehicles available to you, *only* life insurance has the ability to put a substantial, liquid estate together for your heirs by tomorrow if you should die today. You pay for this protection while you live, normally out of your earnings.

Can you afford to be without this coverage? Probably not—especially if you are a young parent who hasn't yet had time to accumulate a sizable estate, but whose family responsibilities are substantial and are likely to remain substantial for the next 10 to 20 years. (Even single men and women with no children should consider their need for life insurance. The benefits of a life insurance policy could be earmarked for a number of purposes—helping parents or other relatives, educational funding, charitable giving, etc.) The good news is that insurance coverage sufficient to meet your family's needs for years after your death is available to you at moderate cost. Consider, for example, the typical yearly premium payments for standard-risk males ages 25–55 who are in good health which are shown in Table 8-1. Rates for a standard-risk female will generally be slightly lower.

Table 8-1. Summary of Average Term Insurance Rates for a
Standard-Risk Male (First Year Premium)

Age	Plan	Premium	Amount	Premium	Amount
25	ART*	$115.00	$100,000	$225.00	$250,000
	10-year level	139.00	100,000	272.50	250,000
	10-year DT**	143.00	100,000	295.00	250,000
35	ART*	$115.00	$100,000	$225.00	$250,000
	10-year level	174.00	100,000	360.00	250,000
	10-year DT**	150.00	100,000	312.50	250,000
45	ART*	$184.00	$100,000	$372.50	$250,000
	10-year level	333.00	100,000	757.50	250,000
	10-year DT**	266.00	100,000	605.00	250,000
55	ART*	$419.00	$100,000	$ 742.50	$250,000
	10-year level	700.00	100,000	1675.00	250,000
	10-year DT**	553.00	100,000	1320.00	250,000

*Annual renewable term.
**Decreasing term.

What Type of Insurance Is "Best"?

The three types of insurance policies available to you are called *term, ordinary* or *whole life,* and *universal life* insurance. Many policy variations exist within these three major categories, such as single payment plans, limited payment plans, and full payment plans. Your selection from the three basic plans offered depends upon your age, your health, your ability to pay, and the purpose of the insurance.

In recent years, a controversy has broken out among financial professionals regarding the comparative desirability of the three basic types of insurance coverage. I am going to stand aside from the fray and simply tell you what my father told me after he had spent 33 years in the life insurance profession: *The "best" kind of insurance you can have is the kind you have on the day you die.* In other words, adequate coverage—coverage that meets your needs and objectives—is far more important than the particular vehicle you use. Table 8-2 provides a brief overview of these insurance types.

Table 8-2. Basic Insurance Types

Type of insurance	What it does for you
Term Life	Provides pure protection only for specified period of time (1 or more years). This type of policy does not build up cash value (has no "savings account" feature). Its sole purpose is to provide an *instant estate* for your family if you should die before accumulating assets sufficient to maintain their lifestyle. Available at low cost. Most economical way to purchase substantial amount of death protection. Coverage must be renewed regularly, and premium increases at renewal time. Think of yourself as "renting" the coverage for a specific period of time.
Whole Life (also called Straight Life and Ordinary Life)	Provides death protection plus a "savings account" feature. Interest earned by this "savings account" is conservative, but some people view it as a good way to save for their old age or a rainy day. Cost per $1000 of death protection is significantly higher than term rates. Designed to be held for the remainder of your life or until a specified age (e.g., 65). Can be canceled at any time, but the earlier you cancel, the less the policy is worth to you in terms of dollars refunded or channeled into another policy. Normally, premiums remain the same throughout the life of the policy. Premium payment period may be reduced by use of dividends. Think of this type as insurance you own.
Universal Life	Universal life is similar to whole life in that it provides a permanent form of life insurance protection. It differs in that it is a so-called interest sensitive policy. By this we mean that the policy values can increase or decrease with current interest rates. Universal life or excess interest plans combine the protection of term life with the cash accumulation benefits of whole life insurance at a higher level of performance for the policyholder. The premium requirements differ from whole life in that it is flexible and may be increased or decreased within certain guidelines. The guarantees of a universal life policy are limited due to the interest-sensitive nature of the policy. The accumulation account and the mortality rates are not guaranteed in most universal life policies. Universal life offers the opportunity to rent and own.

Term Life

Term life insurance offers pure protection for a stated period of time and is based upon your needs. If you die during the term in which the policy is in effect, your heirs collect the entire face amount of the policy. If you live beyond the term of the policy, the premium amount that you have paid for your coverage has simply been one of your expenses, just as the premiums on your automobile insurance and homeowner's insurance policies have been expenses, provided that you have not collected on a claim. Term life policies offer no "savings account" feature, as whole life and universal life policies do. It is useful to think of term insurance as protection that you rent rather than own.

A type of policy called *annual renewable term* (ART) allows you to renew your coverage for another year without undergoing a physical examination. As the years go by, however, your annual rate goes up, because you are growing older and thus becoming more of a risk for the insurance company to assume.

Term insurance policies are available with a number of modifications. Some have a *convertible* feature that allows you to switch from your term policy into a whole life policy at some point, perhaps when you think your children will be old enough to get along without a large, lump-sum cash payment upon your death. A sound plan is to carry substantial term insurance until your children have completed their educations; then you can reduce the amount of your coverage and convert it to a whole life policy that will accumulate cash value. This will also have the effect of fixing your annual premium, since whole life rates do not increase as you get older. Again, remember that whole life policies do not qualify as true investments because of their low interest rates.

In *level term* insurance, you agree to hold the policy for a specified number of years—say 10. Your annual premium payments for this entire period are then calculated actuarially, on the basis of such factors as your age, your health, your occupation, the earnings that the life insurance company expects to realize by investing your money, and the "loading cost" set by the company, which includes sales commissions and servicing charges and mortality experience.

Still another type of policy, called *decreasing term*, has as its main features premium payments that remain level and a death benefit that decreases as the years go by. Because the death benefit gradually drops, the yearly premium you pay is set at a lower level than that of a level term policy. Decreasing term life is especially well suited to the needs of the young family, since it provides a substantial sum of money for the surviving spouse if the insured spouse dies while the couple's children are still young. As the years go by and the couple's need to be assured of the availability of a great deal of ready cash to care for their family diminishes, the death benefit is reduced.

A decreasing term policy can also be linked to your mortgage, with a face amount that is sufficient to pay off whatever you might owe on your home at the time of your death. As your mortgage debt decreases, so does the policy's death benefit.

Universal Life Insurance

This is a new form of policy developed in the 1980s. It is similar to whole life in that it provides lifetime protection and cash values (living values). It differs in that these values are interest sensitive and can fluctuate with interest rates in the marketplace. Universal life or excess interest plans combine the protection of term life with the cash accumulation benefits of whole life insurance at a higher level of performance for the policyholder. The premium requirement differs from whole life in that it is flexible and may be increased or decreased within certain guidelines. The guarantees of a universal life policy are limited because of the interest-sensitive nature of the policy. The accumulation amount and the mortality rates are not guaranteed in most universal life policies.

Whole Life

Also called *ordinary life* and *straight life*, there are many names of policies in this category, such as single premium variable life and joint survivor life, but they still fall in this category and focus around the construction of whole life. This type of policy is based on the assumption that you are going to hold it for the rest of your life. In addition to providing a death benefit, it accumulates cash value through a "forced savings account" feature. If term insurance is thought of as rented protection, then whole life can be described as protection that you own, at least in part. Your percentage of equity ownership increases as your policy's cash value builds.

After they have matured over a period of years, whole life policies can be redeemed for their accumulated cash value. In other words, you don't have to die to collect on a whole life policy.

Because a whole life policy *has* to pay off in some way, either through a death benefit payment to your heirs or a cash-value payment to you, premiums are set at significantly higher levels than those charged for term insurance. The annual rate you must pay, however, remains fixed for your entire life (unlike term rates, which increase as you get older). The younger you are when you buy the policy, the lower your fixed rate will be. Table 8-3 shows the approximate annual premium costs of $10,000 to $1,000,000 in whole life insurance to men between 25 and 50

Table 8-3. Average Annual Whole Life Insurance Rates for a
Standard Risk Male*

| | Amount of insurance | | | | |
Age	$10,000	$25,000	$100,000	$500,000	$1,000,000
25	$132.50	$331.25	$1075.00	$ 5175.00	$10,300.00
35	158.20	423.00	1442.00	7010.00	13,970.00
45	211.20	578.50	2064.00	10,120.00	20,190.00
50	252.10	682.75	2481.00	12,205.00	24,360.00

*Rates for a female would be lower.

who are in good health and have nonhazardous occupations. Rates for
women would be slightly lower.

Remember that as a whole life policy builds cash value, more and
more of the death benefit it carries has been contributed by you, and
less and less by the insurance company. Suppose, for example, that you
were to die when your $10,000 whole life policy contained $3000 in its
built-in "savings account." The company would pay your heirs the full
$10,000, but only $7000 of that total would come from its own coffers;
the other $3000 would be your own money. As whole life policies ma-
ture, the company's "exposure" (in terms of dollars contributed to
death benefit) decreases, and your "exposure" increases.

Since the policy's cash value is yours to use as you wish, you may borrow all or portions of it from time to time at interest rates ranging from
6 percent and up (5 percent on older policies and generally 8 percent
on policies issued recently). You borrow at the lending rate that was in
effect at the time your policy was issued. Currently, most policies are
issued with a variable loan rate. When buying a policy, you should ask
your underwriter to specify the rate that will be charged for loans. A
change in interest rates from fixed to variable has occurred in recent
years. This means that the interest rate charged is not fixed. It can
change from time to time as interest rates fluctuate in the marketplace.
Remember that with current tax laws the interest payments are no
longer deductible on your tax return as an expense.

Joint and Last Survivor

Changes in the tax code in recent years brought about the introduction
of a new policy called *last survivor whole life*. While the concept of a joint
life product has been around for a number of years, it was the Economic Recovery Tax Act of 1981 (ERTA) that created a natural market
for it. Prior to the passage of this act, the maximum marital deduction

was limited to the greater of $250,000 or one half of the client's adjusted gross estate. As a result, there was a need for insurance on almost any wealthy client's life in order to pay the taxes that would be generated by his or her death and to assure that adequate amounts would pass to the surviving spouse.

ERTA changed all of this by allowing an unlimited estate tax deduction for amounts passing to a surviving spouse. Thus, any married client who chooses to do so can reduce the payable estate tax to zero at the first death. This is where the joint life product provides a unique solution: It is designed to provide the cash needed for estate taxes at precisely the moment that current tax law says that it is needed—the death of the surviving spouse.

Aside from this match, the joint life approach also offers two other major advantages involving cost considerations and timing problems. While the numbers will vary according to age and other factors, the premium for a joint life policy may be only one-third to one-half that required to insure either of the lives individually. This is especially significant in dealing with larger estates where the cost of the life insurance solution was previously so exorbitant that it was rarely considered. The reduced costs of the product also help in any situation where the client is asset rich (for example, land, closely held business, etc.) and cash poor; where the client is concerned about acquiring sufficient insurance to cover the taxes generated by future appreciation of estate assets; or where the cost of a single life policy would create insurmountable gift tax problems.

The use of a joint life policy also eliminates the timing problem that occurs when a single life policy is used. Obviously, in deciding which spouse to insure with a traditional policy, we do not know which will be the first to die. The joint life policy eliminates this problem by covering both insureds and the underwriting requirements to issue a contract are much less stringent than applying for single policies.

Nonforfeiture Values

The cash value of your policy is one of its *nonforfeiture values*. That complicated-sounding term describes a very simple concept. It refers to the portion of your permanent life insurance policy that is nonforfeitable, even if you decide to cancel. This is the portion of the policy that you actually own. Naturally, it increases as the years pass; someone who wants to withdraw from a whole life or universal policy at an early stage, say within the first five years, will find that very few nonforfeitable dollars have accumulated, whereas the person who decides to cancel after 10 or 15 years will have a fairly substantial sum coming.

If you decide that a permanent life policy is appropriate for you, you should, in an ideal world, stick by that decision. There is little to be gained from putting your premium dollars into a plan that you do not see through to the end. The earlier you withdraw, the more you will have enriched the insurance company at your own expense. If you have a life insurance policy, it would be a good idea to take a look at the nonforfeiture values shown, and you'll see just what you may lose by opting for one of the nonforfeiture values.

Some circumstances, however, make a change of plans necessary. If events in your life dictate that you cash in your permanent life policy, you need only refer to the *table of nonforfeiture values* provided to you at the time of purchase by your underwriter to determine how much you should receive. There are other options available to you which include extended term insurance and reduced paid up life insurance. Consider the nonforfeiture values offered by a $25,000 whole life policy that was issued on September 9, 1989, to a 25-year-old female.

If the woman who bought this policy wanted to cash it in after holding it for 10 years, she would receive $5300. But wait a minute. This is $7820 less than the amount she paid in, at an annual premium of $1312. Is there any way for her to preserve her investment in the policy and *still* be able to borrow money? Yes, there is. The answer lies in yet another nonforfeiture value: the policy's loan value (which is the same as its cash value). She can borrow up to this amount from her policy and keep the policy in effect as she pays it back.

What if she doesn't really need the cash, but just wants to stop paying that $1312 annual premium? Her policy's nonforfeiture values can be called upon to provide an answer here, too. At the 10-year point, she will be able to stop paying premiums and still have whole life coverage in the amount of $30,600. She will be covered in this amount until she dies, but she will never have to pay another premium.

Yet another option is open. Suppose that she wants to retain the full, original coverage, but doesn't want to make any more premium payments. Another of her policy's nonforfeiture values, at the 10-year mark, is 15 years and 318 days worth of term insurance in the amount of $100,000.

As you can see, these permanent life policies are flexible. You need never feel locked into your policy. If events in your life prompt you to reassess your commitment to a whole life or universal life policy, consider the options available to you under the table of nonforfeiture values.

Some Options

An important variation of the whole life policy is the *limited payment life* policy, which insures you for your entire life, but requires premium payments for only a stated number of years. Since your payments will be made over a condensed period, they will naturally be higher than if they continued for your entire life. Policies with names such as *20-pay life* and *paid-up at 65* are the limited payment type.

Insurance policies today can carry so many riders and options that the rest of this book would have to be devoted to them if we were to outline each one. A rider is simply an addition to your policy that allows you, for extra payment, to have an extra privilege of some sort. For instance, if you are worried that you might become uninsurable at some point because of a beginning health problem, you can buy a rider that will assure you the right of buying additional term or whole life insurance at specified future dates, regardless of your physical condition. Another rider provides that your annual premium will be waived if you become disabled. Insurance companies today offer many riders designed to fill a wide variety of possible future needs.

The most reliable source of counsel on the particular life insurance policy (or combination of policies), plus riders and options, that is best for you and your family is an insurance underwriter (life agent) or financial professional who has taken the time to become familiar with your needs. At the outset of your relationship with an underwriter or any other financial professional, it is up to you to make it clear to your counselors that you expect individualized service. Make sure that your underwriter has a good deal of insight into your present life situation and any situation that is likely to arise in the years ahead before he or she recommends a particular policy. And then ask for an explanation of just how that policy will fill your needs.

This does not mean that most life insurance underwriters are not conscientious in their efforts to serve their clients well. On the contrary, the great majority want nothing more than to be of genuine, lasting service to their clients. But in this age of growing economic pressures and increasingly impersonal contacts between people, there is a tendency in all parts of the business community to accelerate delivery time of goods and services. It is up to you, then, to make sure that any program, insurance or otherwise, that is going to be purchased with your hard-earned money has been fully explained to you, and that its advantages and disadvantages, as they apply to your circumstances, have been completely explored.

Time to Review

There are three basic kinds of life insurance. They are:

1. *Term life, which is pure protection only.* If you have substantial family responsibilities and you have not yet had time to build up an estate

that would meet their needs if you should die prematurely, you should be covered by term life insurance.

2. *Whole life, which combines a death benefit with a "savings account" feature.* Your payments may be spread over your entire life expectancy or they may end much earlier via the use of dividends.

3. *Universal life insurance, which, as we stated earlier, is similar to whole life in many respects.* Its main difference is the interest sensitive nature of its cash value. Also, most universal life policies do not have guaranteed mortality rates. They have a current rate and a guaranteed rate. This gives the company the right to increase the mortality charges if they think it necessary. This in turn could increase your premium payments.

Remember, too, that numerous combinations of these policies can be tailored to your needs by your underwriter. Suppose, for example, that you are thinking of buying a $10,000 whole life policy, but since your children are young you think you really need a higher death benefit, at least for the next few years. A benefit of $100,000 would be more in line with your needs, but you can't afford the premium cost for a $100,000 whole life policy. The solution is simple. Buy the $10,000 whole life policy with a $90,000 term rider. Stipulate that the rider is to be in effect for 10 years—the period of time that your children will need your financial support. At the end of those 10 years, let the rider expire or convert it. You will have been covered to the extent you wished to be during those 10 crucial years, and you will still have your $10,000 whole life policy.

Although term riders must normally be added at the time you purchase a whole life policy, some companies will allow you to add them months and years after you have begun making premium payments. However, the company may require new underwriting. If you currently have whole life coverage and would like to add term coverage, you should look into the possibility of tacking a rider onto your existing policy, since charges you must pay on such an addition are usually lower than normal. If this option is not open to you, and you have a whole life policy that provides a death benefit you consider inadequate in the short run, you can buy a separate term policy to afford your family greater protection.

How Much Is Enough?

How much life insurance should you have? That's hard to say. In the past, underwriters have come up with many different formulas for determining need. Some rely upon a rule-of-thumb figure, such as five times yearly income. The amount of life insurance that you, the reader, need is dependent upon some very personal variables. How old are you, for example? What is your health history? What kind of health and longevity run in your family? What category of work are you in? Does your employer provide you with life insurance coverage? If so, how much? Are you male or female? If you were to die tomorrow, how well would your spouse be able to meet the financial needs of your family? How many children do you have and how old are they? Do you hope to send them to college? Do any of them have special needs that will cost money to fulfill?

Again, your best source of counsel on how much life insurance you need and what form you should buy it in is your life insurance underwriter or financial professional. You may be surprised to learn the extent of the coursework that life insurance underwriters must master before they can put the word "chartered" after their names. To qualify for the Chartered Life Underwriter (CLU) or Chartered Financial Consultant (ChFC) designation, an individual must successfully complete a comprehensive course of study and demonstrate competence by passing a series of college-level examinations in the areas of life and health insurance; pensions; law; trusts; taxation; finance; economics; and business, financial, and estate planning administered by The American College in Bryn Mawr, Pennsylvania, a fully accredited institution.

You normally can have confidence in a life insurance agent who comes to you with this extensive educational background. Another good indication of an underwriter's professionalism and continued involvement in the field is his or her membership in a local chapter of the American Society of Chartered Life Underwriters and Chartered Financial Consultants.

Who Should Own Your Life Insurance?

You may think that this question has an obvious answer: Who else should own your life insurance but you yourself? Stop for a moment and think that over. If you own your life insurance policy, it will become part of your estate when you die, and thus will be subject to taxation. If your estate is substantial, this could pose a serious, yet entirely unnecessary, problem for your heirs. By simply filling out a form, you can transfer ownership of your policy into another person's name or you can make it part of a trust agreement. One of the areas most often overlooked which can have a tremendous impact on the taxation of your estate is the area of fringe benefits provided by your employer or your own business in the form of group life insurance, accidental death benefits while in employment, etc. These do become part of your estate and could be subject to taxation. So be aware of your fringe benefits as they can have an impact on your personal planning.

Should you take this step? This is a judgment that you can make best in consultation with your life insurance underwriter or financial professional, who will help you explore such questions as: How large is my estate right now? How large is it likely to be when I die? At what point do I need to start worrying about federal estate taxes?

Other appropriate questions include: Do I have a sound reason for holding my life insurance in my own name? Would it be advantageous for me to switch ownership to someone else? If so, to whom? In making this last determination, you should take some very personal factors into consideration, particularly the probable durability of your relationship with the person who may become the owner of your life insurance. If this person is your spouse, and if your marriage should end in divorce, you could have created a serious problem for yourself. Since it could be disadvantageous, in terms of taxes, for you to transfer life insurance policy ownership to someone else, be sure to discuss the pros and cons of taking such a step with a knowledgeable professional.

What If You Become Disabled?

Consider the three major financial disasters that can befall you:

1. You can die too soon.
2. You can live too long.
3. You can become disabled and find yourself unable to make a living.

What then? A client recently came in for a review of his situation. He was 55 but looked 75 because of cancer, which had ravaged his body. He and his wife have two sons. Both he and his wife worked for an electronics company—he was making $50,000 annually and she was earning $23,000 annually. As many of you do when you are feeling well, he let several years pass without having any physical examinations. When he turned 55 years of age, he decided that it was time for a physical, although he felt healthy. Unfortunately, the doctors discovered cancer, which even after surgery continued to spread through his body. By December of the same year, his wife had to leave her employment to provide full time care for her husband. Within a period of 9 short months, their family was deprived of both incomes and was facing tremendous medical expenses. In addition, they now had to pay for their medical insurance, $1000 a month, and buy an automobile, which was previously supplied by the company. Their world came to a screeching halt. As he looked at me and talked about facing death, he said in a very weak voice, "Jim, I just never thought it would be me." He is now dead.

Who is to blame for this situation? Anyone can be stricken with disease at any time; that's not the question. Is he to blame because he never thought to review his life insurance or his need for disability insurance? Is the company to blame because they never made it available to employees? Is the insurance company to blame because while they provided medical coverage they didn't offer disability coverage to their clients? The fact is they are all a little guilty. You must think and plan ahead for things not expected but certainly possible.

The insurance company could have provided him with a disability policy which would cover 75 percent of his income with a 6-month elimination period. That simply means that after 6 months the insurance carrier would then begin reimbursing him at 75 percent of his income.

Will you become disabled? Table 8-4 illustrates what the odds are. For example, at age 25 there is a 58 percent chance that you could become disabled for as long as 2.1 years! How many of us have ever considered the possibility of becoming disabled at such a young age?

Is it going to happen to you? I hope not. Is it going to happen to me? Never! We always think it happens to the next guy. Can you prepare for that possibility without paying a fortune? Yes you can.

If the fringe benefit program offered by your current employer does not provide you with disability insurance coverage, you should look into the cost of providing your own coverage. And, by all means, whatever life insurance or disability coverage you have should include a *premium waiver feature*. This means that your life insurance, including disability

Table 8-4. Probability of Disability Before Age 65

Age	Probability	Duration of disabilities that last over 90 days
25	58%	2.1 years
30	54%	2.5 years
35	50%	2.8 years
40	45%	3.1 years
45	40%	3.2 years
50	33%	3.1 years
55	23%	2.6 years

SOURCE: Commissioners Individual Disability A Table.

coverage, will remain in effect even if you become disabled and cannot pay the premiums.

Something about Rates

Despite its seeming omnipresence, inflation has actually missed life insurance rates. This may be difficult to believe, but it is true. You can pick any type of policy, ask the issuing company what rate it carried 10 years ago, and discover, to your pleasure, that it is cheaper today. How has such a miracle been wrought? The answer lies in a staple ingredient of the American economy—competition in the insurance industry. An improvement in our health and life expectancy also contributes. Longer life expectancy means lower life insurance rates that benefit us all.

We've gotten used to thinking of life insurance carriers as steady, conservative, and *safe!* It just isn't so anymore. Investments made yesterday can be tomorrow's death knell for some carriers. You must do your homework and look at the company's long-term philosophy.

There are more than 2000 life insurance companies in existence in this country today. The top 10 companies of the industry have had remarkable market penetration. In fact, they do more business among themselves than do all the hundreds of others together.

You should not conclude, however, that these very large companies are the only ones with which you should deal. In order to survive in the face of such awesome competition, smaller life insurance companies have had to develop some extremely competitive products. If you are considering buying a policy from a lesser known company, investigate the firm in *Best's Insurance Guide* or *Best's Insurance Reports* (A. M. Best, Ambest Road, Oldwick, N.J. 08858), *Standard & Poor's* (Standard & Poor's, 25 Broadway, New York, N.Y. 10004), *Moody's Investors Service* (Moody's Investor Service, 99 Church Ave., New York, N.Y. 10007), *Duff & Phelps* (Duff & Phelps, 55 E. Munroe Street, New York, N.Y. 10007), as well as *Weiss Research* (Weiss Research, P.O. Box 2923, West Palm Beach, Fla. 33402)—the youngest of these raters. These authoritative publications, available at most public libraries, rate insurance companies on a scale of A+ or AAA (excellent) to C (fair) and very weak.

Usually, the first criterion you will consider is the cost. Cost comparisons are important, but they are only one factor. A very important consideration is the financial strength and stability of the insurance company you are considering. The history of a company's performance—its consistency—is more important than a specific yearly rate of return. You need reasonable assurance that you can count on the company's being able to back its product *20–30 years* from the time you buy. Table 8-5 provides guidelines for selecting your insurance com-

Table 8-5. Evaluation Guide for Insurance Companies

1. *Year Chartered*—Look for long-established companies.

2. *Financial Size*—This is an indication of a company's relative size based on its reported policyholder surplus and conditional reserve funds.

3. *Rating*—Refer to Best's, Standard & Poor's, Duff & Phelps, Moody's Investors Service, and Weiss Research. They provide ratings from excellent to very weak in a wide range of areas. All companies do not provide ratings in all the same areas, so you may want to refer to more than one rater.

4. *Net Investment Yield*—What is the company's ability to successfully invest its fund? Is there a consistent performance shown? Consistency of performance is more important than a specific yearly rate of return.

5. *Policy Loans to Company's Assets*—Cash value loaned to policy-owners obviously reduce the company's ability to invest those monies.

6. *Expenses*—The more a company can reduce its expenses, the more funds are available for investment. (Refer to the rating resources shown in item 3.)

7. *Mortality*—Speaks to how carefully the company selects its risk, which ultimately has a significant negative or positive impact on dividends. (Refer to the rating resources shown in item 3.)

8. *Lapses*—Lapses—when you stop paying the premium and cash in the policy—are a loss of income to a company and a cash drain. A low lapse ratio is a positive factor. Increases in the ratio over a short period of time might indicate other problems on the horizon. (Refer to the rating resources shown in item 3.)

9. *Surplus and Reserves to Assets*—The amount of surplus and reserves is an indication of several factors including mortality expenses and a company's ability to successfully invest its assets. Provides a measure of a company's ability to withstand any future negative results such as a downturn in the economy or increased mortality.

10. *Surplus and Reserves to Liabilities*—The larger the percentage the better. This ratio provides a measure of a company's abilities to meet current liabilities.

11. *Junk Bonds to Invested Assets*—Junk bonds are noninvestment-grade bonds. They generally pay a higher yield, but they also carry a higher risk. Obviously the greater the percentage of junk bonds to invested assets, the more severe the potential impact on future investment yield.

12. *Net Gain after Taxes/Dividends*—These figures can indicate a company's ability to run its normal activities at a profit.

13. *Maximum Retention Limit*—This refers to the maximum amount of insurance a company will carry on one life (or joint life) at its own risk. Protection above this amount will be provided by reinsurers. However, a company's ability to obtain reinsurance from a quality company at rates in line with its illustration projections is more important than the limit itself.

14. *Interest Adjusted Indices*The Payment Index and Surrender Cost Index are used as one measure of the cost of owning a life insurance policy. The lower the index number the better. (Refer to the rating resources shown in item 3.)

pany. Review it and use the criteria when making this critical decision.

Life and disability insurance should be just one basic ingredient in your long-range financial plan. Another equally important consideration that we must face today is the fact that we are living longer—and it is costing us more. Let's turn our attention to Chapter 9 and focus on "The Costs of Living Longer."

9

The Cost of Living . . . Longer

There are now 31.3 million Americans age 65 or older. It's estimated that one out of four will require nursing home care, while others will need long-term care at home.

FREEDOM FOCUS

- *What is long-term health care?*
- *Are you prepared for the dramatic increases anticipated in the cost of a nursing home stay?*
- *What are the sources for covering the costs?*
- *What questions should you ask when considering long-term health care insurance?*

Can you imagine what things would be like today if the Spanish explorer, Ponce de Leon, had actually discovered the legendary Fountain of Youth? He probably gave little thought to all the ramifications of living longer. He envisioned a period of immortality—of youth and good health—with never-ending opportunities. From his perspective, good health was a given. The fact is that long-term health care may be the single

most important issue currently facing Americans over 50, yet, until recent years, it has been almost overlooked in the financial planning
arena.

Whoever coined the phrase "golden years" did not understand the
tragedy of a person needing long-term health care. By the year 2030,
the number of Americans age 65 and over will approximately double;
those 85 and over will triple; and one out of every five people in the
United States will be age 65 or over. By this same year, experts expect a
132 percent increase in nursing home residents. The fact is that we *are*
living longer, but not necessarily healthier. Even those who have "taken
care of themselves" through life-long programs of regular exercise, con-
ditioning, and sound nutrition only live so long before the effects of old
age begin to catch up with them. In 1987 the Health Care Financing
Administration reported that one in two people reaching age 85 will
spend some time in a convalescent care facility. According to current
estimates, by the year 2000, about one in four persons age 65 and older
(approximately 7,500,000 Americans) will require some kind of long-
term care—an increase of approximately 56 percent since 1980. Another way of putting it is to picture four of us, each 65 years of age,
sitting down to play bridge. One of us is going to end up in a nursing
home. I know what's going through your mind as you read this chapter:
"I wonder which of the three of *them* will end up in a nursing home."
You never think it will be you—it's always the other person. That thinking somehow allows you to put off planning for this possibility.

Today living longer doesn't guarantee "good health." And in most
cases it isn't cheap either. By the end of 1988, it was estimated that
Americans spent approximately $540 billion, or 11.4 percent of the
Gross Domestic Product (GDP), on the prevention and treatment of illness and injury. According to a study conducted by *50 Plus* in October
1987, each year half a million people use up their life savings for nursing home care—and then go on Medicaid. It's shocking to learn that
half of all elderly people living alone will spend themselves into poverty
after only a 13-week stay (*Chicago Tribune,* March 13, 1989).

Before you read any further, take a minute to review Appendix 9-1.
You've probably heard these terms before, but it is important to understand them as we use them in this chapter.

The U.S. Department of Health and Human Services reports that the
average length of stay in a nursing home is 456 days. Things are not
always what they appear to be, and neither is this statistic. Because over
50 percent of all nursing home stays are for 3 months or less, the 456-
days figure is "pulled down." Over half of the stays tend to be much
longer than 456 days (see Table 9-1).

Table 9-1. Patient Stays in Nursing Homes

Length of stay	Percentage of patients*
0–30 days	31
1–3 months	21
3–6 months	11
6–9 months	7
9–12 months	5
12–24 months	10
24–36 months	5
Over 36 months	11

SOURCE: U.S. Department of Health and Human Services.
*Total equals 101 percent due to rounding.

A study by Baylor University Medical Center gives the following average costs of long-term care services:

Nursing home	$25,000 per year
Home health care	Based on two visits from a registered nurse and three from home health aides per week, $250 per week, or $13,000 per year
Adult day care	$20 to $30 per day
Hospice care	In facility, $300 to $400 per day
	At home, $400 per week

The Brookings Institute in Washington estimates that nursing home care will cost an average of $55,000 by the year 2018. It's also anticipated that by then, $100 billion per year will be spent on the nursing home care of approximately 4 million Americans. With Medicare covering only about 2 percent of the bill, the cost is overwhelming for most. A long stay in a nursing home can quickly wipe out a lifetime of savings. You could end up with $500,000 when you retire and be sent into bankruptcy because of a catastrophic illness or an extended stay in a nursing home. Not only do you bankrupt yourself, but your partner as well.

In looking at the dollars spent, all things are not equal. Statistics show that the older the individual, the higher the cost for treatment and care. Broken down further, the numbers also reveal an increase in the use of medical services brought about by rising incidences of chronic conditions and multiple health problems. In 1984, according to the Ameri-

can Association of Retired Persons (AARP), the 65+ age group represented 12 percent of the U.S. population, but accounted for 30 percent
of all hospital stays, 41 percent of all days of care in hospitals, and 31
percent, or $120 billion, of total personal health care expenditures.
There are now 31.3 million Americans age 65 or older. It's estimated
that one out of four will require nursing home care, while others will
need long-term care at home.

The financial impact of such a reality could well be devastating—even
to the largest estates. Of the $38 billion spent on nursing home care in
1986, $19 billion was paid by Medicaid—a federally funded program re-
served for the poor. The other $19 billion was paid from the pockets of
the patient and/or members of his/her own family.

At the rate of $20,000 to $50,000 a year—for nursing home room
and board care only—a term of treatment of almost any duration could
seriously jeopardize an individual's net worth, as well as the financial
position of the spouse. In several recent years, Americans spent the following on nursing home stays:

1975	$11 billion
1980	$20 billion
1985	$45 billion
1990	$82 billion (estimate)

Many of these individuals and their families, like so many others nationwide, thought that Medicare would pick up the tab. According to an
AARP survey, 79 percent of those interviewed also believed that this federal entitlement program for the aged would cover nursing home care.
*Actually, Medicare and Medicare supplements pay for less than 2 percent of
skilled nursing home care.*

Who actually made those payments? Private insurance accounted for
1 percent while Medicare accounted for approximately 2 percent.
Other government payments totaled 4 percent, with Medicaid paying
approximately 43 percent. The remaining 50 percent was paid for *out of
pocket.*

The Options

Self-Insurance

As the name implies, this risky proposition means that you, personally,
take the place of being the insurance company. Maybe you accomplish
this by setting aside so many dollars each month or year in a special
account to cover medical costs. If you or your spouse require a nursing

home stay, then you and your resources are exposed to all the risks. You become the insurance company. Many people who self-insure and, as a result, begin paying for nursing home care out of their own pockets, find that their savings are not enough to cover lengthy confinements. If they become impoverished after entering a nursing home, they turn to Medicaid to pay the bills.

Another problem of self-insurance is its inflation factor. Between 1975 and 1985, health care costs rose 2 percent faster than the Consumer Price Index as a whole (U.S. Census Bureau). The Health Care Financing Administration estimates that the cost of skilled nursing facilities will rise 2.5 percent a year faster than inflation and home care agencies will beat inflation by 3 percent a year.

Some of the risks of self-insurance include:

- Spending longer (years instead of months) in a nursing home than anticipated

- Not making as high a return as expected on the monies set aside for this purpose

- Encountering a situation that requires the expenditure of these monies

- Exhausting your self-insurance funds, leaving you with no coverage at all

Medicare and Medicaid

The highly touted Medicare Catastrophic Coverage Act was repealed in 1989. As a result, Medicare benefits have changed and could continue to change yearly. Medicare *does not* cover long-term custodial care and other costs associated with long-term health care. Medicare pays for some skilled at-home care but only for short-term unstable conditions and not for the ongoing assistance that many elderly people need.

Medicaid is a public assistance program that pays for health care services to low-income people, including elderly or disabled persons. It pays for long-term nursing home care and for very limited home health services. Among the unfortunate ramifications of being between Medicaid and Medicare (or between a "rock and a hard place") are attempts by individuals to "spend-down"—to use up existing assets to qualify for Medicaid, or to transfer assets to a spouse or children for the same purpose. Each of these efforts (as you would expect) carries a certain amount of risk and legal implications.

The rules of coverage vary from state to state, but they all require using up all life savings before Medicaid starts paying. Also, any source of income, including pensions, is applied toward expenses. Recent legislation has taken steps to ease up on this rule by allowing a healthy spouse to keep assets of up to $60,000 and at least $12,000 and income of at least 122 percent of the federal poverty level for a couple. You should check with your member of Congress for a review of the changes—they are too numerous to cover here. But Medicaid is a state-by-state agency, and the definition of *impoverished* continues to be debated across the country.

Long-Term Care Insurance

The alternatives for a growing number of older Americans sometimes referred to as the "nonpoor," who can't qualify for Medicaid under its current rules, and who need more coverage than the restrictive limits of Medicare provide, are long-term care insurance policies offered by private insurance companies. Children who are facing the financial burdens of caring for their parents should also consider the possibility of long-term care (LTC) insurance.

Like other insurance, LTC insurance allows you to pay a premium that offsets the risk of much larger out-of-pocket expenses. LTC insurance is a relatively new type of private insurance, but more than 130 companies now offer coverage, with frequent additions to the list. You can obtain a free list of all companies offering long-term care policies through: Health Insurance Association of America, Post Office Box 41455, Washington, D.C. 20018. You can also contact your state insurance departments for more information.

These LTC policies generally cover skilled, intermediate, and custodial care in state-licensed nursing homes. They may cover home health services provided by state-licensed and/or Medicare-certified home health agencies. Any policy you consider should cover skilled, intermediate, custodial, and home health services. Many newer policies also cover adult day care in the community.

When considering a policy, ask your agent to explain anything that isn't clear. If the answers don't satisfy you, contact someone else in the company. If you are still not satisfied, call your state insurance department with your questions. If you want to check out a company, you can get general information from the Area Agency of Aging or your Better Business Bureau. But be sure to check their rating by some of the rating services—A. M. Best Company, Moody, Standard & Poor's, or Duff and Phelps. A good insurance agent will want you to know what you are buying and will have no problem disclosing his or her company's rating or providing you with a summary of each policy's benefits and coverage.

Buyer beware! Insurance policies are legal contracts. You must read and compare several policies before you buy one. And *make sure you understand all of the provisions.*

The Policies

Currently, there are approximately 100 different policies, with their own "bells and whistles," featuring varying degrees of benefits, coverage, qualifying requirements, cost, and other pertinent considerations. Picking the right policy requires a diligent review of several critical areas. Some of the things to look for and questions to ask include:

- What is the annual cost to get the coverage you want? (Generally, the younger you are when you sign up, the lower your premiums.)

- Is there a premium waiver once a claim begins? (In the event they have to start paying claims on your policy, do they waive the premium during your period of claim, keeping the policy intact, or do you have to continue paying the premium?) Is it included in the standard policy or is it an "extra cost"?

- How large is the allowable benefit? Is the policy guaranteed renewable? Will the premiums remain fixed, regardless of deteriorating health? What's the position on rate hikes?

- Is prior hospitalization required before you can be admitted to a nursing home? How many hospital days are needed? (No prior hospitalization is preferred.)

- How soon must you check into a nursing home after leaving the hospital?

- What is not covered by your policy? Are there certain limits for preexisting conditions? Are Alzheimer's Disease, Parkinson's, senility, and other organic and nervous system disorders covered under the policy? (Nearly half of all nursing home patients are confined because of these conditions.)

- When do your benefits begin? End? What is the elimination period? What is your daily benefit?

- How long will you receive benefits for skilled, intermediate, custodial, and home care?

- Can you receive home care without first being confined to a nursing home?

To assist you in comparing policies, refer to Appendix 9-2. Use it as a worksheet to give you a side-by-side comparison of policy features.

Given the predictability of getting older, the possibility of needing long-term health care, and the probability that such care will increase in cost with each passing year, it's never really too soon, between the ages of 50 and 80, to consider a long-term health care insurance policy. A number of authorities feel that in one's mid-sixties purchasing a policy that provides for a level premium and guarantees insurability before a disqualifying condition or disease has had a chance to develop is perhaps the most practical approach.

APPENDIX 9-1
Terms and Definitions

Custodial care Nonmedical care that is primarily for the purpose of meeting personal needs (also known as activities of daily living—ADLs) such as help in walking, bathing, dressing, eating, or taking medicine. It can be provided by someone without professional medical skills or training, but for insurance purposes must be based on a doctor's orders.

Home health care A broad range of care received at home, such as part-time skilled nursing care, speech therapy, physical or occupational therapy, part-time services of home health aides, or help from homemakers or chore workers.

Hospice An institution that cares for the terminally ill patient.

Intermediate care Occasional nursing and rehabilitative care that can be performed only by, or under the supervision of, skilled medical personnel. The care received must be based on a doctor's orders.

Intermediate care facility One that is licensed by the state and may be certified by Medicaid to provide intermediate care. It may also provide custodial care. It can provide Medicare- or Medicaid-covered skilled nursing care only if it has been certified to do either one.

Long-term care The day-in, day-out help that you could need if you ever have a chronic illness or disability that lasts a long time and you cannot care for yourself.

Medicaid The joint state and federal program that states have adopted to provide payment for health care services for those with lower incomes or with very high medical bills. It provides benefits for custodial and home health care, *once income and assets have been spent down* to eligibility levels.

Medicare The federal program that is designed to provide those over age 65, some disabled persons, and those with end-stage renal disease with help in paying for hospital and medical expenses. It *does not* provide benefits for long-term care.

Medicare supplement insurance (Medigap) Private insurance that supplements or fills in many of the gaps in Medicare coverage. It *does not* provide benefits for long-term care.

Skilled nursing care Daily nursing and rehabilitative care (this is the only type of coverage that Medicare will pay) that can be performed only by or under the supervision of skilled medical personnel. For insurance purposes, the care received must be based on a doctor's orders.

Skilled nursing facility One licensed by the state that may be certified by Medicare and/or Medicaid to provide skilled nursing care. It may also provide intermediate or custodial care.

Elimination period The number of days before benefits begin.

APPENDIX 9-2
Long-Term Care Policy Checklist*

Policy A: _____

Policy B: _____

	Policy A	Policy B
1. What services are covered?		
Skilled care	_____	_____
Intermediate care	_____	_____
Custodial care	_____	_____
Home health care	_____	_____
Adult day care	_____	_____
Other	_____	_____
2. How much does the policy pay per day for:		
Skilled care	_____	_____
Intermediate care	_____	_____
Custodial care	_____	_____
Home health care	_____	_____
Adult day care	_____	_____
3. How long will benefits last?		
In a nursing home, for		
Skilled nursing care?	_____	_____
Intermediate nursing care?	_____	_____
Custodial care?	_____	_____
At home?	_____	_____
4. Does the policy have a maximum lifetime benefit? If so, what is it?		
For nursing home care?	_____	_____
For home health care?	_____	_____

(Continued)

*This checklist was provided by the Health Association of America, Washington, D.C.

5. **Does the policy have a maximum length of coverage
   for each period of confinement?
   If so, what is it?**
   For nursing home care? _____ _____
   For home health care? _____ _____

6. **How long must I wait
   before preexisting conditions
   are covered?** _____ _____

7. **How many days must I wait before benefits begin?**
   For nursing home care? _____ _____
   For home health care? _____ _____

8. **Are Alzheimer's disease
   and other organic mental
   and nervous disorders covered?** _____ _____

9. **Does this policy require:**
   Physician certification of need? _____ _____
   An assessment of activities of
   daily living? _____ _____
   A prior hospital stay for:
     Nursing home care? _____ _____
     Home health care? _____ _____
   A prior nursing home
     stay for home health
     care coverage? _____ _____
   Other? _____ _____

10. **Is the policy guaranteed
    renewable?** _____ _____

11. **What is the age range for
    enrollment?** _____ _____

12. **Is there a waiver-of-premium provision?**
    For nursing home care? _____ _____
    For home health care? _____ _____

13. **How long must I be confined
    before premiums are waived?** _____ _____

(Continued)

14. **Does the policy offer an inflation adjustment feature?**
    If so:
    What is the rate of increase?   _____   _____
    How often is it applied?   _____   _____
    For how long?   _____   _____
    Is there an additional cost?   _____   _____

15. **What does the policy cost?**
    Per Year?
       With inflation feature   _____   _____
       Without inflation feature   _____   _____
    Per Month?
       With inflation feature   _____   _____
       Without inflation feature   _____   _____

16. **Is there a 30-day free look?**   _____   _____

10

The Magic of Mutual Funds

Mutual funds have become the nation's third largest financial service.

FREEDOM FOCUS

- *How do mutual funds operate?*
- *What are the investment objectives of funds?*
- *What services are offered by funds?*
- *Are there any regulatory agencies?*
- *Where can you get more information?*

By now you know there are only two sources of money—people at work and money at work. And by now you also know that there is no question in my mind which lasts longer. Human beings wear out; money doesn't. If it's handled properly, it perpetuates not just for your generation, but for other generations. The name of the game is to have your money constantly working for *you* just as hard as you have worked for *it*. Probably your next thought is that you don't have the time or the training to manage your money on a full-time basis. What to do?

Mutual funds have become the nation's third largest financial service. Why not hire a full-time, highly skilled portfolio manager who will provide the luxuries of diversification, income, and growth of your investments, and even do much of the bookkeeping? This manager will keep reinvesting your dividends and capital gains for as long as you wish. When you need ready cash, this manager will send you a check, or wire to your bank, whatever amount you require. The conveniences are unbelievable. Your investment will be so liquid that you will be able to get a check simply by asking for it by letter or phone.

That's what most mutual funds can do for you. So who are mutual funds for? They're for the person who has $100 (sometimes less) to $100,000 (or more) to start with. But how many people have the kind of time it takes to manage their investments on a full-time basis—the doctor who divides time between the office and the operating room? The lawyer tied up with case work? Or the company president with all those board and management meetings?

At one time mutual funds were promoted for the "small" investor. However this came about, it was a misconception. Maybe that was because of their accessibility to individuals who could only make a small initial investment. But as for being for the "small" investor, remember that mutual fund managers handle sizable amounts of money for many of the nation's largest pension funds, major college endowment funds, and other institutional investors. This means that the portfolio managers, market analysts, and technicians who must satisfy the directors of a *Fortune* 500 company's pension fund are the same managers, analysts, and technicians who handle the $1000, $10,000, or $100,000+ you might put into a mutual fund.

Are you thinking that maybe mutual funds just aren't your kind of investment? Do you know what kinds of mutual funds there are? There are open- and closed-end funds; income funds, which include money market, short-term, long-term, high-yield, taxable and tax-exempt, insured and uninsured funds; and there are equity funds, which include income-oriented, balanced, growth and income, growth, large/small company, sector, asset allocation, domestic, international, global, and indexed funds, and more!

Consider one fund out of the thousands available and compare its investment portfolio to yours. The Delaware Group DelCap Fund–Concept I Series, according to financial statements at this writing, contained the following portfolio mix:

Common stock totaled 72.64% of the portfolio invested as follows:

Services	4.22
Capital goods	2.72

Consumer growth	11.55
Communications	1.12
Media/publishing/cable	4.37
Entertainment	2.07
Environmental services	3.01
Energy	0.65
Restaurants	3.74
Health care	14.59
Retailing	9.08
Technology hardware	6.56
Technology software	8.96
Preferred stock	0.36
U.S. Treasury obligations	9.59
Short-term investments	14.80

Is it possible to have such diversity within your own portfolio? Do you own such stock as: Novell, Toys R Us, Seagate Technology, Aldus, Equifax, Nike, Hormel, Cellular, King World Productions, Chili's, Biomet, SciMed Life Systems, Circuit City, Home Depot, Tiffany & Company, etc.? Probably not, but that diversity is part of the beauty of mutual funds.

Let's look at mutual funds in yet another light: If you own 20 or 30 stocks, *you are a mutual fund yourself.* Your private fund may be doing very well for itself at the moment. But how diversified are you? How do you keep up with developments in five or six industries—perhaps even more? Or, if you aren't that diversified, what will happen if your primary industry suddenly encounters serious difficulties? And what if something happens to you, the portfolio manager? Who would look after your investments should you become either temporarily or permanently unable to attend to them yourself? Or suppose that you should die and the market dips considerably while your estate is in probate— what then? Are you really willing to risk these consequences for yourself and your heirs? If not, you should look into mutual funds.

The same money management companies that offer mutual funds may also offer *individual managed accounts.* These accounts are put together specifically for you by a mutual fund company or other investment firm. Some of them have minimum requirements. As an example, many of these money management companies have a minimum investment requirement of $10,000,000 for these accounts. However, lately we are seeing individually managed accounts with much lower minimum investment amounts. This specialized service is attractive to the person who doesn't want to pool his or her funds with other people's money for investment purposes; instead, this client is willing to pay for personalized attention. Any investment adviser can tell you how to go about setting up an individual managed account if this option interests you.

What Is a Mutual Fund?

Mutual funds found their beginnings in Boston in 1924 when the first fund, Massachusetts Investors' Trust, was organized by a company called Massachusetts Financial Services. That fund and those that followed were somewhat patterned after the "trusts" formed by British investment companies—a concept which originated in nineteenth-century England. Several funds were created during the 1920s, but after the crash of '29 they remained almost dormant for a decade. However, even in the face of this disaster, many of them continued to grow as a result of their efficient management.

The industry has continued to grow because of the popularity and accessibility of mutual fund investing. In 1940 there were 68 mutual funds with $448 million in assets and 296,000 shareholder accounts. By 1945 the industry reached $1 billion in assets, and by 1951 it consisted of 1,000,000 accounts. By the end of 1989, there were more than 2900 mutual funds with assets of more than $900 billion (see Figure 10-1). As we move into the 1990s, funds are still experiencing phenomenal popularity and growth—not only with the individual investor, but with institutions and pension funds (see Figure 10-2).

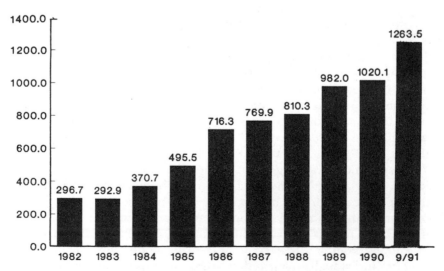

Figure 10-1. Dollars invested in all types of mutual funds. (Assets in billions.)

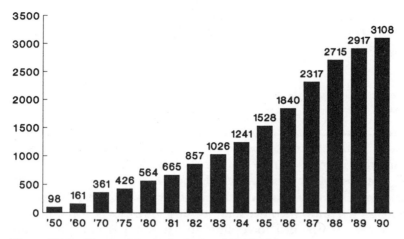

Figure 10-2. Growth of the fund industry—1950–1990.

The standard definition of a mutual fund is a company that combines the investment funds of many people whose investment goals are similar, and, in turn, invests those funds in a wide variety of securities—stocks, bonds, money market securities. Investing in a mutual fund simply means buying shares of the fund. When you buy, you own. You would own the shares of the mutual fund just as you own the shares of stock of a large corporation. There is a difference, though. The fund you purchased is in the business of investing in securities, so the price of its shares is directly related to the value of the securities (the fund's portfolio) the fund owns.

How Do Mutual Funds Work?

Mutual funds are owned by the shareholders, who might number in the thousands. The shareholders elect a board of directors whose responsibility is to make sure that the fund is being operated according to its investment policies and objectives, described in the prospectus. In order to manage the day-to-day operation of a fund the board appoints officers or delegates that responsibility to a management company. Often, the management company is the organization that creates the fund as well as serving as its investment adviser. The investment adviser employs a professional portfolio manager whose responsibility is to decide where to invest the fund's assets.

Fund managers perform extensive research and evaluation of basic economic trends. Their economic and financial research helps them to develop data which will assist them in making intelligent investing decisions. The buy and sell decisions for their portfolio are based on this research and the fund's investment objective.

Importance of Investment Objectives

Mutual funds are usually categorized by a stated investment objective (described in the fund's prospectus), which describes the funds' goals—and that is precisely how you should shop for it. This investment objective is extremely important. It tells you where you are going with the fund and will give you an indication of the risk of the ride. Those goals generally include income, stability, or growth, or a combination thereof. See Appendix 10-1 for definitions. It is important for the investor to know what the fund's objective is in order to decide if its goals are in line with the investor's. If your concern is preservation of capital, then you would want to stay away from a high-risk fund offering potentially higher rates of return. Conversely, if you are just starting out and your goals are long-term, you should consider an aggressive growth fund.

Remember that there is not one single fund that will meet all your objectives; that's why it's best to use a combination of different types of funds with different types of objectives. This is called achieving *portfolio optimization* in your mutual funds.

Consider the following case history, which is typical of what I see most often. A couple will come in and ask me to review their portfolio of mutual funds and I'll see perhaps a Fidelity government security fund, a Delaware government security fund, an Oppenheimer government security fund, a Massachusetts Financial Services, government security fund. When I say to them that they are not diversified, they may reply, " . . . but we bought four different funds." What they bought was four different fund companies. But each fund has basically the same objectives and each fund manager is doing basically the same thing to reach his or her objectives. So it's very important to understand the objective of a fund as well as its track record and who was responsible for that track record. Understanding the risk/reward nature of a fund is vital. Again, you must understand that there is no single fund that will meet the needs of every stage—spring, summer, fall, and winter—of your life.

Young professionals, about 30 years of age, are young money machines, sometimes making a substantial amount of money. One of their considerations is that, as money machines, somewhere along the line they will wear out. They are also concerned about giving a considerable amount of their earned money back to the federal government in income taxes. Obviously they should take advantage of a deferral program, because if they can defer taxes and not pay them in the current year, but rather 20 or 30 years out, they will end up with more money than the person who bought the same investment, but paid current taxes each year on the investment. Some deferral programs include variable or fixed annuities, 401(k) programs, pension/profit sharing, and IRA programs. Perhaps their objective is to be able to retire, financially secure enough to travel for extended periods of time, at age 60. That gives them 30 years (this is a long-term goal) to accumulate the funds they need. We know by all our indications and history, that you make more money by investing in the IBMs of the world before the world has identified them as IBMs. Does that mean you have to try to identify those areas? No—but it *does* mean that you would want to invest in a fund that does that for you, such as emerging growth funds or aggressive growth funds. They have the expertise and research to pick out the Home Depots, Costcos, Toys R Us, etc. of the world. With 30 years ahead, you have time on your side to counter the higher level of risk. So the younger person with long-term growth on their side should be placing more of their money in the emerging/aggressive growth areas.

Perhaps your objective is to be able to provide for a college education for your child who is currently 2 years of age. That means you have 16 years to work with—and with that amount of time you may want to put 50 percent in the emerging/aggressive growth areas and 50 percent in a growth and income fund which offers more stability and lower risk.

I have a client who is 75 years old. She told me that she doesn't even buy green bananas—too long-term. While she was just kidding, she did get across *her* view of long-term. We each have to work from our personal frame of reference. Although she didn't have long-term goals at this stage in her life (she was living comfortably and was actually in pretty good shape), she did want to be able to leave something to her children and grandchildren. And, more importantly, she wanted to be able to sleep at night—she did not want to take a high level of risk. The solution for her was a balanced fund with a three-part objective:

1. To conserve her initial principal

2. To pay current income

3. To promote long-term growth of both principal and income

You may have a different scenario than any of the cases we just discussed. For a quick look at mutual fund objectives, refer to Appendix 10-1.

As you look for a mutual fund to fit your investment plans you will

Table 10-1. Diversity of One Fund Family—How One Company Has Organized the Funds in Its Family by Goals and Investment Philosophy

Maximum current return

Aggressively seeking higher-than-average yields without undue risk to principal.

1. A high-yield trust that seeks high current income from a diversified portfolio of lower rated corporate bonds.

2. An option income trust that seeks high current return from common stocks on which call options are written.

High current income and stability

A conservative approach, aimed at producing a high current return, consistent with prudent risk and stability of principal.

1. A daily dividend trust that seeks income with liquidity from short-term "money market" securities.

2. A tax-exempt income fund that seeks income largely exempt from federal tax through quality municipal bonds.

3. An income fund that seeks current income consistent with prudent risk, emphasizing quality corporate bonds.

Growth plus current income

Securities selected both for capital appreciation and dividend or interest payout. Risks are relatively modest, with reasonable stability of principal.

1. A fund that is "balanced" for current income, preservation of principal, and possible capital growth.

2. A convertible fund that puts equal emphasis on appreciation and income from convertible bonds and stocks.

Long-term growth

Common stocks, generally of established, highly rated companies, selected for growth potential over the longer term. Risks are moderate; some income can be expected.

1. A growth fund based upon a broadly diversified common stock portfolio seeking growth and some income.

2. An investor's fund based upon a concentrated portfolio of quality stocks geared for growth and some income.

Growth through technology and energy resources

Seeks growth of capital and some income by investing in companies active in science, research, and the development of energy resources.

1. A fund based upon a high-quality portfolio focusing on stocks of larger science-oriented companies.

2. A fund emphasizing smaller science- and technology-oriented companies with unusual opportunities for growth.

Table 10-1. (*Continued*)

Growth through technology and energy resources (*Continued*)

3. A fund seeking capital appreciation through investments in companies believed to be responsive to domestic and worldwide energy needs.

Maximum capital appreciation

Aggressively seeking capital growth from common stocks. Regarded as high-risk/high-reward investment; income is not a consideration.

1. A fund based upon an internationally diversified portfolio that may invest up to 70 percent in foreign stocks.

2. A fund that seeks out companies with above-average earnings growth; allowed to invest borrowed money.

3. A fund that looks for stocks that appear to be undervalued by the market.

also notice that many funds are part of a *family of funds*. It is preferable to buy a fund from a family because most families—and you should confirm this before you buy—offer exchange privileges, either for free or a very small fee. This means that with either a telephone call (often on a toll-free number) or a letter, you can switch your money from one of the family's funds into another that might be performing better.

Table 10-1 shows how one company has organized the funds in its family by goal and investment philosophy. Most large families provide similar charts of their funds that rate each one in terms of growth, income, and stability (or volatility).

Keep in mind that once you have invested in a fund, you are hiring the fund manager to diversify your investment within the framework of the fund's objective and the fund manager's expertise.

Buying Mutual Funds

Mutual funds are easy to buy. The price you pay for a share can change from day to day, depending on the value of the securities it holds. The share price is also called the net asset value (NAV). Funds can be purchased directly from the company—if you write or call any of these funds, an agent of the fund will contact you and guide you through your purchase. Or you can purchase funds through certain financial institutions or an investment adviser.

Mutual funds are either sold by a broker (registered representative) with a "load" or sales charge, or sold directly to the public through advertising campaigns without a load. Any fees charged by a fund are described in the prospectus.

Sales charges on funds that carry loads vary, but the usual amount on smaller investments ranges around 4 to 5 percent of net asset value. Larger investors are given discounts. Load discounts are also allowed by certain funds that offer:

Letter of intent privileges. You obtain the discount by stating your intent to invest the amount qualifying for a discount over a set period, such as 13 months.

Right of accumulation. You already own shares in the fund or the fund family, and your current purchase will bring you up to discount level.

Combined purchase privilege. You are buying into a fund as part of a group that qualifies for a discount.

Your broker will have full details on the circumstances under which discounts are available; they are also outlined in each fund's prospectus.

No-load funds often advertise in popular financial publications. To buy one, you either write or call for a prospectus and sales material. Then you fill out a form and mail it to the company with your check.

There are many high-quality no-load funds, but don't let your decision to buy hinge on whether the fund you are considering carries a sales charge. Remember that someone has to pay for all those marketing campaigns that no-load funds run, even if they do not charge a sales fee. In some cases their management fees and assessed expenses might be higher than those charged by a load fund. Instead of focusing on the sales charge, you should try to make an accurate judgment of how well a given fund is likely to perform for you, in terms of your objectives, over the period of time that you expect to hold it.

Always check on performance. Don't avoid this important task. Many large stock brokerage firms now have their own mutual funds, some of which are excellent. You will be more confident about any purchase, however, if you personally investigate the fund's track record. We must also point out to you that this is not the only basis for selecting a fund. What if the fund manager, who guided the fund so successfully in its past, is no longer there? You must also look at who made that record and what is happening in the economy at this point in time. You'll find much of this information in the bond's prospectus and annual reports. Another point of consideration is the fund type—is it still in favor? Finding this information requires you to take a look at where the fund is invested. A fund could be out of favor because it invests in activities that spoil the environment, or in products that are no longer in demand, such as Nehru jackets, or South African gold. You cannot drive an automobile by looking at the rear-view mirror—you must look forward and sideways as well. When you select a fund, make sure the objective fits in with your own objectives.

Who Regulates Mutual Funds?

Investment companies are regulated by four major federal statutes. The Securities Act of 1933 requires filing with the SEC a registration statement that contains extensive information regarding the fund. This act also requires that a prospectus be given to potential investors. The objective of a mutual fund's prospectus is to provide the reader with full and complete disclosure. It is a legal requirement that you be given the prospectus of any fund to read before you purchase that fund. It should always cover the following key points:

- The fund's investment objective and financial goals
- The investment methods used to achieve these goals
- The name and address of its investment adviser
- A brief description of the adviser's experience
- The level of investment risk the fund will assume to reach its investment objective (ranges from maximum to minimum risk)
- Investments that the fund will *not* make
- Tax consequences of the fund to the investor
- How to purchase shares
- Any costs or fees involved in purchasing shares

The Securities Exchange Act of 1934 provides anti-fraud guidelines regarding the purchase and sale of mutual fund shares and all securities. Distributors of mutual funds are regulated by the Securities and Exchange Commission (SEC) and the National Association of Securities Dealers (NASD), pursuant to the 1934 act.

The Investment Advisors Act of 1940 regulates the activities of investment advisers.

But perhaps the most important act is the highly detailed regulatory Investment Company Act of 1940, which requires mutual funds to register with the SEC. Industry professionals worked closely with the SEC to draft the 1940 act and then decided to form a permanent committee. This permanent committee's function was to work with the SEC in formulating rules and regulations that would implement the new law. It was called the National Committee of Investment Companies. As their activities increased they changed their name in 1941 to the National

Association of Investment Companies. It took on the responsibilities of promoting public education, acting as a liaison with the SEC, and monitoring legislation affecting mutual funds. In 1961 it changed its name to the Investment Company Institute (ICI).

The ICI gathers an enormous amount of research and information on the mutual fund industry each year and publishes it in the form of the *Mutual Fund Fact Book*. This directory and a number of other information pieces can be purchased directly from ICI by writing to them at 1600 M. Street, N.W., Suite 600, Washington, DC 20036.

In addition to the regulatory agencies, four major organizations track mutual funds. They are Wiesenberger Investment Companies, Standard and Poor's Corporation, Lipper Analytical Services, and Morningstar Corporation. Each of these organizations publish their research.

Diversity Is Built In

By law, an investment in a mutual fund must buy shares in at least 20 different companies. In reality, most funds spread their money much further, seeking diversity among various types of industries and within certain industries.

The following examples show how several funds diversify their holdings while seeking different objectives. The type of holdings listed are taken from the funds' annual reports and, since they are managed funds, their portfolios vary from month to month and year to year, depending on market conditions.

Example 1: Bond Fund

If you want to begin on the conservative side, find common stocks unnerving, and desire a relatively safe place to invest your money at a good rate of return, you might consider one of the bond funds. Again, you must understand just what "safe" means to you. Does it mean you want your exact principal to be delivered to you 10 years out? That means safety of principal, but it does not mean safety of purchasing power. What you really have to try to understand is that there is no such thing as total safety in the investment business or in your life.

Because all funds are not equal, it's very important to look at the expense ratio (see Glossary, page 302) of the bond fund. What is it costing you? What are the sales charges and management fees? Bond funds, by their nature, do not normally have a great chance for appreciation, so expense factors are very important when you are buying a debt fund (Ginnie Maes, government security funds, bond funds, tax-free bond funds, etc.). Please understand that I am *not* saying you should avoid bonds or bond funds completely. They are appropriate bottom-of-the-pyramid holdings, particularly for people whose investment comfort zones are firmly rooted at the conservative end of the spectrum. Remember, however, you must calculate the total cost of your investments, as measured in terms of taxes and inflation, before you can calculate their worth—or cost—to you.

Our hypothetical example is described by its management as a fund for "the conservative, income-minded investor." It seeks high current return from a mix of quality bonds, government securities, and prime-rated commercial paper and certificates of deposit. Suppose you are just becoming acquainted with the mutual fund market and decide to invest $1000. Here's what that money buys:

Government obligations	
United States	$ 396
Canada	86
Corporate notes (none rated less than A)	
Banks/holding companies	36
Basic industries	33
Chemicals	8
Conglomerates	29
Data processing	13
Electric utilities	114
Finance	77
Retail	8
Telephone	30
Transportation	14
Money market instruments	171
TOTAL INVESTMENTS	1015.40
Other assets minus liabilities	(15.40)
NET ASSETS	$1000.00

Example 2: Growth Fund

If you are willing to trade some security for capital growth and some income for capital gains—and you should be—you will look for a growth fund. Our example comes from the AIM Weingarten Fund (according to financial statements at this writing), which is described as a fund seeking long-term growth of capital (future income rather than current income) by investing in large capitalization (refers to large corporations such as IBM, Ford Motors, Exxon, etc.) equities. Your $1000 would be invested like this:

Short-term notes	$ 127.20
Common stocks	
Basic industries	21.20
Business services	117.80
Capital goods	69.30
Consumer durables	54.10
Consumer nondurables	369.40
Consumer services	16.80
Energy	15.20
Financial	54.70
Retail	126.30
Utilities	5.00
Wholesale	12.20
Other	26.20
TOTAL INVESTMENTS	1015.40
Other assets minus liabilities	(15.40)
NET ASSETS	$1000.00

Example 3:
Aggressive Growth Fund

Another type of fund is the "aggressive growth" category. Here, your investment goal would be capital appreciation with very little income. Our example can be described as an aggressive mutual fund seeking capital appreciation. (These funds invest in companies like Gap, Home Depot, Toys R Us, etc. that are growing at a much faster rate than the norm.) Rather than restricting ourselves strictly to *America's aggressive growth companies* (this cuts out 70 percent of the investment opportunities available to us), let's look at an aggressive fund company called Templeton Smaller Companies Growth Fund, Inc. (according to financial statements at this writing). Your $1000 would be invested as follows:

Common stocks	
Energy sources	$ 16.00
Utilities	5.00

Building materials and components	2.00
Chemicals	1.00
Forest products and paper	82.00
Mining and metals	3.00
Construction and housing	52.00
Data processing and reproduction	1.00
Electrical and electronics	14.00
Electrical components and instruments	16.00
Industrial components	11.00
Machinery and engineering	11.00
Appliances and household durables	24.00
Automobiles	3.00
Food and household products	11.00
Health and personal care	11.00
Recreation, other consumer goods	3.00
Textiles and apparel	22.00
Broadcasting and publishing	18.00
Business and public services	47.00
Leisure and tourism	1.00
Merchandising	49.00
Telecommunications	87.00
Transportation	101.00
Wholesale and international trade	29.00
Banking	90.00
Financial services	50.00
Insurance	41.00
Real estate	7.00
Multi-industries	61.00
Bonds	12.00
Short-term obligations	120.00
TOTAL INVESTMENTS	1001.00
Other Assets minus liabilities	(1.00)
NET ASSETS	$1000.00

Example 4: Specialty Fund

The investor who wants to speculate in a specialty fund might consider a gold-mining fund. Here's what your $1000 might look like in a hypothetical fund:

Common stocks

Long-life gold mines	$ 314
Gold mining finance	136
Medium-life gold mines	171
Silver/other mines	69
Short-life gold mines	57
Developing gold/silver mines	11
Other industries	36

Other

Treasury bills	103
Short-term money market investments	94
Overseas bonds	24.40
TOTAL INVESTMENTS	1015.40
Other assets minus liabilities	(15.40)
NET ASSETS	$1000.00

To repeat: As a lone investor with $1000, or even $100,000, you could not obtain this sort of diversity on your own, even if you resorted to buying expensive odd lots of common stocks.

Looking Over Management's Performance

Anyone can randomly compile a diversified portfolio of investments. The trick is to find the profitable stocks, over the long or short run. When considering a mutual fund, you should look over the stock selection track record of its management.

If you were to visit the offices of a large fund, you would find a variety of financial experts and technicians at work. Most funds have their own analysts who study companies' performances, spend several days on-site going over the books, and then compare their findings with those of analysts from major brokerage houses. The fund analysts make recommendations to the portfolio manager, who makes the final decision on whether to buy or pass. Portfolio managers also decide when a stock holding should be sold. These professional money managers are objective in their approach and have no sentimental attachment whatever to the stocks they purchase. When a stock fails to meet certain computer-checked performance criteria, it is jettisoned from the portfolio. Unlike some individual investors, a portfolio manager will never hang onto a sinking stock because "XYZ stock has always been our family," or "Dad had faith in it, so I should too."

The portfolio manager must defend his or her buy-and-sell choices before a review committee, usually on a weekly basis. If performance isn't satisfactory, he or she may be looking for another job. The ultimate responsibility for a fund lies with its board of directors, some of whom are independent of the fund's management.

A report on management's track record is as close as your public library. You should become familiar with using at least one of the services that chart mutual fund performance. The most common of these are the mutual fund section in the back of Standard & Poor's *Stock Guide,* Morningstar, the monthly and annual reports of Wiesenberger Investment Services, *Business Week*'s annual scoreboard issue, Lipper Analytical Services' *Mutual Fund Performance Analysis*—all of these can usually be found in your public library. Look at the total return of a fund, capital gains distributions (a capital gain is the increase in value of an asset from date of purchase to date of sale), dividends (yield on investments), and increases in net asset value (the worth of each share) over the past few years.

Benefits of Fund Ownership

One of the time-savers a mutual fund will offer you is a single 1099 form for your tax bookkeeping. Instead of having to contend with the myriad forms a large portfolio can produce, you will have just one that neatly summarizes your long-term capital gains and tells you which dividends qualify for tax exclusion and which do not. The fund handles all the paperwork.

Other conveniences to look for in a fund's prospectus include:

Access to Your Money. By law, an open-ended mutual fund must stand ready on any given day to redeem (buy back) any or all of your shares at their current net asset value.

Automatic Investment. Some funds offer a payroll deduction type plan, or you can arrange to make regular contributions to your fund by authorizing it to withdraw a specified amount from your bank account.

Automatic Reinvestment.   Most funds offer this feature. It allows you to reinvest all or part of your fund income (dividends or capital gain distributions) into additional shares. You may cancel this arrangement at any time.

Automatic Withdrawal.   This feature allows you to take your income as it is earned in check form, or you can specify a set amount that you would like to receive each month. This system works particularly well for retirees.

Exchange Privileges.   This is the right to switch out of one fund and into another in the same family. The service is performed free or for a nominal charge. Some funds include *telephone exchange privileges*.

Redemption.   This allows you to sell your shares, or part of them, back to the fund by following a stipulated redemption procedure. (This usually requires the help of your broker or bank or can be accomplished through a letter.) Payment for your shares is to be mailed to you within seven days of notification.

Retirement Plans.   This is one of the best uses to which you can put a mutual fund. The Internal Revenue Service has qualified most of them to be custodians of programs such as Individual Retirement Accounts (IRAs), Keogh plans, and corporate pension and profit-sharing plans. Some of them can be used in conjunction with a variable annuity plan.

Additional Purchases.   All funds have a minimum initial investment amount, usually $500 or $1000. Most will permit you to make additional, smaller investments whenever you wish.

Checkwriting.   This is a relatively recent innovation that allows you to write checks and obtain credit card advances against the value of your investment in a fund. Most funds with this feature are money market funds.

Newsletters.   Many funds keep in touch through newsletters which provide a wealth of practical and easy to understand information on a variety of subjects.

A Recommendation?

Mutual funds can fit almost anywhere in an investment portfolio. You can buy into a fund that specializes in high-grade, tax-exempt municipal bonds that, while not risk-free by any means (remember the bond market debacle of 1980?), are at the conservative end of the risk spectrum. The growth potential of the capital you put into such an investment is quite limited, however, and in some cases may not exist at all. At the other extreme, you can buy a mutual fund with little dividend yield but very high capital appreciation, such as a fund specializing in South African gold mines. This would be considered a high-risk venture. Most funds, however, fall somewhere in between in terms of their mix of risk, income, and capital gains.

I'm not going to tell you what mutual fund to buy. I can only tell you the type of fund I prefer and why I think you should consider it, unless you are investing for the short term.

I like common stock funds that seek capital growth. Why? Remember that in investing there are two types of money: equity and debt. Equity money means that you own a piece of the business, a piece of the action. It is common sense to me that if my children and their children buy clothes at certain stores, drink certain sodas, then I want to own some of that. You can "own what you buy" through a well-diversified portfolio of a mutual fund. This kind of investment should provide you with some dividend return, but, more important, it should allow your money to grow. In the face of today's rates of inflation and taxation, growth must be the name of the game. As I have pointed out before, since 1954 there has never been a single year of deflation! Obviously, there is risk in common stocks, as there is risk in anything in life. Remember, there is no such thing as a risk-less anything, only degrees of risk.

In a debt-based investment such as a bond fund, you are actually making a loan and later getting that money back with some interest. But your dollars become worth less and less as inflation chips away at them, so you should seriously question whether the principal plus the interest you will collect some years down the road is, in reality, more than what you've lent. Remember, too, that the interest you receive can be fully taxable.

The one consideration that we must factor in is the emotional side of the equation when investing money. Even though I might say that bonds provide no long-term hedge against inflation and that they fluctuate tremendously based on interest rates, if you sleep soundly at night invested only in government security funds, then you must do what you can live with. If moving your money into a more diversified position makes your stomach roll, then don't do it. But if you are able to understand risk/reward and the importance of long-term investing, you will be able to understand why equity ownership, in my opinion, is the key.

The thing to remember is that mutual funds can fit practically anywhere in an investment portfolio. To make it easier for you to get started, I've included Appendix 10-2, A Sampling Directory of Mutual Fund Listings, which lists many mutual fund companies and how to contact them.

APPENDIX 10-1
Mutual Fund Investment Objectives

The Investment Company Institute, the national association of the American investment company industry, serves as a clearinghouse of information on the mutual fund industry in the United States. They have classified mutual funds into 22 broad categories according to their basic objectives.

Fund objective	Definition
Aggressive Growth Funds	Seek maximum capital gains as their investment objective. Current income is not a significant factor. Some may invest in stocks of businesses that are somewhat out of the mainstream. Some may use specialized investment techniques such as option writing or short-term trading.
Balanced Funds	Generally have a three-part investment objective: (1) to conserve the investor's initial principal, (2) to pay current income, and (3) to promote long-term growth of both this principal and income. Balanced funds have a portfolio mix of bonds, preferred stocks, and common stocks.
Corporate Bond Funds	Seek a high level of income by buying bonds of corporations for the majority of the fund's portfolio. The rest of the portfolio may be in U.S. Treasury bonds or bonds issued by a federal agency.
Flexible Portfolio Funds	May be 100 percent invested in stocks or bonds or money market instruments, depending on market conditions. These funds give the money managers the greatest flexibility in anticipating or responding to economic changes.
GNMA or Ginnie Mae Funds	Invest in mortgage securities backed by the Government National Mortgage Association (GNMA). To qualify for this category, the majority of the portfolio must always be invested in mortgage-backed securities.
Global Bond Funds	Invest in the debt securities of companies and countries worldwide, including the United States.

Fund objective	Definition
Global Equity Funds	Invest in securities traded worldwide, including the United States. Compared to direct investments, global funds offer investors an easier avenue to investing abroad. The funds' professional money managers handle the trading and recordkeeping details and deal with differences in currencies, languages, time zones, laws, and regulations, and business customs and practices. In addition to another layer of diversification, global funds add another layer of risk—exchange-rate risk.
Growth Funds	Invest in the common stock of well-established companies. Their primary aim is to produce an increase in the value of their investments (capital gains) rather than a flow of dividends. Investors who buy a growth fund are more interested in seeing the fund's share price rise than in receiving income from dividends.
Growth and Income Funds	Invest mainly in the common stock of companies that have had increasing share value but also a solid record of paying dividends. This type of fund attempts to combine long-term capital growth with a steady stream of income.
High-Yield Bond Funds	Maintain at least two-thirds of their portfolios in lower-rated corporate bonds (Baa or lower by Moody's rating service and BBB or lower by Standard and Poor's rating service). In return for a generally higher yield, investors must bear a greater degree of risk than for higher-rated bonds.
Income-Bond Funds	Seek a higher level of current income for their shareholders by investing at all times in a mix of corporate and government bonds.
Income Equity Funds	Seek a high level of current income for their shareholders by investing primarily in equity securities of companies with good dividend-paying records.
Income-Mixed Funds	Seek a high level of current income for their shareholders by investing in income-producing securities, including both equities and debt instruments.
International Funds	Invest in equity securities of companies located outside the United States. Two-thirds of their portfolios must be so invested at all times to be categorized here.
Long-Term Municipal Bond Funds	Invest in bonds issued by states and municipalities to finance schools, highways, hospitals, airports, bridges, water and sewer works, and other public projects. In most cases, income earned on these securities is not taxed by the federal government, but may be taxed under state and local laws. For some taxpayers, portions of income earned on these securities may be subject to the federal alternative minimum tax.

Fund objective	Definition
Money Market Mutual Funds	Invest in the short-term securities sold in the money market. These are generally the safest, most stable securities available, including Treasury bills, certificates of deposit of large banks, and commercial paper (the short-term IOUs of large U.S. corporations).
Option/Income Funds	Seek a higher current return by investing primarily in dividend-paying common stocks on which call options are traded on national securities exchanges. Current return generally consists of dividends, premiums from writing options, net short-term gains from sales of portfolio securities on exercises of options or otherwise, and any profits from closing purchase transactions.
Precious Metals/Gold Funds	Maintain two-thirds of their portfolios invested in securities associated with gold, silver, and other precious metals.
Short-Term Municipal Bond Funds	Invest in municipal securities with relatively short maturities. These are also known as tax-exempt money market funds. For some taxpayers, portions of income from these securities may be subject to the federal alternative minimum tax.
State Municipal Bond Funds	
Long-term	Work just like other long-term municipal bond funds (see above) except their portfolios contain the issues of only one state. A resident of that state has the advantage of receiving income free of both federal and state tax. For some taxpayers, portions of income from these securities may be subject to the federal alternative minimum tax.
Short-term	Work just like other short-term municipal bond funds (see above) except their portfolios contain the issues of only one state. A resident of that state has the advantage of receiving income free of both federal and state tax. For some taxpayers, portions of income from these securities may be subject to the federal alternative minimum tax.
U.S. Government Income Funds	Invest in a variety of government securities. These include U.S. Treasury bonds, federally guaranteed mortgage-backed securities, and other government notes.

APPENDIX 10-2
A Sampling Directory of
Mutual Fund Listings

The following mutual fund groups or families of funds are only a representative sampling of the funds available for purchase. In the cases of funds' not listing an 800 number, we have listed area codes and telephone numbers. The majority of mutual fund groups have toll-free numbers. If you are interested in a fund that is not listed, call 1-800-555-1212 and ask for the fund's toll-free number.

Mutual fund company	Telephone number
ABT Fund Group	800 441-6580
ADTEK Fund, Inc.	414 257-1842
Aetna Funds	203 273-4806
AIM Group	800 347-1919
Alliance Group	800 221-5672
AMA Family of Funds	800 AMA-FUND
AMCAP Fund, Inc.	800 421-0180
American Capital Group	800 421-5666
Anchor Series Trust	800 858-8850
Axe-Houghton Funds	800 323-USFG
Bankers National Funds	800 888-4918
Bartlett Capital Trust Funds	800 543-0863
Bedford Group	800 523-7798
Benham Group	800 321-8321
Boston Company Funds	800 343-6324
Bull & Bear Funds	800 847-4200
Burnham Funds	800 874-FUND
Calvert Funds	800 368-2745
Carnegie Funds	800 321-2322
Chubb Funds	603 224-7741
Colonial Group	800 426-3750
Common Sense Group	800 544-5445
Compass Capital Group	800 451-8371
Conestoga Family of Funds	800 344-2716

Mutual fund company	Telephone number
Daiwa Money Funds	212 945-0100
Dean Witter Funds	800 869-3863
Delaware Group	800 523-4650
Dreyfus Group	800 645-6561
Eaton Vance Group	800 225-6265
Enterprise Group of Funds	800 432-4320
EquiFund	800 225-6265
Equitable Funds	800 852-6860
Equitec Siebel Fund Group	800 869-8900
Evergreen Group	800 235-0064
FBL Series Funds	800 247-4170
Federated Funds	800 245-2423
Fidelity Funds	800 544-8888
Financial Strategic Portfolios	800 525-8085
First Investors Funds	800 221-3846
Franklin Funds	800 632-2180
General Group	800 242-8621
Goldman-Sachs Group	800 621-2550
G. T. Global Funds	800 824-1580
Guardian Funds	800 221-3253
GW Sierra Trust Funds	800 331-3426
Harbor Funds	800 422-1050
Heartland Group	800 432-7856
Helmsman Funds	800 338-4345
Heritage Funds	813 573-3800
IAI Funds	800 927-3863
IDS Funds	800 328-8300
Independence Capital Group of Funds	800 833-4264
International Cash Portfolios	800 826-0188
INVESCO Funds	800 554-1156
IVY Funds	800 235-3322
Janus Group	800 525-3713
John Hancock Group	800 225-5291
J. W. Gant Fund	407 241-3846

Mutual fund company	Telephone number
Kemper Group	800 621-1148
Keystone Group	800 225-1587
Kidder, Peabody Group	212 510-5552
LBVIP Group	800 328-4552
Legg Mason Funds	800 822-5544
Lexington Group	800 526-0056
Lord Abbett Funds	800 223-4224
MacKay-Shields Group	800 522-4204
Mackenzie Funds	800 456-5111
Mariner Funds	800 421-8878
Massachusetts Financial Group	800 343-2829
Merrill Lynch Funds	800 637-3863
Midwest Group	800 543-8721
MONY Funds	201 907-6669
NASL Series Trust Group	800 344-1029
National Funds	800 237-1718
Neuberger & Berman Group	800 877-9700
OLDE Group	313 961-6666
Olympus Funds	800 626-FUND
Oppenheimer Group	800 525-7048
Overland Express Funds	800 458-6589
Pacific Horizon Funds	800 367-6075
PaineWebber Group	800 544-9300
Parkstone Group	800 451-8377
Phoenix Group	800 243-1574
Pioneer Group	800 225-6292
Prudential-Bache Group	800 225-1852
Putnam Group	800 225-2465
Quantum Fund	606 491-4271
Quest Group	800 232-FUND
Rightime Funds	800 242-1421
Rodney Square Funds	800 225-5084
Royce Funds	800 221-4268

Mutual fund company	Telephone number
SAFECO Group	800 426-6730
SafeGuard Group	800 523-7798
Salem Funds	800 245-2423
Scudder Group	800 225-5163
Seligman Group	800 221-2450
Sentinel Group	800 282-3863
Shearson Lehman Funds	800 334-4636
Smith Barney Funds	800 544-7836
State Street Group	617 482-3920
Strong Group	800 368-3863
Templeton Funds	800 237-0738
Thomson Fund Group	800 628-1237
Transamerica Group	800 999-3863
T. Rowe Price Group	800 638-5660
Twentieth Century Group	800 345-2021
Unified Funds	800 862-7283
United Funds	800 366-5465
USAA Group	800 531-8181
U.S. Eagle Funds	800 622-3363
Value Line Group	800 223-0818
Vanguard Group	800 662-7447
Van Kampen Group	800 225-2222
Venture Group	800 279-0279
Voyager Group	800 553-2143
Wasatch Funds	800 345-7460
Weiss, Peck & Greer Group	800 223-3332
Wright Managed Group	800 225-6265
Yamaichi Funds	212 466-6800
Zweig Funds	800 272-2700

11

The Annuity Advantage

Under normal circumstances, the average individual in our society stops producing money through work at age 60 or 65.

FREEDOM FOCUS

- *What is an annuity?*
- *How do you fund an annuity?*
- *What types of annuities are there?*
- *What are the tax advantages of annuities?*
- *How do annuities fit into your freedom strategy?*

Through the miraculous advancement of civilization, almost all of the insurmountable health and welfare problems that plagued our ancestors have today been reduced to chapters in history books. But out of this also comes the reality that you and I will live longer and better than our counterparts of a century or so ago—and an increasingly important and challenging stage of life is retirement. Our country has never had a group of retired individuals so large and diverse. You have a choice to make when faced with this reality: You can choose to plan for what will probably be a lengthened retirement, or you can choose to rely on fixed resources such as social security and pensions, assuming they remain available for the length of your retirement. If you choose to plan properly, every year of your long life can be full and satisfying. But your plan must be adequate and complete, or your retirement years may be strained and stressful rather than the pleasurable time which we all envision.

People at Work versus Money at Work

Under normal circumstances, the average individual in our society stops producing money through work at age 60 or 65. You, and whoever might be dependent upon you at that time, will have to rely on the income-generating capabilities of your investments, plus whatever retirement income you may have. People at work versus money at work: The latter will always outlast the former, so you must put your money into vehicles that are going to turn in good performances over the long run.

Currently, American men age 65 have an average life expectancy of 15 more years, and women of the same age can look forward, on the average, to 18–20 more years. By the time younger Americans reach retirement age, those figures probably will have gone up. The message you should be getting is this: *The chances are very good that money you invest now will have to support you through a substantial part of your retirement. You must find ways to maximize the productivity of your investment dollars.*

Consider this scenario: You are in your early thirties and looking for a sound investment that will promise you some retirement income. After carefully analyzing your budget, you decide that you will be able to invest $50 a week in this program. Do you know what your investment will be worth 35 years from now if you place it in a variable annuity that averages a total annual return of 15 percent, tax-deferred? (Caution, I am not referring to a fixed annuity, but rather a variable annuity utilizing equities.) Take a deep breath before you read the next number because it may knock the wind out of you: *$3,260,946.* Yes, *nearly 3.3 million dollars!*

Pensions, profit-sharing plans, social security—all of these can provide part of the income you will need when you stop working. But will those sources of revenue, generally fixed in nature, provide enough income for you to keep pace with increases in food, shelter, clothing, health care—in other words, with the costs of inflation.

This chapter introduces investment vehicles that are frequently overlooked, despite their high degree of safety, affordability, and money-making potential: *annuities.*

Annuities, unlike an insurance policy that is intended to provide financial protection to your beneficiaries if you die too soon, are designed to protect you from living too long. That is, living beyond your financial resources. Annuities offer tax deferral, compound earnings, payout flexibility, an umbrella for a variety of other investment vehicles, and an excellent means of supplementing your retirement pension through private sector sources.

Annuities are not new. The Roman Empire provided us with the first fixed-annuity contract when the emperor rewarded loyal senators possessing long service records with a contract of income for the remainder of the senators' lives. Today there are several variations of annuities designed to meet an individual's future income needs.

What Is an Annuity?

Annuities are among the oldest financial instruments in existence. Even the version that we consider the newest, the variable annuity, dates at least to 1265, when Robert Norman and his son Baudoin, entrepreneurs in Utrecht, Holland, arranged for a survivorship annuity in Parisian livres that was to be paid back in Tournai sous if the purchasing power of the Parisian livre declined.

In its traditional form, the annuity is a contract that is purchased from a life insurance company for the purpose of providing the annuitant (the purchaser) with a guaranteed monthly income for life. This income can begin immediately after purchase of the annuity or upon retirement. The purchase may be made in installments or all at once (single premium), and the payback varies according to the amount you have put into the annuity and your life expectancy, as determined actuarially by an insurance company. Some annuities run out after a specified period, but the vast majority of them pay a monthly income until the holder's death. In buying an annuity you are betting that you will live longer than the insurance company thinks you will.

A "qualified" annuity is one that meets IRS requirements for inclusion in tax-favored group pension plans, Keogh retirement plans, and IRAs (Individual Retirement Accounts). You are permitted to buy these annuities with pretax dollars. "Nonqualified" annuities do not enjoy this advantage, but their earnings are tax-deferred.

Annuity Advantages

Among the annuity's features are tax-deferred accumulation, a choice of variable or fixed rate returns, and a flexibility that may appeal to a variety of situations.

With tax deferral, the annuity's principal and earnings are allowed to accumulate through compounding, without being diminished by taxes. The absence of such pressure allows the account to earn more on more money than would be possible if this were a taxable investment. Just how much more depends on the principal amount, term of maturity, and the corresponding rate of return.

For example, an individual making annual payments of $2000 over a 30-year period, in a *taxable* investment earning a 12 percent rate of return compounded annually, would accumulate $276,985. In a tax-deferred annuity using the same annual contribution amount, frequency, and rate of return, the individual would accumulate $540,585.

Likewise, a *lump-sum* investment in a tax-deferred annuity would register greater growth over time. Consider that a $100,000 investment earning 12 percent over 30 years would grow to $1,201,414 in a taxable investment—assuming a 28 percent tax bracket—while reaching $2,995,992 when taxes are deferred.

If you can't make a lump-sum investment and opt to invest, for example, at a rate of $50 a week, continuously, there are definite rewards to reap. Even if you are no longer in your thirties, your investment will still grow to $769,786 if you can invest for 30 years, or $412,969 if you have 25 years to work with. Table 11-1 illustrates what weekly investments of $15, $25, $50, $75, and $100 can grow to in a tax-deferred annuity with an average annual total return of 12 percent.

Can't afford $50 a week? Cut that back to $15 a week, and you will still have about $1.3 million at the end of 35 years, providing that your variable annuity has averaged a 16 percent range or better. Like most other

Table 11-1. Weekly Deposits into Tax-Deferred Plan*

End of year	Amount of weekly deposits				
	$15	$25	$50	$75	$100
	$ 15	$ 25	$ 50	$ 75	$ 100
1	830	1,383	2,765	4,139	5,531
5	5,348	8,913	17,826	26,740	35,653
10	15,086	25,143	50,286	75,428	100,571
15	32,817	54,695	109,389	164,084	218,779
20	65,103	108,505	217,009	325,514	434,018
25	123,891	206,485	412,969	619,454	825,939
30	230,936	384,892	769,786	1,154,678	1,539,571
35	425,849	709,749	1,419,498	2,129,247	2,838,996

*Assumes average annual total return of 12 percent.

investments with a high reward potential, an element of risk is always there. My point is that with a variable annuity, such earnings are *possible*.

Most annuities also offer a choice of interest-earning behavior. Depending upon your level of risk tolerance and other personal preferences, you may select either a fixed or variable rate of return.

In an annuity that earns a *fixed rate* you are given a guaranteed rate of return, and both your principal and the interest earned are guaranteed against loss.

This type of contract is frequently attractive in the early development of an individual's financial plan, when guaranteed performance is important and/or when interest rates are high. Under the fixed-rate annuity, almost all of the risk, including that associated with mortality, administrative and other expenses, and investment performance, is borne by the issuing company.

With a *variable annuity* your rate of return is tied to the performance of the underlying investments used. Neither the principal nor the earnings generated are guaranteed during the annuitant's lifetime.

The selection of a variable annuity may be attractive to both the young or older investor for the same reason—the opportunity to capitalize on potentially positive investment performance, while generating a return that outpaces inflation. In addition, there is usually a broad range of investments to select from, as well as the ability to move from one selection to another as personal preference and market conditions warrant without creating a taxable event. While the insurance company continues to guarantee the risk in mortality and expense accumulation, the individual now assumes the investment risk.

Also left to individual discretion is how the money goes in and comes out of the annuity until the contract is annuitized. You determine the amount and frequency of payments, as well as the method of disbursements. (But pay attention to age requirements and tax consequences.)

Before you leave this subject, I'd like to give you an example of another of the variable annuity's advantages. Suppose that you have a $10,000 variable annuity contract that takes a beating in the stock market and drops to a value of $8000. And then suppose you die. What would your heirs receive? The devalued contract amount? No. They would inherit the full $10,000. Upon your death, your contract would return to its original value, even if it lost ground during your lifetime. Although your principal can fluctuate in a variable annuity, your heirs will not be affected by any bad luck you might encounter in the investment arena. All variable annuities have some form of minimum death benefit. In general, the beneficiary cannot receive less than what was put into the contract. However, there are slight variations among the various companies, so be sure to check this out when considering an annuity purchase.

Funding the Annuity

Typically, annuities can be purchased through life insurance underwriters, financial planning professionals, stock brokers, banks, and other financial institutions. Surprisingly enough, you can open an account with as little as $250, and some annuities qualify as IRA programs. Some of you may have thought that annuities were just for the wealthy who are looking to shelter money.

In funding an annuity you may do one of the following:

- Make installment premium payments of a set amount on a monthly, quarterly, semi-annual, or annual basis.
- Make flexible premium payments with the amount and premium varying.
- Make a single-premium annuity payment in one lump sum.

While funding for the first two methods frequently comes from earned income, the availability of a lump-sum amount as a single-premium payment may come from a variety of sources including a payout from a pension or profit-sharing plan, the distribution of proceeds from a life insurance policy, a 1035 "tax-free exchange," or an unexpected windfall (i.e., lottery winnings, inheritance, etc.).

Additionally, one of the most popular sources for annuity funding in a lump-sum fashion comes from existing monies that have been accumulating elsewhere (possibly in CDs, money market accounts) and are currently subject to taxation. Rather than continue to pay taxes on these funds (not needed for cash flow) individuals often opt to transfer a portion of them (as a premium) to an annuity's tax-deferred environment. The move expectedly creates the potential for a tax reduction on the individual's overall income tax base, plus the potential benefit for increased earnings growth on monies sheltered in a tax-deferred environment.

The actual payout of the annuity, whether it goes to you or your designated annuitant, may be on a deferred or an immediate basis. In the case of deferred, the payout will begin (according to your wishes) at some future date which is more than one year after purchase, while payouts from the immediate annuity will begin as stated within the first year. The respective payment(s) may be made in a lump-sum or installment fashion, according to the selected option.

For example, you may request a payout schedule that simply provides you with an income for the rest of your life. Under this schedule, payments may be made monthly, quarterly, semiannually, or annually.

However, if you're married you may want to consider a joint and survivor life option that will provide monthly payments for as long as either you or your spouse live.

Beyond these options there exist additional opportunities for structuring the annuity's payout behavior. Ultimately, the payout amount may vary with the age and the sex of the individual covered by the annuity (annuitant) and the option selected.

Liquidity

While the tax-deferred annuity is ideally used to hold and retain monies for an extended period of time, free from any current tax liability, the funds are available—if needed—without IRS penalty, under certain conditions, and with or without a company withdrawal charge.

According to IRS regulations, withdrawals are governed by a variety of factors, requiring an individualized evaluation for determining the existence and/or the amount of the corresponding penalty. (This determination is best left to your tax or insurance specialist or your financial adviser.)

In general, withdrawals made from an annuity prior to age 59½, except in the case of disability or death of the annuitant, are subject to a 10 percent IRS penalty in addition to ordinary income taxes on the earnings. However, a further exception to the rule may be when the individual's distribution is part of a series of substantially equal periodic payments for a minimum of 5 years (over the annuitant's life expectancy). Once in place, you cannot deviate from your plan.

From the standpoint of the issuing company, withdrawals, made under certain conditions that are likely to vary from one annuity policy issuer to another, may be permitted without charge. And, in certain instances, the amount of the charge may diminish according to the length of time the money has been in the account.

As an alternative to taking a withdrawal, needed monies (within certain types of annuity programs) may also be obtained by pledging the annuity contract as collateral for a loan.

Types of Annuities

Annuities may be classified as

- Fixed or variable
- Single-premium or flexible premium
- Deferred or immediate

The *variable annuity,* for reasons that follow, is the preferable plan. These annuities shelter your money during the crucial income-building process, an advantage that can be worth literally thousands of dollars to you. When you buy one of these products, in essence you are repositioning your money from a currently taxable status to a currently tax-deferred status. It is generally suited to those individuals who have the time to allow their money to grow tax-deferred in a variable account, with some measure of investment risk.

Variable annuities are intended to be used as long-term retirement vehicles, but you may, if you wish, withdraw all or part of your investment before annuitization. This annuity contract, for example, usually permits you to withdraw up to 10 percent of your original purchase payment during any one year without charge. Additional withdrawals are allowed, but they may carry penalty fees.

Remember, though, that one of the secrets of the variable annuity's success is the access to equity investments (to maximize growth) on a tax-deferred basis. Anytime that you can take a single dollar bill and not pay taxes on it until a later date, you end up with substantially more money than the person who takes the same dollar bill and pays current income taxes on it. One of the most significant advantages of an annuity is the substantial tax savings it provides for retirement. Of course, both the rate of return you receive and your personal tax circumstances would have an impact on the actual tax results. Deferred programs are a very integral part of building and preserving wealth.

A variable annuity also offers the flexibility to choose the investment mix to improve the total return potential, instead of having to accept the interest rate stated by an insurance company in a fixed annuity. How can this be? Because variable annuities, like many families of mutual funds, allow you the privilege of switching all or part of your money from one investment alternative to another, as you see fit. One such alternative is usually a money market fund and another is often a stock fund. (You should note at this point that your investment can erode as well as increase in value.) Another advantage is that the various investment programs are all under the expert management of a mutual fund company. The variable annuity is offered for sale by brokerage houses and life insurance companies through their registered representatives, who are properly licensed.

To learn how these interesting instruments work, let's look closely at one example. You need to invest the minimum in the contracts described here; there is, however, no limit on how many variable annuity contracts you may own, so you can buy another one every time you have an additional minimum amount to invest. Or, you can, in many cases, add to the value of the annuity contract you are holding. (That $3.3 million figure we were talking about a few paragraphs back is based on your repeated purchase of variable annuity contracts or your addition to an existing contract with your weekly savings.) Here are the investment vehicles that this particular variable annuity opens up for you, on a tax-deferred basis:

- A fund that invests mainly in high-quality, fixed income securities. It is designed for conservative investors who seek above average income, consistent with prudent investment techniques.
- A fund that invests in lower-rated fixed income securities to provide greater yields than a higher-grade portfolio. It seeks to control risk through careful selection and broad diversification.
- A fund that writes covered call options on high-quality dividend-paying stocks, providing some of the long-term growth benefits of an equity investment, but with less volatility and greater current income.
- A fund that contains a concentrated portfolio of quality stocks, with superior prospects for long-term earnings growth and high potential for use in tax-qualified retirement programs.
- A fund that is composed of high-grade, high-yielding money market instruments of short maturity. This trust seeks high current income while preserving capital and maintaining liquidity.

The *fixed annuity*, designed to assure the buyer of a lifetime of payments of a guaranteed fixed amount for a chosen period of time, generally offers no market risk while at the same time offering the traditional deferral of taxes on an annuity contract. Fixed annuities are frequently used to form the basis of retirement planning. With a fixed annuity you can obtain a guarantee of a high interest rate and concurrently enjoy a tax deferral. This product guarantees an initial interest rate, usually for a period of between 1 and 10 years, then the rate is adjusted typically on an annual basis (called the *renewal rate*). Some contracts have a *bailout provision* that allows the contract holder the right to surrender the contract without any sales charges if the renewal rate offered by the insurance company falls below the *bailout rate* stated in the contract. Most fixed annuities also have a minimum guaranteed renewal rate (called a *floor rate*) to protect the buyer from extremely low renewal rates.

The reputation of fixed annuities was tarnished in 1983 when Baldwin-United Corporation filed for bankruptcy protection. More recently, failures by Executive Life, First Capital, Fidelity Bankers, and a few others have caused a great deal of concern about fixed annuities. The risk involved with fixed annuities is that the money invested into these products goes directly into the insurance company's general investment portfolio, unlike money entering variable annuity contracts, which are held in separate accounts outside of the insurance company.

A *deferred annuity* is purchased in a lump sum (or in installments) and defers annuity payments to commence at a future date.

Immediate annuities are often bought by individuals with lump-sum payments received from pension or profit-sharing plans or from savings accumulated otherwise. If you buy an immediate annuity, your periodic checks will begin soon after you purchase the annuity, or within one year of making the purchase.

The *single premium deferred annuity* (SPDA) is for a lump-sum investment, while a *flexible premium deferred annuity* (FPDA) allows for additional deposits into the contract.

Although annuities make excellent components of a retirement plan, you need not look at them exclusively in this light. They also make sense for those individuals who have lost pension benefits, since many small businesses are eliminating pensions and profit-sharing entirely. Because of the annuity's versatility and its long-range advantages, it's also a viable vehicle for individuals seeking to provide financial support for a financially incompetent or handicapped child, dependent parents, and/or a favorite charity. It can also be used to fund Individual Retirement Accounts (IRAs). The fixed annuity and the variable annuity can be used to meet shorter-term investment objectives, too. They are truly investments for all seasons. *Do not,* however, confuse them with the old-style annuities that commonly turned in unexciting or disappointing performances.

Tax Treatment

By adhering to the annuity policy's parameters, you begin to pay taxes on the policy's proceeds as *withdrawals* are made with a deferred annuity.

At the time of the annuity *payout,* chances are you will be in a lower tax bracket than you were when the annuity (accumulation phase) payments were made. Each payment to you, when you annuitize, is part principal and part income and therefore only partially taxable.

Remember, payouts are the payments made to you from your annuity, whereas withdrawals occur when you take funds from your annuity (to meet short-term needs that may arise) that are not part of your annuity's scheduled payout plan.

Probate Protection

With a stated beneficiary included in the annuity contract, the policy is able to avoid the scrutiny and legal and administrative costs of probate.

As such, monies will be able to be moved more quickly (and quietly) to designated individuals.

Fees

The annuity fee structure varies from company to company. However, a fairly common element is the absence of an initial sales charge. Charges that are likely to be billed over the life of the annuity involve maintenance and administrative costs, mortality and expense risks, and (in the case of a variable annuity) management fees.

Tax-Free Exchange

Like your financial plan as a whole, investment vehicles should be routinely evaluated and monitored. Approaches and instruments selected earlier in a financial life cycle may not now be appropriate. Nor may they reflect the maximum benefit available in today's financial programs and products. Certain annuity and life insurance policies purchased years ago may offer far less in their advantages and benefits when compared with current selections.

Through the use of a 1035 "tax-free exchange" an individual may upgrade an existing annuity policy for another, or convert a current life insurance policy to an annuity—without causing a taxable event.

Creditor-Proof Potential

Another important point to note is that in some states, like Florida, annuities are sheltered from lawsuits from creditors. Check with your state's regulatory authority (generally under the Department of Insurance) to see what protection you might have from potential lawsuits.

Evaluating Annuities

Among the areas to be considered in evaluating and selecting a particular annuity are the following:

1. Examine the issuing company's reputation. Look for a long record of financial strength and stability. Check the company's standing in *Best's Insurance Guide, Best's Insurance Reports, Moody's, Standard and Poor's,* and *Duff and Phelps.* All are in most public libraries.

2. Remain diversified. While an annuity may offer specific advantages, you should not place all of your monies in it. Other investment/savings opportunities should be reviewed for handling additional aspects of your financial needs.

3. Review your options. Since annuity requirements and benefits are likely to vary between companies, individual policies should be reviewed for the best rate, most flexible terms, demonstrated stability, etc. Further, the trend today is to look closely at the "soundness" of the company in which you are thinking of investing. This point really cannot be overemphasized.

4. Look at the rate of return. A fixed or variable rate of return should be carefully considered in light of long-term suitability and risk tolerance.

5. Evaluate continually. With the annuity normally targeted to the future, particulars such as the annuitant and beneficiary designations should be reviewed periodically.

In Summary

Although most tax-deferred annuity programs offer a variety of advantages, both in their flexibility of programs and their favorable tax position, they are not totally without limitations. For this reason you may wish to consult a financial professional during the decision-making process.

There are some down-sides to annuities. First is that they may very well be subject to new tax law changes (some are being considered at this writing). Second, they are deferral programs, not a tax-free program, so they may subject you to estate tax (transfer tax at death) and income tax obligations.

If you buy a fixed annuity (one that guarantees an interest rate for a specific period of time) versus a variable annuity, your funds are commingled with the insurance company's funds. If the insurance company has financial difficulties, you would also bear the financial difficulties. A variable annuity is a segregated account. Thus, I prefer the variable annuity over the fixed annuity.

As we have discussed, an annuity can be a valuable vehicle on your road to financial freedom. Although they are not the all-encompassing vehicle that some proponents claim them to be, they certainly do serve their place in the investment arena. The range of uses for annuities— from funding a college education to funding retirement—is broad and they may have a place in your planning.

12

Fixed Income Investments

*Like all investments, bonds and
other fixed income instruments
should be judged on their real total
return—dividends plus capital gains
minus inflation and taxes.*

FREEDOM FOCUS

- *What is a fixed income investment?*
- *What are the three major areas of fixed income investments?*
- *How do money pools fit in with fixed income investments?*
- *What are six strategies for investing in fixed income areas?*

Rising interest rates are the biggest enemy of fixed income investments. When interest rates go up, the market value of bonds goes down because they were purchased at a lower rate, meaning that if bondholders want to dispose of their bonds at that point, they have to sell them at a loss. Inflation reduces the purchasing power of the income that bonds produce and the purchasing power of the principal when the bond is redeemed.

Even so, there is still a possibility that bonds and other fixed income investments may be right for you. You should, at the very least, learn about them so that you can make an informed nonemotional decision about this investment option.

What Is a Fixed Income Investment?

Fixed income investments include government and corporate bonds, bond mutual funds, money market funds, Treasury bills and notes, Ginnie Maes, CDs, collateralized mortgage obligations (CMOs), zero coupon bonds, and many others.

The common characteristic of these investments is that they are *debt instruments*. Through a fixed income investment, you lend money to a governmental unit or a company and, in return, you normally receive a guaranteed, fixed rate of return. While this enables you to avoid the risk of *equity ownership* (stock ownership) in a corporation, it also prevents you from benefiting financially from the company's growth because your return is *fixed* in nature.

In the past, the fixed income area was looked upon as the ultimate safe harbor for investment dollars. For decades, American couples entered their retirement years serenely, secure in the knowledge that their principal and interest were both guaranteed and that the mailman could be relied upon to deliver a steady stream of checks to their door that would replace the earned income of their working years. In some people's minds, this scenario still exists, and some people are more than happy to take part in it. If your prime concern is to be sure that a certain amount of money flows into your household on a regular basis, then you might be satisfied with an investment in bonds. You buy bonds with the hope that the erosion on both principal and interest that will take place over time will occur slowly, while you are provided with a means of obtaining a steady, predictable, long-term income. This feature is of significant value to some investors. But please keep in mind that since 1954 there has never been a single year of deflation in our country—every year since 1954 has been inflationary in nature. And, remember that the only purpose of money is its purchasing power. So you can't ignore the effect that inflation has on the purchasing power of a fixed investment when the same amount of dollars is being delivered at a later date.

Anyone who needs guaranteed principal and interest, however, should consider investing only in high-quality bonds. (Information on bond ratings appears further on in this chapter.) As in all investment decisions, you should confer with a qualified adviser before you make a bond or other fixed income purchase.

Bonds, as fixed income investments, fluctuate wildly at times based on interest rate swings. However, bond holders normally do not look daily at the value of their holdings. Rather, they look at the maturity value, that is, what the bond is worth when it matures in the year 2000, for example. An investor in the stock market tends to look daily at fluctuations in the stock market. I suggest to you, however, that bonds fluctuate as greatly as common stocks do, based on the interest rates. People perceive bonds to be guaranteed. In reality, their market value fluctuates depending on the interest rate the bond was purchased at versus the interest rate available at present.

The Yardstick: Total Return

Like all investments, bonds and other fixed income instruments should be judged on their real total return—dividends plus capital gains minus inflation and taxes. As a general rule, remember that when interest rates go up, the value of the bond goes down, although the price will recover to the face value at maturity or when the bond is called away from you. By buying bonds at a discount, a new purchaser will then receive a rate of return close to current interest rates since bonds are made to match current market forces.

Should prevailing interest rates fall, the value of the bonds will increase, and the purchaser can realize a capital gain should the purchaser sell those bonds prior to maturity. Historically, over the long period of time, bonds have not been as good a hedge against inflation as equity ownership. In reality, when you purchase bonds, you are loaning your money. What did I say earlier? Be an owner, not a loaner.

Dividend Reinvestment

Another way to make money through fixed income investments is to reinvest your dividends, compounding your interest. The "Rule of 72" comes in handy here. Simply divide any interest rate into 72 and you will know how long it will take to double your money. If your certificate of deposit is compounding at an annual rate of 6 percent, for example, it will take 12 years to double your money.

This is simply pure return of money and does not take into consideration taxation.

The Rating Services

You should be aware that many fixed income instruments are rated for their creditworthiness by Standard & Poor's and Moody's investors' services. Find out the rating from both services before you buy. The services also rate commercial paper (short-term unsecured promissory notes issued by corporations to finance short-term credit needs, usually sold on a discount basis with a maturity at the time of issuance not exceeding nine months), with Prime-1 being Moody's top rating and A-1 being Standard & Poor's best. Other good rating sources to check are Fitch Financial Services and Duff & Phelps.

Most investors should stick to the three highest ratings from Moody's (Aaa, Aa, A) and Standard & Poor's (AAA, AA, A) since the bond market will seldom reward an investment in lower quality bonds with enough yield to offset the increased credit risk of buying lower quality paper. If a bond service assigns the rating NR (no rating) it means the service felt there was insufficient information on which to base a rating. (For bond rating explanations, see Table 12-1.)

Uses of Fixed Income Investments

Although I would be reluctant to counsel you to put a major portion of your investments into fixed income securities, you should understand what is available to you and how to use these vehicles to your best advantage.

These investments are most commonly used because of their excellent track record in providing timely payments of interest and preserving capital (at maturity in the case of bonds and mortgages), in addition to their perceived safety and liquidity. Like most individuals, you probably own two fixed income investments right now: a checking account and a savings account. In today's economy, both are costing you money. You are willing to pay inflation's toll on these accounts in order to maintain some liquidity, but you should be monitoring the amounts you have in these positions.

Should your checking and savings account totals be more than your monthly cash needs plus a small cushion, you should look for some *cash management* tools. These investments, such as short-term notes and money market funds, put your idle cash to work while you are shopping for other investments or hiding from the stock market. Money market funds became very popular in the mid to late 1970s because they offered a safe harbor when the stock market was having a stormy time.

Another use of fixed income investments is, of course, *investment*, but

Table 12-1. Bond Rating Explanations*

Rating	Explanation
Aaa** (AAA = S&P)†	Bonds with this rating are generally referred to as gilt-edge—the best bonds. It indicates that interest payments are protected by a large or very stable margin and the principal is secure. The issuing entity is considered stable enough to withstand any changes by the issuer.
Aa (AA = S&P)	These ratings indicate high quality bonds by all standards. The group generally known as high grade bonds consists of these and the Aaa group. The Aa rating indicates that their margins for protection are not quite as large as the Aaa and their possibility for fluctuation may be greater.
A (A = S&P)	Bonds in this category are considered upper-medium-grade obligations. Although the security for payback of both principal and interest is considered adequate, such areas as their consistent profitability could leave them susceptible to impairment at some time in the future.
Baa (BBB = S&P)	These bonds are considered medium-grade obligations. The security of principal and interest payments cannot be projected for a substantial period of time. They generally lack outstanding investment characteristics. Under the rules of law, bonds rated Baa or higher are considered "prudent-man" investments.
Ba (BB = S&P)	This rating indicates speculative elements that leave questions as to their future. They generally lack strong protection of interest and principal, leaving them somewhat vulnerable during hard times.
B (B = S&P)	These bonds are generally lacking in the characteristics of desirable investments. Over a sustained period of time, it is questionable whether the interest and principal payments, or maintenance of other terms of the bond's contract, could be sustained.
Caa (CCC = S&P)	These bonds have a poor standing. They could be in default or present elements of risk in terms of paying interest or principal.
Ca (CC = S&P)	Bonds rated Ca are definitely speculative. These issues are often in default or have serious problems.
C (C = S&P)	Moody's lowest rated class of bonds are C bonds. They are considered very poor possibilities for any real investment purposes.
CI (S&P)	This is S&P's rating for income bonds which are paying no interest at the present time.
D (S&P)	S&P's rating for bonds that are in default of payment of interest and/or for which the repayment of principal is in arrears.

*Although referring to these ratings is helpful, even ratings have limitations. The quality of most bonds is not fixed or steady and tends to change over a period of time. So even a bond with the highest rating carries the potential for change in risk.

**Moody's rating.

†S&P refers to the rating given by Standard & Poor's.

please remember again that bond prices can fluctuate just as much as common stocks. While your interest income may not fluctuate in terms of "constant" dollars as much as dividends on common stock might, the value of your investment will be affected by changes in interest rates, tax laws, the creditworthiness of the issuer, and the supply and demand forces of the market.

Kinds of Fixed Income Investments

Banks: Checking, Passbook Accounts, Certificates of Deposit

Banks and savings and loan associations are the most widely used fixed interest investment institutions. Shop around to see what services banks and S&Ls in your area offer and what they charge. They are now under great competitive pressures and are being squeezed by rising costs. You do not want to break off a good relationship with a banker to chase penny savings, but you do want to make sure the banker is close to the competition. Do not use your checking account to hold money. It is a cash-flow device.

As for passbook saving accounts, these are strictly for short-term needs like new tires for the automobile and children's birthday checks. The amount of "rainy day" money you set aside depends upon your judgment and comfort zone. There are other higher yielding, liquid investments such as money market funds. The only advantage of the passbook account is that it is covered up to $100,000 by the Federal Deposit Insurance Company (FDIC) (which, incidentally, may not cover a state bank). If you do have a passbook account, make sure that it is insured.

Federal insurance is also a reason that people put substantial amounts of money into certificates of deposit. Certificates lock up your money with severe early withdrawal penalties. The most attractive certificates are the money market certificates pegged to the going rate of Treasury bills, but you should realize that the interest on the shorter term certificates is straight, not compounded, and the minimum for best return is currently $10,000. Some banks do issue "jumbo" certificates for $100,000, with negotiable interest rates and terms.

Your bank can offer you some other profitable, although less frequently used, short-term investments if you have a large sum of money. One is *commercial paper*, which is a short-term, unsecured loan carrying an interest rate above certificates and Treasury bills. These loans go to businesses with high cash demands and fast turnover such as your local car dealer. For a small fee, you can purchase from some banks commercial paper with terms of 30 to 270 days in various denominations.

Another high deposit investment is *bankers acceptances,* which offer a return close to a prime rate for investments that are generally of $100,000 plus. These are backed by the bank and the borrower and usually finance international trade or currency exchanges.

Government Securities

With deficit financing now the American way of government, you are offered a variety of enticements to lend your money to Uncle Sam or City Hall. Some of these are good cash management vehicles for the short term—parking places for your money. Others offer you tax advantages in exchange for long-term investment. Federal obligations are considered virtually credit-risk-free, but will still decline in market value when interest rates rise.

The Treasury issues a variety of bills, notes, and bonds that are sheltered from state and local income taxes (except in Tennessee) and, except for savings bonds, are marketable.

For cash management purposes, you may wish to look at *Treasury bills,* now available weekly through the Federal Reserve Bank or, for a fee, through your banker. T-bill yields are stated at the time of purchase and are published in *Barron's* and *The Wall Street Journal.* T-bills can be purchased in denominations starting at $10,000 for terms of 13 to 26 weeks. The yield fluctuates from week to week and can be slightly below the nongovernment market.

Treasury notes and *bonds* are long-term investments issued at face value with interest paid at fixed rates, usually on a semiannual basis. Treasury notes have 1- to 10-year maturities, while Treasury bonds have a duration of 10 years or longer. Denominations in bonds and notes can start as low as $1000 to $5000. You can buy older bonds, notes, and bills through brokers at a discount or premium depending on prevailing market conditions.

The federal government also issues bonds and securities through such agencies as the Tennessee Valley Authority, the Farm Credit Bank, the Home Loan Bank, and the Federal National Mortgage Association (FNMA, or Fannie Mae). Most of these obligations are not sheltered from state and local taxes.

Somewhat different from bonds are the securities issued by the Government National Mortgage Association, known as *Ginnie Maes* (GNMA). Ginnie Maes are pools of mortgages underwritten by agencies such as the Veterans Administration. The minimum investment is

$25,000. Ginnie Mae's monthly check to you will include both interest and principal, increasing your cash flow—a useful feature if you are retired or perhaps edging your way into another investment. Ginnie Maes are marketable and are affected by changes in interest rates. The disadvantages of GNMAs are that if interest rates go up, the value of your investment declines, and if interest rates go down, the probability is that more and more of the mortgagees represented in the pool will refinance their mortgages or increase their prepayments of principal, forcing you to reinvest larger return-of-principal distributions into other fixed income investments at lower rates.

A recently developed offshoot of GNMAs that has become one of the hottest-selling fixed income products today is called a Collateralized Mortgage Obligation (CMO). CMOs are made up of slices (called "tranches" in the business) of GNMAs, FNMAs, and FHLMCs that are packaged by major Wall Street firms. Fixed income investors buy CMOs today in an attempt to salvage investment yield as interest rates fall. Although CMOs have virtually no credit risk, they do pose risks because of their extreme complexity and often volatile reactions to interest rate swings. The complexity inherent in an investment that combines bits and pieces of various mortgages creates an uncertainty as to the predictability of cash flow and resulting effective rate of return on a CMO.

The government security that seems to have the most appeal for beginning investors is the tax-exempt *municipal bond*. Municipal bonds are issued by cities, counties, school districts, utility authorities, states, and other political subdivisions. They are used to build and maintain public works and are paid back by taxes (for general obligation bonds) or the revenue of the project (for revenue bonds). Their interest income is tax exempt on your Federal Form 1040 and usually exempt from state taxes, should you live in the state in which the bond was issued. If you buy a municipal bond at a discount (except for an original issue discount bond or a tax-free zero coupon bond) and hold it to maturity, you will pay a capital gains tax on the increase in principal. The tax would also apply to a municipal bond sold at a higher price than the purchase price. Some types of bonds, such as industrial development revenue bonds and pollution control revenue bonds, may be subject to the Alternative Minimum Tax (AMT). Bonds issued outside your home state (except for tax-free bonds from Puerto Rico) may be subject to state and local taxes.

So intriguing is the idea of tax-free investment that some investors forget to measure it against the yardstick of total return. Many people who own municipals should not. Why? A municipal (except for zero coupon municipals) is designed to produce tax-exempt income, rather than growth. The purchasing power of the interest payments and the principal is eroded by inflation.

It is essential that you understand the difference between *yield to maturity, yield to the call,* and *current yield* if you are planning to buy bonds. *Yield to maturity* reflects the current interest *plus* the change in value from the time of purchase to the stated maturity date. *Yield to the call* includes interest received *plus* the change in principal value to the call date (a date on which the issuer has the right to call in the bond prior to maturity). Generally, discount bonds are sold based on the yield to maturity, while bonds selling at a premium are usually priced to the call date. The *current yield* is simply the annual interest rate of the bond divided by the purchase price.

If you bought an 8 percent bond that matures on January 1, 2013 and is callable at par (100) on January 1, 2003 and you paid 105 ($10,500 for a face amount of $10,000), what would the current return, yield to maturity, and yield to the call be?

The yield to maturity (your annualized rate of return if the bond lasts until maturity) is reduced from the 8 percent rate stated on the bond to 7.51 percent.

The yield to call (the annualized rate of return on the investment if the bond is taken away from you by the issuer on the call date) is even lower, at 7.29 percent. This is because the loss of premium (from a 105 bond price down to 100) occurs faster than if the bond goes to maturity.

The current return is 7.62 percent. This is calculated by simply dividing the income stream received during the year ($800) by the actual price ($10,500). The yield to call and yield to maturity are more important that the current return because they provide a better picture of the total return of the bond, and not just the current income rate.

Corporate Obligations

Just to make sure the distinction is clear, let's quickly review the difference between stocks and bonds. When you buy common stock in a company, you own part of the business. When you buy a *corporate bond,* you are buying a debt—that is, you are lending your money to the company. As a bondholder, your investment is considered more secure because you are near the top of the list of those to be repaid (a creditor of the company) if the company fails. If the company should be a roaring success, however, your interest checks won't reflect this, while holders of common stock will enjoy fatter and fatter dividends. Similarly, success won't mean as much to the real dollar value of your bond as will the effects of inflation and interest rates. Common stock, on the other hand, can be rewarded with dramatic gains in value.

Most corporate bonds offer fixed rates of return over a fixed length of time, although many also include a provision for early redemption (call) and some companies issue variable rate bonds. The key to analyzing the credit quality of a bond comes by examining the security behind the bond, if any. Among the secured bonds are *first mortgages,* usually offered by utilities with a lien against property, and equipment trusts issued by companies such as airlines and railroads with liens against specific pieces of equipment. Sinking funds are designed to retire a certain percentage of the issue each year, beginning in a designed year. Eurobonds can be secured by equipment or a sinking fund (or nothing at all) and are issued by European corporations and the overseas subsidiaries of American corporations. Debentures generally are not secured by more than the full faith and credit of the company, leaving bondholders with a claim on assets after mortgages have been satisfied. Subordinated debentures are further down the list of creditors.

What bonds you buy depends largely on what your crystal ball tells you about interest rates. Should you have reason to believe that interest rates will decline, you should buy long-term noncallable zero coupon bonds. The reason is that since these types of bonds pay no current interest, all of the total return is reflected in price appreciation only, which can be dramatic when rates fall. Also, in general, long-term bonds move more in price than short-term issues and the noncallable feature assures the investor of retaining the yield all the way to the maturity date. If you think rates will keep going higher, you will want to consider very short maturity bonds, T-bills, or money market funds.

What you should avoid, unless you are speculating with money you can afford to lose, are *junk bonds.* These are deeply discounted bonds of companies with poor or no ratings. This can be a very treacherous market, as many banks, savings and loans, and insurance companies have recently discovered. Prices can fluctuate wildly, and when an issue goes into default, the bond seldom resumes the payment of interest, while the market price often nosedives with little hope of recovery. There have been junk bonds that have turned out to be rewarding investments too. Just understand that, for most people, the increased yield is not worth the increased risk of principal loss.

Debentures may include a *convertible feature.* That means the company will trade the security for common stock at a specified ratio of shares until a fixed date. Convertibles are supposed to offer the best of both worlds: the steady fixed income of a bond, and the growth possibilities of common stock. You pay slightly more for a convertible in the hope that, with the growth of the company, common stock dividends will eventually approach your interest payment, making it profitable for you to trade. As a practical matter, your interest income on a convertible will be less than that from a straight bond and the market value will reflect the common stock market. While the price of nonconvertible securities is supposed to act as a price floor for convertibles, convertibles can suffer in a bear market. In a rising market, investors can do well with convertibles, and long-term investors can realize the potential of converting. Overall, convertibles require patience and good advice. Convertibles have historically performed better than stocks during weak stock market periods, but tend to underperform stocks in rising markets.

Money Pools

Historically, the fixed income market generally favored the large investor who could buy in quantity. One reason was government policy designed to keep denominations of various securities large to protect S&Ls and banks from the loss of savings deposits. The other reason was practical: Corporations and institutions do not want the overhead of dealing with $500 investors, especially in short-term loans.

When small investors pulled out of the bear market of the 1970s, they had few places to turn. That led to the outstanding growth of *money market funds*. These funds are interesting in that they have a totally different purpose from most other fixed interest instruments. For one thing, instead of being designed to yield predictable amounts over the long term, money market funds are short-term, cash management vehicles. They are excellent financial planning tools that allow you to "park" your money in a safe haven while you wait for market conditions to stabilize sufficiently to allow you to move into other areas.

Money market funds are offered not only by mutual fund companies, but also by major stock brokerages and investment firms. They have very short-term loans, such as commercial paper, government securities from the United States and overseas, and large certificates of deposit. Many of them offer check-writing privileges for amounts of $500 or more and redemption by telephone or telegram, making the money markets almost as liquid as regular checking accounts. Most have minimum investment requirements, although a handful have no minimums.

To invest in a money market fund, phone or write the company that you have selected for a prospectus and application. The prospectus will tell you how the fund invests and how much risk it takes. Standard guides such as the one published by Wiesenberger's Investment Services, available in most public libraries, will give you the addresses. Check your daily paper or *The Wall Street Journal* for current yields. Money markets do not charge a sales fee, but do levy a small management fee.

As for longer-term investments, you have a choice of mutual funds or unit trusts. *Mutual funds*, as you know, may specialize in almost any type of securities, including corporate bonds, government obligations, Ginnie Maes, and tax-free municipal bonds. There are even a few funds that handle nothing but preferred stocks, passing on the tax deduction to corporations that invest in the fund. Like other mutual funds, you pay management fees and, in the case of "load" funds, a sales charge. Mutual funds offer diversification and professional management and are discussed in Chapter 10, The Magic of Mutual Funds.

Unit trusts, on the other hand, are "closed-end" funds. They are invested in such securities as government obligations, corporate bonds, or municipal bonds, but once the purchase is made there is no further buying and selling of securities or reinvestment of principal into new securities as the bonds or mortgages mature. Unit trusts are redeemable, usually through any brokerage firm or directly to the unit trust company. Should you sell one, you may make a profit or take a loss; it could go either way.

Six Fixed Income Investment Strategies

1. Just as most investors considering stocks should buy them indirectly through mutual funds, fixed income investors should seek the professional expertise and portfolio diversification that mutual funds can provide.

2. When choosing fixed income funds, compare several different funds for the long-term historical performance, fund expenses, quality of the portfolio, average maturity of the portfolio, and the length of time the fund manager has been managing the fund.

3. Compare the after-tax yield of taxable products to tax-free investment yields before investing to see which type will give you a higher net yield.

4. When buying municipal housing bonds, be aware that if you pay a premium for the bond and the bond is called away from you before the regular call date, you could experience a low yield or even a negative return on your investment. (Most housing bonds can be called in at any time, usually beginning 18 months after issue, due to unexpended proceeds or refinancing of the underlying mortgages.) This caution also applies to any premium bond that has a sinking fund provision.

5. When short-term rates are higher than long-term rates (an inverted yield curve) buy long-term noncallable bonds and sell them at a profit as interest rates go down.

6. When buying into mortgage pools, such as Ginnie Maes or CMOs, keep in mind that if you sell your investment before it matures, you may see a significantly large spread between the bid and asked price of your investment, since certain pools can sometimes be infrequently traded (especially for CMOs) in the secondary market.

As you can see, there are many ways for you to invest in fixed income instruments if your taste runs in this direction. As always, it is most important for you to be aware of the advantages and drawbacks of this type of investment, to know where they fit on your personal investment pyramid, and to make your decisions accordingly.

13

IRAs, Keoghs, and Other Retirement Plans

The first thing you must do in planning for retirement is to dismiss Social Security from your thinking.

FREEDOM FOCUS

- *Is a Keogh plan right for you?*
- *What can you expect from an IRA account?*
- *Do you qualify for 401(k) or 403(b) plans?*
- *Would a SAR/SEP plan be suitable for you?*

Retirement can be a frightening prospect for those who have not had the foresight to plan for it. But for those of us who are wise enough to know that we should lay the groundwork for our post-career periods as carefully as we prepared ourselves for our life's work, this period of our lives can truly be the best of times. Please understand that this chapter is an introduction to these plans; it is not intended to be an encyclopedia of retirement plans. When you have completed it, you will have the basic understanding you need to seek further information.

Note that retirement planning carries substantial preretirement advantages, too. When we are talking about retirement plans, we are also talking about current tax savings—one of the few breaks you and I can get from Uncle Sam. You can never be too young, too rich, or too busy to think about current tax savings, especially the kind that add appreciably to your net worth.

This chapter covers the retirement plans available to individuals—individual retirement accounts (IRAs), Keogh plans (HR-10s), mini Keogh plans, simplified employee pensions (SEPs), 403(b) plans, 401(k) plans, and IRA rollover accounts. Don't worry—all of them will soon be translated into English. Just don't ask me to explain why the government does what it does: Why is a doctor allowed a more liberal plan than a wage-earner? Why can a missionary use retirement funds to send his or her children to college and not a businessperson? Why can a factory worker include a spouse in an IRA, whereas a shop owner can't include a spouse in a Keogh?

Chapter 14 will deal with corporate pension and profit-sharing plans. Even if you are now in a plan, corporate or individual, you should carefully read both chapters to understand fully your options, both present and future.

The first thing you must do in planning for retirement is to dismiss social security from your thinking. As your FICA tax zooms skyward, the government attempts to make reassuring noises about your future benefits. Should inflation average just a modest 5 percent a year for the next 20 years, you would need a monthly income of $6633 to buy what that $2500 buys today. (See Table 7-2, page 111.)

An important consideration in retirement planning is present tax advantages. Most of the money contributed to a qualified plan is tax deductible (an exception would be any extra, voluntary donations) and the dividends and the earnings are tax-deferred. In addition, any money left in some types of retirement plans at your death receive special tax treatment, depending on how your heirs wish to receive the funds.

If you were in the 30 percent tax bracket, your investment in a retirement account would, in effect, produce an immediate 30 percent return for you on each dollar you put in. (However, all monies will be taxed when they are withdrawn, according to the tax bracket you are in, which is normally a lower tax bracket at your retirement.) Whatever gains your investment makes are not taxable until you take the money out, and then it will be taxed at your retirement income level. Since the investment comes off the top of your gross income just like a business expense, you should also realize tax savings by bumping yourself into a lower bracket.

Here is an example of the kind of tax benefits that an investment in a retirement account can bring. Consider the worker who stays in the 28 percent tax bracket for 25 years. Before the worker pays taxes each year, he or she would like to put $1500 aside for old age. If the money is put into a qualified retirement plan, the entire $1500 will go to work earning on a tax-deferred basis. But if it's put into a regular savings account, the worker will have only $1080 in post-tax dollars, and then the IRS will take a cut of the annual earnings. (See Table 13-1.)

Investments in a tax-deferred IRA amount to much more when compared to the same amounts invested in a fully taxable account, because your earnings are not taxed during this critical retirement-building period. You benefit not only by avoiding the payment of taxes on these earnings until you begin to withdraw the money, but by reinvesting those earnings in additional shares of your IRA. Of course, distributions from an IRA are taxable as ordinary income when they are withdrawn at retirement (assuming they were eligible for pre-tax contribution—otherwise only the earnings are taxable, not the contributions).

This means that you can try to avoid the effects of inflation by seeking the best returns for the particular economic conditions with which you are coping or by splitting your account among investments of varying risk and return. You should never think of retirement plans as a way to tuck money away under a loose floorboard. Quite to the contrary, your retirement plan affords you a golden opportunity to launch a dynamic investment program.

You should know, however, that your investment in these plans must meet government requirements. With few exceptions, and those may be subject to capital gains taxes, you may not transfer or sell stocks or property you now own to a retirement account. You may not use the account as collateral for a loan of any kind. The only way you can use your retire-

Table 13-1. Tax-Deferred Compounding versus Taxable Compounding*

Investment period	Tax deferred	Taxable at 31 percent	Taxable at 28 percent	Taxable at 15 percent
10 years	$ 25,937	$ 19,488	$ 20,042	$ 22,610
20 years	$ 67,275	$ 37,980	$ 40,169	$ 51,120
30 years	$174,494	$ 74,017	$ 80,509	$115,583
40 years	$452,593	$144,247	$161,358	$261,330

*These figures are calculated on a rate of return of 10 percent on $10,000 and assume reinvestment of all distributions, no fluctuations in the value of the principal and no fees or sales charges.

ment funds for current business or personal expenses is to pay a 10 percent penalty (if under age 59½), plus current income taxes on them. They are, for the most part, protected from court judgments and they are reflected on statements of your net worth. One exception to the rule is a series of substantially equal payments over a period of 5 years.

Before we delve into various plans, two caveats are in order: First, these plans are subject to changes by Congress, the IRS, and the courts. This means that what is true today may not be so in the future. *Be sure to consult a qualified professional who keeps up with changes in the tax area.* Second, a number of existing regulations apply to people in special circumstances. The exceptions to the general rule are too numerous to list here, so you should be sure to inquire about them when you discuss retirement planning with a financial professional.

Keogh Plans

These are plans primarily for self-employed (full or part-time) professionals, owners of unincorporated businesses, and their employees. They work much like IRAs, but you have the advantage of being allowed to put much more money into them and deducting it all from your taxable income. Self-employed moonlighters can shelter part of their income after regular hours under a Keogh plan, even if they also participate in corporate or government retirement plans at work. This applies, for example, to the corporate lawyer who writes wills at night for private clients, the government clerk who plays jazz on Saturday nights, or the graphic designer who works out of the home. It now applies even to inside corporate directors, who may shelter part of the directors' fees they receive from their companies while at the same time participating in the corporate retirement plan based on their salaries.

You can contribute up to 25 percent (under the defined contribution plan) of your income from self-employment, up to a maximum contribution of $30,000 yearly. The same limits apply to your spouse if he or she meets the self-employment qualifications. Under a Keogh plan, you may not receive any benefits until you are 59½ or disabled. Otherwise, you must pay a 10 percent penalty. Exceptions to the penalty may be granted for disability or hardship. You must start making withdrawals (in amounts calculated on the basis of your life expectancy) by the April 15th of the year following your attainment of age 70½ or be subject to a 50 percent penalty on the underwithdrawal.

Holders of Keogh plans must also include all full-time employees who have worked for them for two years or since the business was started, whichever is less. Employee contributions must be the same percentage of earnings—or benefits—as the employer's, and the employer may not reduce employee salaries to make up for the employer's contribution.

Employees become vested in their Keogh plans immediately for the full sum of the employer's contribution.

Your Keogh plan must be opened by December 31st of the taxable year, but then contributions may be made up to the April 15th (or August 15th, if you get an extension) tax filing deadline, or any extension date. The earlier your contribution is made, the sooner it starts generating tax-deferred earnings.

Keogh plans offer two programs: a defined contribution program (the more popular of the two) and a defined benefit program.

Some Keogh Pros and Cons:
Defined Benefit versus
Defined Contribution

Very basically, a *defined benefit plan* is a qualified retirement plan which entitles an employee to receive a specific dollar amount (defined benefit) each year. A *defined contribution plan* is a qualified retirement plan which requires an employer to contribute to it a pre-set percentage (defined contribution) of compensation each year. (See the sections in Chapter 14 entitled Defined Benefit Plan and Defined Contribution Plan for a fuller discussion of these types of plans.)

Under a defined benefit plan you may be able to shelter more income than under a defined contribution plan. You may, however, have to make large contributions at the beginning of your plan and then, if the investment income exceeds expectations, your contribution—and deduction—will shrink. In a defined contribution plan, upon your death what is left goes to your beneficiary, either in installments or as a lump sum that can be placed in tax-deferred annuities.

In a defined contribution plan, your benefits are limited only by your wisdom with regard to investments and the vicissitudes of the economy. You can make more money than with a defined benefit plan, but you can also make less. You can outlive your benefits, but as you grow older you can refigure your withdrawals. After retirement, you can also tap your defined contribution plan for emergencies, a privilege you do not enjoy under a defined benefit plan.

Keogh plans may be invested in savings accounts or certificates, annuities, mutual funds, or a variety of limited partnerships. (Keep in mind that partnerships are nonliquid.)

In general, Keogh plans are a good idea for any self-employed person, especially one who is just starting, moonlighting, or expecting growth in income. Before you decide to start a Keogh plan or remain in one, you should study the advantages of incorporating and having a corporate pension or profit-sharing plan.

Individual Retirement Accounts (IRAs)

An Individual Retirement Account (IRA) is especially suitable for a person who is not covered by a qualified pension or profit-sharing plan at work. It is available to both the individual tax payer and his or her nonworking spouse. You may use an IRA if you are self-employed and don't wish to cover your employees. In many respects, it is simpler than a Keogh plan, but far less generous in its provisions.

To qualify, an individual must be under 70½ years old and receive earned income during the year which is at least equal to the IRA contribution.

At the moment, the top contribution you may make to an IRA is $2000 per working individual. Restrictions on the amount of contributions apply if either you or your spouse is covered by an employer pension plan, or if your income exceeds certain levels. You can contribute $2250 to a marital IRA if your spouse does not work at all during the taxable year. This contribution may be split between your account and your spouse's in any manner you see fit as long as the contribution to either one does not exceed $2000.

As in a Keogh, you must be 59½ or disabled to make withdrawals without penalty, and you must start regular withdrawals at 70½ or be penalized. There is a *50 percent* excise tax penalty if you are not receiving distributions by April 1st of the calendar year following the year in which you attain age 70½. Provisions are made for distributions without the 10 percent tax penalty for reasons of death, permanent disability, periodic payments based on a life expectancy formula which cannot be modified for a specified period of time, attainment of age 59½, or transfer of assets from a participant's IRA to spouse's or former spouse's IRA pursuant to a divorce or separation instrument. All distributions from any type of IRA are taxed as ordinary income except for distributions of nondeductible contributions which are considered a nontaxable return of principal.

An IRA offers the same choice of investments as a Keogh defined contribution plan—savings accounts or certificates, fixed or variable annuities, mutual funds, and trust arrangements covering a variety of investments.

Simplified Employee Pensions (SEPs)

This is a hybrid IRA plan to which your employer can contribute under Keogh limits. (The SEP/IRA is also discussed in Chapter 14.) It allows your employer to contribute the lesser of 15 percent of your compensation or $30,000.

Your employer may deduct from its contribution the amount paid into Social Security for you. This is called integration of benefits. It tends to reduce the employer's costs and favors owners and employees on the high end of the company's salary scale. Whatever your employer does contribute to your plan will be included on your W-2 form as income. You then take a deduction, even if you are using the standard deduction forms.

You may pick the investment you want for your plan from among the standard IRA vehicles and submit it to your employer. As its name implies, the simplified employee pension (SEP) is easier for an employer to administer than a Keogh plan. The paperwork is substantially reduced. Also, certain types of SEPs may be integrated with Social Security more readily than a Keogh plan, thus reducing the financial burden on the employer. Note that although the SEP holds a number of advantages for employers, employees do not necessarily gain more from this kind of plan than from a Keogh. SEP distributions, for instance, do not qualify for capital gains tax treatment and 10-year forward averaging, as certain Keogh distributions do.

SAR/SEP Plans

The Salary Reduction Simplified Employee Pension Plan allows participants to contribute by deferring part of their salary or bonus. The employer may not have more than 25 eligible employees and at least 50 percent of the eligible employees must participate.

Participants cannot currently defer more than $8728 (indexed annually for inflation) and there are limits for compensated employees.

401(k) Plans

A 401(k) is a very flexible retirement plan that has become popular with employers as an alternative to potentially more costly profit-sharing and pension plans.

Contributions to the plan may be made through direct payments by the employer, pre-tax (salary reduction) payments by the employee, or a combination. Contributions by the company are limited to the lesser of 15 percent of wages or $30,000 inclusive of the $8728 employee salary reduction limit. 401(k) plans are discussed in detail in Chapter 14.

403(b) Plans

A 403(b) is a retirement plan for people who are employed by a non-profit [tax-exempt according to Internal Revenue code section 501(c)(3)] organization or public school system, either full-time or part-time. It has its own rules and is more generous than Keogh and IRA in some respects.

Under a 403(b), your employer makes the contribution either through a reduction in your salary or by withholding a raise, if you request this latter course of action. He or she must give you several choices of investment vehicles among mutual funds and annuities, either fixed or variable. (See also Chapter 14.)

IRA Rollovers

These accounts are for anyone whose plan, corporate or individual, has been terminated either because they have retired, quit, or been fired, or because their plan has been terminated by an employer or investment company. If you inherit money from your spouse's qualified retirement plan, you may also put these funds into an IRA rollover account to avoid current taxes. SEP/IRAs can also be rolled over.

Should any of the above circumstances occur and you find that a large amount of money is coming to you from a retirement account, you will have to make some important decisions. If you are retired and receiving your funds in regular periodic payments, you may simply wish to add to these payments.

What do you do when a company or other plan virtually insists upon giving you a lump sum? Or what if your plan is an investment that "safely" yields 4 percent while inflation is running 5 percent and higher?

Since the amount of money involved—and tax consequences—may be sizable, you should consult an expert in such cases. Under a Keogh plan or corporate plan, you may be able to use 10-year forward averaging on your income tax if you receive a lump sum (everything).

Still another alternative, taking taxes and your lifestyle into consideration, may be an *IRA rollover*. That means taking your money and putting it into a new tax-sheltered account. Rollover accounts have the same 59½ to 70½ withdrawal rules and penalties as the standard IRA.

To start a rollover IRA, you must comply with some specific rules. In general, these are:

1. The plan must have been terminated or you must have been separated from service from that employer.

2. You must receive all funds due you within a single taxable year.

3. You must put these funds or part of them into a rollover account within 60 days.

This sounds simple enough. Yet there are many pitfalls to avoid. Should your rollover fail (be disqualified by the IRS), you will face immediate taxation, and in the event of a preretirement rollover, you will be subject to the 10 percent penalty. Professional help is imperative here, as the following examples illustrate.

Consider the 60-day provision. What if your qualified profit-sharing plan includes shares in a closely held corporation? You may need considerable time to plan for the sale before your 60 days from distribution to rollover begin. Because the limit is inflexible, advance planning is essential. Any last minute capital gains can be placed in your rollover without current tax. Then, of course, you can't deduct any losses.

What are the problems in receiving a lump sum? You can't roll over any contributions you have made to the plan, but your rollover can retain the inflation factor and any gains your contributions have earned. What about dividends on stocks in your plan that might not be paid until the next taxable year? In general, your IRA rollover is valid, but you can't put this money into the account. That brings up the point that if you take a lump sum and put only a part of it into an IRA rollover, the remainder is taxed as ordinary income without any favorable averaging.

Another problem might arise if you are 55, want to retire and take your pension funds with you, but have agreed to be a consultant to your company. Is that considered terminating your employment, or will you be penalized on the grounds that you are making an early withdrawal of funds? If your consultancy contract is standard for the industry, the IRS will accept your rollover. In any case, check all options carefully.

You may use a rollover no more than once a year. There are many other ways to move your money around without worrying about rollover provisions. You can take your funds from one employer's account and transfer them to a second employer if his or her plan permits it. If you don't handle the money, you can transfer your funds between fiduciaries—a savings account with a bank to a mutual fund, for example. You can simply leave your money in one type of account and join another.

If you have a Keogh plan, for instance, and then go to work for a firm with a corporate plan, you may leave your Keogh intact and allow it to keep making money. You can at that point, or years later, transfer your Keogh plan from investment to investment as you see fit. You just can't add any money to it until you are eligible to do so again.

For investment purposes, IRA rollovers are treated like other IRAs and Keoghs.

Investments

Whatever you do, don't think of your retirement account as a sacred treasure to be set aside and admired once a year. Your retirement plan is an investment aimed at giving you both a comfortable retirement and a larger estate. If you fail to invest in such a program, you will have little to show for your years of hard work.

As always, your investments should be based on your ability, personal and financial, to withstand risk. You may choose to spread your investment among several accounts with varying degrees of risk. You may also switch your investments through "trustee-to-trustee" transfers. As long as you never touch the money, it will not be taxed; you will, however, be subject to certain costs such as brokerage fees. Beware of plans sold with all the fees payable during the first few years. Should you want to drop that kind of plan, you will find that most of your initial investment dollars will have gone toward the fees.

Except for 403(b) plans, which are limited to annuities and mutual funds, four types of investments have traditionally been used in retirement plans: savings instruments, annuities, U.S. government bonds (see Chapter 12), and mutual funds.

Savings Instruments

Savings accounts are insured up to the bank or savings association limits, now $100,000. Your principal cannot appreciate except through interest. You are also somewhat restricted in the size of savings certificate your total investment will buy. To get into one, just stop by your bank or savings and loan association. Other savings instruments include certificates of deposit (CDs) and U.S. Treasury bills.

Annuities

Many annuities are available that offer a variety of investment options, including equity funds. For information, write a mutual fund, insurance company, or see your financial professional. Fixed annuities can be eaten alive by inflation. Variable annuities offer more options to the investor than fixed annuities. Once you start receiving benefits, it is impossible to transfer or roll over into another type of investment. Annuities are fully discussed in Chapter 11.

Mutual Funds

Retirement plans are generally a good place to use mutual funds. If you have bought into a "family of funds," there are no IRS limits on how many times you may reposition your investment. If your mutual fund family introduces a new, more attractive fund, or if the stock market

becomes depressed and you want to switch into money market accounts, you are restricted only by the fund's regulations. The lack of a
guarantee on your investment, however, could be a disadvantage should
you receive benefits during a bear market. There are no problems for
beneficiaries and you can move from mutual funds to other investments. Mutual funds are discussed fully in Chapter 10.

Retirement planning is an essential ingredient in your financial freedom planning. It is something you must begin to consider as soon as
you begin earning an income. In many cases, when you think about re-
tiring, you may be thinking about income to provide for more than just
your needs: What about your spouse or other dependents? So it is essential for you to understand all the plans that are available for your use
now, as tax-deferral vehicles, and later, as retirement income programs.
There are numerous books, publications, and other literature available
to you by purchase or loan through your public library that can answer
questions which you might have. Of course, a qualified professional
with whom you might be working will be happy to discuss your questions. Remember, the only dumb question is the one that is not asked!

14

Pension and Profit-Sharing Plans

Experts estimate that retirees need 60 to 70 percent of preretirement, pretax income to maintain their current standard of living.

FREEDOM FOCUS

- *What are defined benefit plans?*
- *What are defined contribution plans?*
- *Which deferred compensation plans are most suitable for nonprofit organizations?*
- *What is a 401(k) plan?*

Flip open the classified section of any Sunday newspaper and you're guaranteed to see a bumper crop of boxed ads offering "liberal retirement benefits" to potential employees. In recent years, the benefit package has become an important addition to employers' bargaining arsenals; often, this factor is the "scale-tipper" that brings a job-seeker under one corporate umbrella rather than another. Such packages normally include more than retirement benefits, of course, but we will limit our discussion to the major types of retirement plans that companies are offering today.

First, let's deal with the subject of employer motivation. Why would a large employer who pays competitive wages choose to sweeten the pot even more for employees by offering them a retirement plan? Keeping up with the competition is just part of the answer. Another motivating factor (and this is undoubtedly the most compelling one) is that in almost all instances *the employer and other top-ranking executives in the company stand to benefit most from a well-constructed retirement plan.* This fact should not disturb you if you happen to be an employee rather than an employer. Why? *Because you, too, can benefit substantially from such a program.*

Corporate retirement plans are among the best deals going. Think about it for a moment: Where else can you find an investment opportunity that

1. Is set up for you with company funds
2. Gives you big-money leverage in the marketplace
3. Is professionally managed
4. Allows you, in some cases, to make voluntary contributions that can accumulate tax-deferred earnings

If this is a good deal for you, it's a super deal for your company's owners and top-level executives. Through corporate retirement plans, employers can channel thousands of their company's pretax dollars into a safe, legal tax haven each year. In addition, that money can compound earnings without creating a tax liability for the company. But don't lose sight of safety values in quest of higher returns. Don't forget the junk bond debacle we've recently suffered or the not-so-safe havens for your money such as Executive Life Insurance (an insurance company out of California which went into receivership as a result of bad investments, including junk bonds).

Although we are about to examine some retirement plans that are available today, *this will not be a definitive treatment of the subject.* If you are a business owner who is considering putting a retirement program into effect for yourself and your employees, you *must* consult professionals that specialize in fitting such plans to companies' needs. (Some firms will design a plan especially for you, while others will simply sell you a prototype plan that has been approved by the IRS. For the names of several firms in your area that provide pension plan consultation services, check your Yellow Pages, your Chamber of Commerce, or professional associations.)

Most corporate retirement plans come in two basic types: *defined benefit plans* and *defined contribution plans.* In the general category of defined contribution plans you will find *money-purchase pension plans, profit-sharing plans,* and *401(k) plans,* which have much in common, along with *target* (or *assumed*) *benefit* plans, which are a combination of defined benefit and money-purchase pension plans.

Defined Benefit Plans

Although not used as frequently as some other plans, this type of plan guarantees participants a certain percentage of their preretirement salaries in retirement benefits. In order to make sure that the promised retirement funds (the defined benefit) will be available to all covered employees, the company must make a specific contribution to the plan annually. The program is evaluated by an actuary every year to make sure that the plan's dollar intake remains adequate to meet its obligations—in other words, a lot of governmental red tape is involved.

Funds in this type of plan are invested, but the portfolio's performance rarely has any effect upon the amount of income retirees receive. Instead, a high-yield portfolio will reduce the annual company contributions required in future years, while disappointing investments will increase the amount of these contributions.

In the defined benefit plan, the retirement benefit is commonly expressed as a percentage of participants' salaries. This percentage is often set with an eye toward giving the boss the kind of income that *he or she* wants to retire on. Suppose, for example, that the president of your company is currently earning $100,000 a year, and wants $50,000 a year in retirement benefits. Since the law requires pension and profit-sharing plans to treat all participants equally, everyone in the plan will retire on 50 percent of salary. (In practice, this calculation is based upon the average amount of annual compensation that has been received by each employee—including the employer—over a certain number of years before retirement.) In other words, defined benefit plans are designed primarily to fill the needs of employers and highly compensated employees. Your share of the retirement fund will increase in direct proportion to the size of your salary at retirement, which often is related to length of service.

The amount of the contribution that the company must make annually may be discounted to allow for anticipated investment earnings and anticipated forfeitures. A *forfeiture* occurs when an employee covered by the retirement plan leaves the company before he or she is fully *vested.* Vested benefits are those benefits that belong to the employee outright.

Vesting normally takes place gradually, until, after a period of years, the employee is entitled to 100 percent of his or her part of the retirement account even though employment is terminated. Any employee who leaves the company prior to becoming 100 percent vested forfeits some plan money, and this money is used by the company to reduce its annual contribution.

Defined Contribution Plans

Defined contribution means that the amount of money that a company must put into its retirement plan every year remains stable. This type of program does *not* promise participants any particular percentage of salary in retirement benefits; the payout depends entirely on the plan's investment returns. (In practice, retirement benefits paid through a defined contribution plan are almost always substantially higher than those paid through a defined benefit plan, particularly for workers on the middle and lower rungs of the salary ladder.)

Consider now the two most frequently used types of defined contribution plans, *money-purchase pension plans* and *profit-sharing plans,* along with another popular full service plan, the *401(k) plan.*

Profit-Sharing Plans, Money-Purchase Pension Plans, and 401(k) Plans

A *profit-sharing plan* permits employers to make tax-deductible contributions on behalf of their employees. These plans are well suited for businesses where cash flow and income are somewhat variable. Contributions may be based on business profits (as a percentage of payroll) or an amount that is determined each year. A *money-purchase pension plan* also permits employers to make tax-deductible contributions on behalf of their employees. Contributions are based on a fixed contribution formula predetermined by the employer. These plans are well suited for businesses with substantial income. Both plans bear a strong resemblance to one another and are also suitable for small firms or corporations, "S" corporations, partnerships, sole proprietors (self-employed), and nonprofit organizations (pension and profit-sharing only), but there is at least one important difference between them: Companies offering money-purchase pension plans *must* contribute a certain percentage of each employee's salary to the plan each year, regardless of whether they have realized a profit or not. Firms with profit-sharing programs do not have to make contributions. Thus a profit-sharing program has a discretionary factor, which many companies find extremely attractive. (Incidentally, profit sharing need not be used solely as a retirement plan; sometimes it is used simply as a means of sharing a company's wealth with employees, a kind of bonus system. The kind of profit-sharing plan being discussed here, however, is linked to retirement. When profits are up, the retirement account receives larger contributions—up to a maximum of 15 percent of the salaries of covered employees. When profits are down, contributions drop and sometimes even dry up altogether.)

In addition to the annual contribution, at least two other major differences exist between money-purchase pensions and profit-sharing plans. The employer is allowed to put the maximum deductible amount of the lesser of 25 percent of each participant's compensation or $30,000 into a money-purchase plan annually, but the deductible contribution to profit-sharing plans is limited to the lesser of 15 percent of each participant's compensation or $30,000. With profit-sharing plans, employer contributions are discretionary and can be based on, but not limited to, profits. Under a money-purchase pension plan the employer contributes a predetermined percentage each year. Contributions are mandatory regardless of profits. In both cases, forfeitures may reduce the company's annual contribution to money-purchase pensions or may be distributed proportionately among the remaining participants. Thus, companies with high employee turnover rates can have a constant stream of forfeiture money for their own use or for channeling these forfeitures to the employees who remain on board.

Both plans must be set up on or before the last day of the employer's fiscal year for the year in which the deduction is taken. Funding must be on or before the date the employer's federal income tax return is due, plus extensions.

Employees who meet the age and service requirements are eligible to participate in the plans, and the employer must include employees who have reached age 21 and who have completed the required number of years of service. Part-time employees, those who have worked less than 1000 hours during the year, can generally be excluded from the plans.

Employers save on taxes because the money they contribute for their employees is deducted from their taxable business profits, thereby reducing the company's federal tax liability.

Table 14-1 provides a summary of the major characteristics of defined benefit pensions, money-purchase pensions, and profit-sharing plans.

401(k) Plans

A 401(k) plan permits employers to make tax-deductible contributions on behalf of their employees. It also has a salary deferral feature that

Table 14-1. Major Characteristics of Three Types of Pension and Profit-Sharing Plans

Defined benefit pensions	Money-purchase pensions	Profit-sharing plans
How company's contribution is determined		
Mathematically determined in advance; must be adequate to fund benefit.	Established by plan formula; can utilize lesser of 25 percent of covered compensation or $30,000 per participant. Contribution must be made with or without profits.	Set by formula and action of board of directors; can utilize lesser of 15 percent of covered compensation or $30,000 per participant. Contributions are made only in profitable years.
Where company's contribution goes		
Larger shares to owner and longer-service, more highly paid employees.	Distributed proportionately according to salary and length of service.	Distributed proportionately according to salary and length of service.
Effect of investment gains and losses		
Above assumed rate: Reduces company deposit. Below assumed rate: Increases company deposit.	Benefits increase or decrease accordingly.	Benefits increase or decrease accordingly.
Effect of forfeitures		
Above assumed rate: Reduces company deposit. Below assumed rate: Increases company deposit.	Reduces company deposit.	Reallocated proportionately to remaining participants.
How plan pays benefits		
Each participant's benefit predetermined mathematically. (Benefit is generally lower than in defined contribution plans.)	Vested funds due participants upon termination of employment.	Vested funds due participants upon termination of employment.
Benefit is a function of		
Plan-stipulated percentage of final average salary; related to pay level/length of service.	Years of participation, contributions, investment results.	Years of participation, contributions, investment results, forfeitures.

permits employees to defer a portion of their salary into the plan on a pre-tax basis through payroll deduction. 401(k) plans differ in that the maximum deductible amount is the lesser of 15 percent of each participant's compensation or $30,000. (This figure includes employer basic, employer match, and $8475 employee salary reduction.) It is flexible in that employer contributions are discretionary and can be based on, but not limited to, profits. Currently, the maximum salary deferral amount cannot exceed $8475 (indexed by inflation every year) and is included in the maximum contribution limit. Nondeductible voluntary contributions are included in the maximum contribution limit. The set-up, funding, and filing requirements are the same as those listed for profit-sharing plans. The 401(k) works well for the larger firm where the majority of employees wish to defer a portion of their salaries, and for businesses wishing to contribute on a match basis.

It should be noted that combined pension and profit-sharing or pension and 401(k) are subject to a single maximum deductible limit of 25 percent of compensation.

Cafeteria Plans

Cafeteria plans allow a participant to choose from two or more benefits consisting of cash and qualified benefits. To be a participant in a cafeteria plan, you must be an employee. Generally, once participants make their selections, they are not permitted to revoke those selections, except in specified situations.

Cafeteria plans can include contributions made by the employer under a salary reduction agreement (but it must relate to compensation that has not been received). They may also offer such qualified benefits as group-term life insurance, certain coverage under an accident or health plan, or dependent-care assistance programs.

If your employer offers a cafeteria plan, carefully weigh each option with your retirement needs in mind.

Target Benefit Plans

The *target benefit plan* (also called the assumed benefit plan) is a combination of the defined benefit and money-purchase pension plans. As its name indicates, this type of plan *targets* a particular benefit for participants, but does not promise to deliver it as the defined benefit plan does. The company's contributions can thus remain level from year to year, regardless of such variables as portfolio performance and employee forfeitures.

Plans for Nonprofit Organizations

Since there are no tax benefits to the nonprofit organization, the employer should focus on the retirement benefits the employer receives as a participant in the plan. A few of the plans we'll discuss here include the 403(b), 457 deferred compensation plans, and the SEP/IRA.

A *403(b) plan* allows employees of tax-exempt [as defined by IRS Code section 501(c)—religious, charitable, scientific, literary, educational, etc.] organizations and public education institutions [as defined by IRS Code section 170(b)] to defer a portion of their salaries into the plan on a pre-tax basis through payroll deduction. These plans can be set up and funded any time during the calendar year and can consist of employer contributions, salary deferral contributions only, and can allow "catch-up" contributions. These plans are used by many school teachers and employees of universities, colleges, hospitals, churches, and other nonprofit organizations.

A *457 deferred compensation plan* permits employees to defer a portion of their salaries into the plan on a pre-tax basis through payroll deduction. These plans are available to state and local governments and their agencies, state political subdivisions and their agencies, and tax-exempt organizations (other than a governmental unit). Employees or contractors with earned compensation from a qualifying employer are eligible. The employer is the owner of the assets until payments commence. There are many special rules which apply to 457s.

The *SEP/IRA plan* must include employees who have reached age 21; who have worked 3 or more of the last 5 preceding years; and who have annual compensation of at least $363 (in 1991). *All* eligible employees must participate in the plan. Employer contributions are limited to the lesser of 15 percent of each participant's compensation or $30,000. SEP/IRAs must be set up and funded on or before the employer's tax filing deadline plus extensions and may be maintained on a calendar or fiscal year basis.

Nonqualified Deferred Compensation Plans

Even if you are covered by a pension and/or profit-sharing plan, you may want to explore the advantages of entering into a *nonqualified deferred compensation plan* with your employer. That means simply this: You agree to take part of your income at a later date—either upon your retirement or when you leave your present employment. This money can then earn investment income for you on a tax-deferred basis (and we already know the great advantage of that). You pay *no* tax until you take receipt of your deferred income, either in a lump sum or through regular monthly payments. But the employee should have reasonable assurance that the company will still be around at the employee's retirement.

What can your company gain from such an arrangement? For one thing, your employer will never have to pay either Social Security or federal unemployment tax on deferred compensation dollars. (You pay no Social Security tax on it either, yet your Social Security benefits are not reduced.) The company will not be able to take federal income tax deductions while it is paying into a nonqualified deferred compensation program, but once payout begins, such deductions *are* allowed.

One of the greatest advantages of this type of plan is that it doesn't come wrapped up in the miles of government red tape that accompany qualified retirement programs. You and your employer simply strike a deal together, carry it out together, and enjoy the benefits together, without having to examine reams of IRS regulations. Since it isn't a qualified plan, it doesn't have to treat all employees equally. This means that the company may select certain employees for inclusion and exclude others.

Some General Considerations

Split-funding is another option that is available to employers. A split-funded pension or profit-sharing plan channels some of its assets into term and whole life insurance. Although whole life insurance does not perform well as an investment, its inclusion in a retirement plan could be of substantial value to employees (and employers) who are in poor health and unable to obtain insurance by any other means. Life insurance policies may be issued as part of a retirement plan without physical examinations upon purchase or renewal. Death benefits, up to certain limits, can go to participant's beneficiaries without being subject to probate administration if properly distributed.

Upon retirement or termination of employment for other reasons, participants in vested pension plans and profit-sharing plans may receive their benefits in *lump sum payments, installment payments,* or through purchase of *annuities.* Should you leave a retirement program when you are partially vested, you should be aware of your options and if you aren't sure of what course to take, consult a financial professional. These options include rolling your account over into an IRA, taking a lump sum payment, or taking monthly distributions. The financial professional will be able to guide you toward the course of action that is best suited to your case.

As an employee, you can prove the real value that a company-offered pension or profit-sharing plan has for you by asking questions such as these:

1. What are the eligibility provisions of my company's retirement plan?
2. Are loans to participants permitted? If so, how much?
3. What is the vesting schedule?
4. If the company has a profit-sharing or money-purchase plan, are earmarked investments allowed?
5. How are the funds invested and by whom?
6. Can employee participants make voluntary contributions to the plan?

Voluntary contributions to any retirement plan may be withdrawn by the employee to meet cash needs that may crop up before retirement, such as illness-related expenses or costs involved in sending a child through college, buying a new home, adding to your present home (and thus increasing its value), and so forth. Your voluntary contributions become a type of savings account that you may tap at any time or save for use during your retirement. Because this feature is so valuable to you, you should find out when you join a company whether the retirement program the firm offers will permit you to make voluntary contributions.

We have covered considerable ground since we first turned our attention to the subject of retirement. As we have seen, opportunities for you to put aside substantial sums in tax-favored programs are in plentiful supply. If you want to make your retirement years "the best of times" and enjoy certain current advantages too, you should make certain that you are covered by a retirement program that meets your needs. As I said before, retirement planning is a very necessary ingredient in your financial freedom planning.

PART 3
Action...

15
Tax-Time Tactics

Next to being shot at and missed,
nothing is really quite as satisfying
as an income tax refund.

F. J. RAYMOND

FREEDOM FOCUS

- *What are 12 commonly overlooked areas on your 1040 form?*
- *Who is most likely to be audited?*
- *What are the questions IRS examiners ask before*
  they evaluate computer- selected returns for audit?
- *Do you know what tax publications are available*
  from the IRS and the toll-free numbers
  to call for free information?
- *What is the Taypayers' Bill of Rights?*

Oliver Wendell Holmes said it, and our friends at the IRS have been happily echoing it ever since: "Taxes are the price we pay for a civilized society." But I'd like to show you some ways that will help you keep your hard-earned money where it belongs—in your own pocket.

Tax manuals do not make the most compelling reading, and I certainly do not intend to create my own version of one here. I'm sure you'll stay awake much longer and benefit a good deal more if I simply point out some of the pitfalls that dot the landscape of your 1040 form.

First of all, let's clear the air on one point. It is absolutely acceptable for you to use every legal means at your disposal to minimize your tax bill. No less an authority than Judge Learned Hand said,

> Over and over again, courts have said that there is nothing sinister in so arranging one's affairs as to keep taxes as low as possible. Everybody does so, rich or poor; and all do right, for nobody owes any public duty to pay more tax than the law demands; taxes are enforced exactions, not voluntary contributions.

Before we discuss how you can keep those "exactions" to a minimum, you should recall the advice of another chapter: *The time to begin your tax planning is January 1, not the last few weeks of the taxable year.* Ducking into a hastily located tax shelter just before Christmas is a lot like taking refuge under a tree during an electrical storm; your "shelter" could leak badly when subjected to IRS scrutiny and could even attract a bolt of lightning—in the form of disallowed deductions. Tax planning should *always* be a beginning-of-the-year task for you and your advisers.

There are three basic rules that apply to your income tax preparation:

1. *Be meticulous about documentation and recordkeeping.* The IRS clearly spells out the types of documentation you need for backup of your 1040. Lack of documentation leaves you in a vulnerable position should you be audited. Lack of records, or poorly kept records, could cost you actual dollars in the form of deductions.

2. *Check and recheck your figures.* Many returns are flagged each year due to incorrect addition and subtraction. Checking figures applies to all schedules you file with your return as well as forms provided to you from outside sources, such as form 1099.

3. *Use a professional.* Unless you fall into one of the very simple "short-form" categories, take advantage of professional guidance not only to prepare your return, but to assist you in tax planning for the future.

By adhering to these three simple rules you can save yourself potential headaches and possibly tax dollars.

Twelve Commonly Overlooked Deductions on Your 1040 Form

In order to realize maximum advantages from the preparation of your tax return each year, you must keep abreast of changes in the regulations. You can do this by buying one of the tax preparation guides that are privately published each year, and by carefully reading the instruction booklet issued by the IRS with your reporting forms. You also might consider subscribing to one of the many "tax tip" newsletters in circulation. Your accountant or financial planner will probably be able to give you the name of one that can be understood by the lay person. One such newsletter is *Research Institute Recommendations,* published by the Research Institute of America, Inc., 589 Fifth Avenue, New York, New York 10017. There is a small subscription fee.

Here are some frequently overlooked deductions and credits that are allowable as of this writing, in 1992. If you have deductions over and above the standard deduction you may deduct the excess from your taxable income.

1. *Separate returns or joint.* In some cases you can significantly reduce overall taxes by filing separate returns. This tactic usually involves the bunching of medical expenses as a deduction by one spouse, thus utilizing a lower amount (7.5 percent) from which to start taking deductions.

2. *Medical and charitable mileage.* Many people who claim medical deductions forget that they are also permitted to take 9 cents a mile for transportation to and from the doctor's office. And if you are a charitable volunteer, you can deduct 12 cents a mile for driving related to this work.

3. *Losses.* Any losses to nonbusiness property (casualty, theft, or embezzlement) in excess of $100 that you have sustained that have not been paid for by an insurance policy or other source of reimbursement may be claimed on your 1040 form, and are deductible to the extent they exceed 10 percent of your adjusted gross income. In order for a loss from theft to be deductible, you must be able to prove that a theft has taken place, so make sure you file reports with the police that list evidence of the theft. If they investigate, you should retain your case number in your records with any other pertinent information.

4. *Securities.* If you own securities (stocks, bonds, and so on), costs related to maintaining your portfolio are tax deductible. Such costs can include fees you have paid for financial advice, accounting charges, tax preparation costs, safe deposit box rental—and, yes, the price of this book. As "miscellaneous" expenses they are subject to a floor amount. To be deductible as a miscellaneous expense on Schedule A, the expenses must either be connected to producing income or be incurred for a tax related matter. Other deductions which have been allowed include the following:

- Trustee's commission for administering a revocable trust
- Transportation and parking costs on trips to the taxpayer's stock-broker
- Depreciation on a safe used to store securities and other financial certificates
- Service charges subtracted from cash dividends before the dividends are reinvested
- Postage related to investment activities

5. *Capital gains and losses.* Many taxpayers fail to claim costs such as broker's fees that they incur during investment transactions that lead to capital gains or losses. These fees reduce the amount of gain you'll be taxed on or increase the loss you may take.

6. *Dependent parent or other family members.* Even if you do not contribute over 50 percent of the cost of maintaining a parent or other relative, you may take a *$2300* (at this writing) exemption if other members of your family who also contribute to the person's support agree that you may do so. This means, of course, that no one else will be able to claim this person as a dependent.

7. *Tax breaks on your car.* If you buy a car for business use, you can claim actual expenses, including depreciation, related to business use. This could be better for you than the standard deduction of 27.5 (at this writing) cents a mile. If you incur expenses as an employee, seek any reimbursement you are entitled to from your employer. Transportation expenses such as taxi fares and auto operation may not be deducted directly by an employee unless the amount of the expenses exceeds the reimbursement. These rules apply equally to self-employed persons and to employees who purchase cars for business use. However, employees must reduce such unreimbursed business expenses and other miscellaneous itemized deductions by 2 percent of their adjusted gross income.

8. *Dividend and interest income.* Be sure to take a careful look at your 1099 (dividend reporting form). In some cases, particularly with utility stocks, dividends are either tax-free or are taxed at the more favorable capital-gains rate. Read the small print on your 1099 and carefully review any supplemental material that you might receive from the corporation. Incidentally, the IRS contends that the figures shown on Form 1099 are correct in the reported amount of interest income paid to you—the burden of proof rests with you. (Remember check and double-check!) Interest earned in a Keogh plan, a qualified pension or profit-sharing plan, or on your own voluntary contributions to a qualified profit-sharing plan is not tax-

able as long as you make no withdrawal. Income earned is reported and taxed when withdrawals are made.

9. *IRAs and Keoghs.* If you are eligible to set up an IRA (Individual Retirement Account) or Keogh Plan for yourself and have not yet done so, you should give serious consideration right now to seizing the tax benefits that these plans afford you. IRAs are for employees who are not active participants in qualified retirement plans at their places of work, and Keoghs are for self-employed individuals. Refer to Chapter 13 for more detailed information on IRA accounts. An IRA may permit you to put 100 percent of your pretax income, to a maximum of $2000 a year, into a special retirement fund. The Keogh limit is set at 25 percent of your earnings from self-employment, up to $30,000.

10. *"Bunching" your deductions.* Anytime your deductible personal expenses fall below the standard deduction for a year, those actual deductions are not doing you any good. It is sometimes possible to "bunch" deductible expenses that you may have planned to incur over, say, a two-year period into a single year. Then, in the second year when your expenses drop off, you can simply take the standard deduction.

11. *Interest deductions.* If you have purchased a home during the taxable year, be sure to claim the "points" you have paid the bank. Home mortgage interest is deductible. It is interest you pay on a loan secured by your home, including a mortgage, second mortgage, line of credit, and a home equity loan. If the interest is on a debt that is secured by property that is your qualified home, you may deduct all of it. Careful planning is necessary to maximize the deduction of investment interest. Investment interest expenses and income must be matched and portions of the interest expense may be disallowed. Consult a tax professional for planning strategy in reporting of deductions.

12. *Passive activity losses.* Special rules prevent "sheltering" current earned income and investment income with losses from rental property and limited partnerships. The governing regulations are extremely complex and require expert assistance to avoid technical problems.

Nine Additional Overlooked Deductions

The listing below is just a reminder of deductions which are often overlooked. It is not intended to be all inclusive. If you have a specific question, present it to the professionals who prepare your returns, or take advantage of the toll-free IRS Tele-Tax information service. (See Appendix 15-1.)

1. Accounting fees for IRS audits and tax preparation services
2. Treatment for alcoholism or drug abuse
3. Fees to an employment agency
4. Plastic surgery; seeing-eye dog; special foods or diet; hair transplant; wigs essential to mental health; medical transportation, including standard mileage deduction; hearing devices; braille books and magazines; air conditioner allergy relief
5. Points on a home mortgage and certain refinancings
6. Passport fee for business trip
7. Amortization of premium on taxable bonds
8. Appreciation on property donated to a charity
9. Moving expenses, including those related to house-hunting, selling your old home, or settling an unexpired lease, and travel (including lodgings and meals) as a result of your employment

Will You Be Audited?

One of the rites of spring in our society is the annual agonizing that taxpayers large and small go through as they wonder, "Will this be the year I get called in for an audit?" All of this anxiety must surely rank as one of the country's greatest energy drains. As long as you can show the IRS why you claimed what you claimed, you don't need to lie awake nights participating in this national pastime. Your basic rules of thumb should be: (1) start your tax planning early in the year, (2) obtain competent, trustworthy advice on investments that purportedly carry tax advantages, and (3) keep accurate records and documentation. You are required to keep your copy of the 1040 statement and all supporting documents and records for three years after the filing date. Records on capital items should be kept for at least three years after sale. However, many financial planning professionals recommend keeping these records for six years.

Returns that become candidates for audit are selected by IRS computers programmed with a highly confidential scoring system. These returns are then reviewed by human screeners, who make recommendations either for or against an audit.

Here are the questions that these screeners, according to an IRS directive, are to ask themselves as they evaluate computer-selected returns:

1. Is the income sufficient to support the exemptions claimed?
2. Does the refund appear to be out of line when considering the gross income and exemptions?
3. Is there a possibility that income may be underreported?
4. Could the taxpayer be moonlighting, earning tips, or have other types of income not subject to withholding tax?
5. Is the taxpayer engaged in the type of business or profession normally considered to be more profitable than reflected by the return?
6. Is the taxpayer's yield (net profit) on his/her investment (equity in assets) less than he/she could have realized by depositing the same amount in a savings account?
7. Is the standard deduction used with high gross and low net shown on a business schedule? Experience has shown that the incidence of fraud is greater on low business returns when the return reflects large receipts ($100,000 or more) and a sizable investment, and when the standard deduction is used.

For 1989, if you earned less than $25,000 and didn't itemize deductions, the IRS figures your chances of being audited are about 1 in 164. If you itemized and earned more than $50,000, the odds become about 1 in 143. It gets worse. If you file Schedule C with gross receipts of more than $100,000, you have a 1 in 24 chance of being audited. The message seems to be that increased wealth is accompanied by an increased chance of being audited. This should not, of course, deter you from seeking increased wealth.

In 1989, 199,567,366 returns were filed. Of those, 1,200,949 returns were audited. Accordingly, your chances of being audited are approximately 1 in 100. Will you be audited? Who can say? But you can increase your chances of being audited by sending up "red flags." There are three entries that accountants say consistently cause problems. They are

1. *Business use of a car.* The red flag here is that people guess how far they drove and the IRS knows they can usually catch someone on this. *Keep a log or diary of destinations and distances.*
2. *Noncash contributions.* This requires you to file a Form 8283 (another red flag). IRS will question you on how you arrived at the

value. Make sure your value is determined legitimately and, of course, keep documentation of valuation or appraisal.

3. *Home office deductions.*   The IRS loves this flag. The rule is very simple—the area you claim as home office space must be dedicated to office use only. A home office which is in space that includes any other activity (such as bedroom, dining room, etc.) would be very questionable.

What to Do If You Are Audited

Why do we fear audits so much? Maybe it's because we know the chances of our having to write a check for additional money are in the IRS's favor. Maybe it's because we think there may be gray areas on our returns. Or perhaps it's simply because we have a general feeling of loss of control when we become part of an audit.

Let's examine these fears one by one. According to the IRS, for 1989 only 6 percent of all audits resulted in more taxes; 25 percent produced no change; and 6 percent resulted in refunds. The average penalty for returns examined by an auditor was $1827. So the odds are not really stacked against you. As for those gray areas, work with a professional and if it is still a questionable matter, contact the IRS for clarification. Weigh the benefit versus the risk, then make a decision and be prepared to accept the consequences. Personally, if I have a serious doubt, I leave it out. Although I don't believe he was actually referring to taxes, J. R. R. Tolkien said it best, "It does not do to leave a dragon out of your calculations if you live near him."

Your control over the situation begins with proper tax planning, not in December, but in January; it extends to proper recordkeeping and documentation by you. Control can further be exercised through the selection of the tax professional and the completion of your return. The fact is that you do have control, even to the point of bringing a professional to represent you at the audit.

Should you be one of those audited it is very important to remember a few things. When you receive your notice, call the IRS to schedule your meeting during a time when no one will be rushed. If they tell you it will only take a couple of hours, breathe easier—but if they suggest you set aside a week, then you can expect the "super" audit, a very serious review. However, when you schedule your meeting, insist that it be held at either the IRS offices or the offices of your preparer. Allowing them into your home will only provide the auditor a more complete picture of your economic situation.

Of course, the most important element of your audit will be the records and documentation you present to back up your deductions. In fact, it is possible that you could end up asking for additional deductions. Additionally, your attitude will influence the auditor, so be polite. Give simple and direct responses to the questions you are asked and answer only those questions you are asked—don't volunteer information.

Be prepared. Review your return with your tax preparer and have that person come with you to the audit. It's well worth the fee for time, and having a professional with you who knows what kinds of answers the auditor is looking for could potentially save you several times the amount of the fee.

If you think the auditor assigned to you is abusive, request another, but do not become rude or belligerent toward your auditor. If you are dissatisfied with the results of your audit, appeal on the spot to the auditor's supervisor who can make his or her own conclusions (see Figure 15-1). Still unhappy? You have 30 days to request that an IRS appeals officer hear your case. The appeals officer has the authority to weigh the cost of a possible court battle in determining how much, if anything, you should pay. This flexibility *allows* them to concede some or all the issues that your auditor raised.

If you and your tax professional still believe that you have a case to be heard, and the benefits outweigh the risks, you can further appeal to the U.S. tax court, district court, or claims court. These cases don't generally favor the taxpayer.

We have all heard the horror stories. You come home to find your front door and all the windows boarded up; you can no longer write checks from your checking account or withdraw money from your savings account. Your credit cards are canceled and, basically, anything with equity is seized. No doubt it has happened in the past, but not as a rule, and not based on one audit. Because of the horror stories, a Taxpayers' Bill of Rights was enacted. If you feel that you are being treated unfairly, you do have rights to call upon. As a taxpayer, you have the right to be treated fairly, professionally, promptly, and courteously by IRS employees and you have certain rights at each step of the IRS audit and collection process. Know your rights: General Guide 1, Your Rights as a Taxpayer, is shown as Appendix 15-2. For a listing of publications available to you at no charge, refer to Appendix 15-3, IRS Tax Publications.

To paraphrase a ruling by Judge Learned Hand, it is the legal right of a taxpayer to reduce or eliminate his or her taxes. The benefits of such tax deferral or avoidance cannot be underestimated when making your investment decisions on your way to financial freedom.

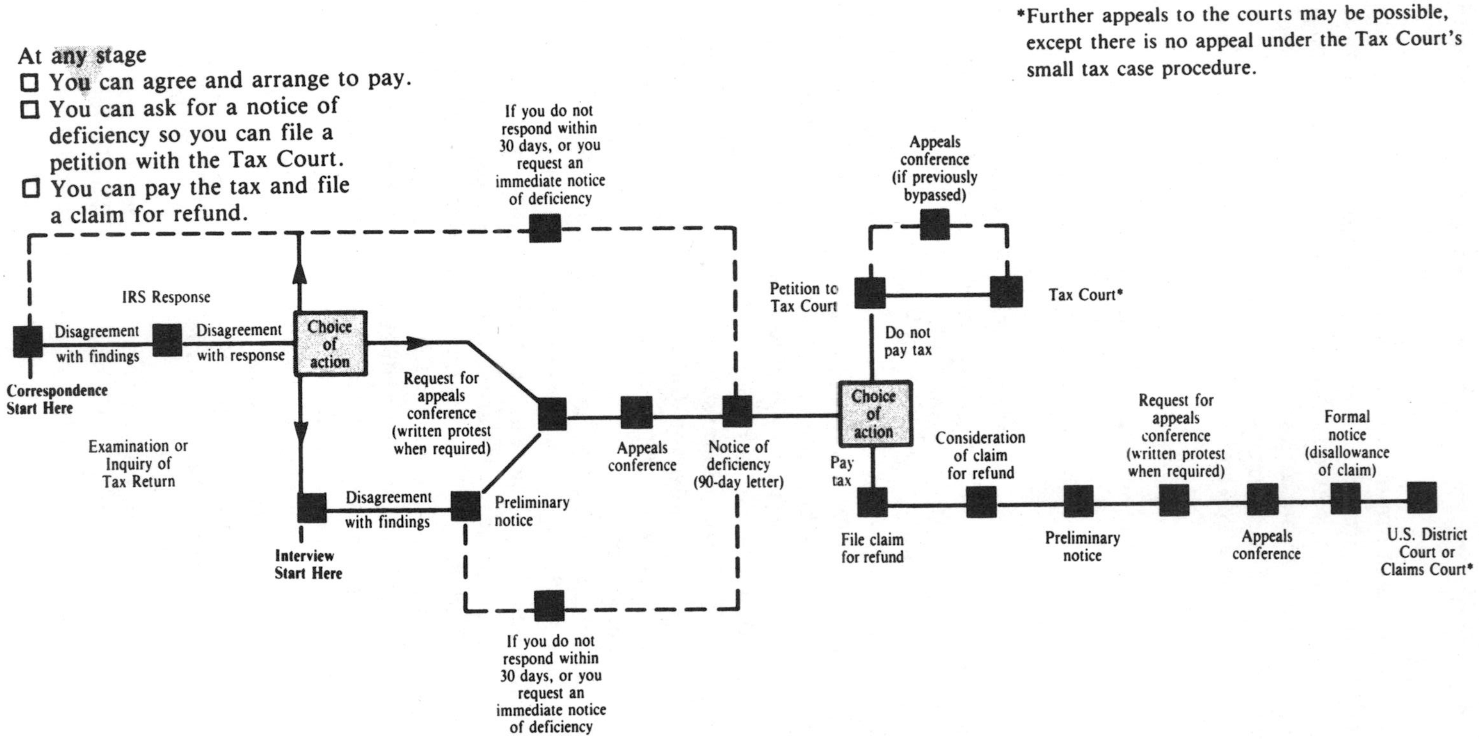

At any stage
☐ You can agree and arrange to pay.
☐ You can ask for a notice of deficiency so you can file a petition with the Tax Court.
☐ You can pay the tax and file a claim for refund.

*Further appeals to the courts may be possible, except there is no appeal under the Tax Court's small tax case procedure.

Figure 15-1. Income tax appeal procedure. *(Courtesy of the Internal Revenue Service.)*

APPENDIX 15-1
IRS Tele-Tax
Information Service

Tele-Tax is recorded tax information on approximately 140 topics that answer many federal tax questions. You can hear up to three topics on each call you make.

Call Tele-Tax toll free, but use only the numbers listed for your area. Long distance charges apply if you call from outside the local dialing area of the numbers listed. *Do not dial 1-800 when using a local number.* But when dialing from an area that does not have a local number, be sure to dial 1-800 before calling the toll free number.

How Do You Use Tele-Tax?

Topic numbers are effective January 1, 1992. Push button (tone signaling) service is available 24 hours a day, 7 days a week. Rotary (dial)/ push button (pulse dial) service is available Monday through Friday during regular office hours. (In Hawaii from 6:30 a.m. to 1:00 p.m.) Select by number the topic you want to hear. For the directory of topics, listen to topic 323. Have paper and pencil handy to take notes. Call the appropriate phone number listed and follow the directions given to you.

Automated Refund Information?

Be sure to have a copy of your tax return available since you will need to know the first social security number shown on your return, the filing status, and the *exact* amount of your refund. Then call the appropriate phone number listed and follow the recorded instructions. IRS updates refund information every 7 days. If you call to find out about the status of your refund and do not receive a refund mailing date, please wait 7 days before calling back.

- Push button (tone signaling) service is available Monday through Friday, 7:00 a.m. through 11:30 p.m. (hours may vary in your area).

- Rotary (dial)/push button (pulse dial) service is available Monday through Friday by calling during regular office hours. (In Hawaii, from 6:30 a.m. to 1:00 p.m.)

Alabama	1-800-829-4477
Alaska	1-800-829-4477
Arizona	
Phoenix	252-4909
Elsewhere	1-800-829-4477
Arkansas	1-800-829-4477
California	
Counties of Amador, Calaveras, Contra Costa, Marin, and San Joaquin	1-800-829-4032
Los Angeles	617-3177
Oakland	839-4245
Elsewhere	1-800-829-4477
Colorado	
Denver	592-1118
Elsewhere	1-800-829-4477
Connecticut	1-800-829-4477
Delaware	1-800-829-4477
District of Columbia	882-1040
Florida	1-800-829-4477
Georgia	
Atlanta	331-6572
Elsewhere	1-800-829-4477
Hawaii	1-800-829-4477
Idaho	1-800-829-4477
Illinois	
Chicago	886-9614
In area code 708	1-312-886-9614
Springfield	789-0489
Elsewhere	1-800-829-4477
Indiana	
Indianapolis	631-1010
Elsewhere	1-800-829-4477
Iowa	
Des Moines	284-7454
Elsewhere	1-800-829-4477
Kansas	1-800-829-4477
Kentucky	1-800-829-4477

Louisiana	1-800-829-4477
Maine	1-800-829-4477
Maryland	
Baltimore	466-1040
Elsewhere	1-800-829-4477
Massachusetts	
Boston	523-8602
Elsewhere	1-800-829-4477
Michigan	
Detroit	961-4282
Elsewhere	1-800-829-4477
Minnesota	
St. Paul	644-7748
Elsewhere	1-800-829-4477
Mississippi	1-800-829-4477
Missouri	
St. Louis	241-4700
Elsewhere	1-800-829-4477
Montana	1-800-829-4477
Nebraska	
Omaha	221-3324
Elsewhere	1-800-829-4477
Nevada	1-800-829-4477
New Hampshire	1-800-829-4477
New Jersey	1-800-829-4477
New Mexico	1-800-829-4477
New York	
Bronx	406-4080
Brooklyn	858-4461
Buffalo	856-9320
Manhattan	406-4080
Queens	858-4461
Staten Island	858-4461
Elsewhere	1-800-829-4477
North Carolina	1-800-829-4477
North Dakota	1-800-829-4477
Ohio	
Cincinnati	421-0329

Cleveland	522-3037
Elsewhere	1-800-829-4477
Oklahoma	1-800-829-4477
Oregon	
Portland	294-5363
Elsewhere	1-800-829-4477
Pennsylvania	
Philadelphia	627-1040
Pittsburgh	261-1040
Elsewhere	1-800-829-4477
Puerto Rico	1-800-829-4477
Rhode Island	1-800-829-4477
South Carolina	1-800-829-4477
South Dakota	1-800-829-4477
Tennessee	
Nashville	242-1541
Elsewhere	1-800-829-4477
Texas	
Dallas	767-1792
Houston	850-8801
Elsewhere	1-800-829-4477
Utah	1-800-829-4477
Vermont	1-800-829-4477
Virginia	
Richmond	783-1569
Elsewhere	1-800-829-4477
Washington	
Seattle	343-7221
Elsewhere	1-800-829-4477
West Virginia	1-800-829-4477
Wisconsin	
Milwaukee	273-8100
Elsewhere	1-800-829-4477
Wyoming	1-800-829-4477

APPENDIX 15-2
Your Rights as a Taxpayer*

As a taxpayer, you have the right to be treated fairly, professionally, promptly, and courteously by Internal Revenue Service employees.

Free Information and Help in Preparing Returns. You have the right to information and help in complying with the tax laws. In addition to the basic instructions provided with the tax forms, a great deal of other information is available.

- Taxpayer publications
- Walk-in assistance
- Recorded telephone information through Tele-Tax
- Materials available in braille and in Spanish
- Informational videotapes
- Education programs for specific groups of taxpayers
- Copies of previous forms

Privacy and Confidentiality. You have the right to have your personal and financial information kept confidential. People who prepare your return or represent you *must* keep your information confidential. You have the right to know why the IRS is asking for information, how it will be used, and what will happen if you don't give it.

Courtesy and Consideration. You are entitled to courteous and considerate treatment from IRS employees.

Representation and Recordings. In your dealings with the IRS you have the right to representation or to represent yourself. If during an interview you want to consult an attorney, a certified public accountant, an enrolled agent or other person permitted to represent a taxpayer during an interview for examining a tax return or collecting tax, the IRS will stop and reschedule the interview. If you notify the IRS 10 days prior to a

*Department of the Treasury, Internal Revenue Service, Publication No. 1 (6-89).

meeting, you can generally make an audio recording of an interview with their collection or examination officer.

Payment of Only the Required Tax.   You have the right to plan your business and personal finances so that you will pay the least tax that is due under the law.

If Your Return Is Questioned

- Many examinations and inquiries can be handled entirely by mail. You have the right to write for an explanation of anything you don't understand, or you can request a personal interview. You can appeal through the IRS and the courts.

- If examination is by interview, you have the right to ask that the examination take place at a reasonable time and place that is convenient for both you and the IRS.

- To avoid repeat examinations of the same items, if the IRS examined your tax return for the same items in either of the two previous years and proposed no change to your tax liability, contact them and probably avoid repeat examinations.

- You have the right to an explanation of any changes proposed to your return.

- If an IRS error caused a delay in your case, and this was grossly unfair, they may reduce the amount of interest on additional tax you owe.

- Business taxpayers are generally covered by the rights explained herein. In some cases special rules apply to the examination of your returns. Request Publication 556, Examination of Returns, Appeal Rights, and Claims for Refund.

An Appeal of the Examination Findings.   You have the right to appeal; Publication 5, Appeal Rights and Preparation of Protests for Unagreed Cases, explains your rights.

- You can appeal the findings of an examination with the IRS through the Appeals Office.

- Depending on whether you first pay the disputed tax, you can take your case to the U.S. Tax Court, the U.S. Claims Court, or your U.S. District Court.

- If the court agrees with you on most issues in your case, and finds that the IRS position was largely unjustified, you may be able to recover some of your administrative and litigation costs.

Fair Collection of Tax. If you owe tax, the IRS will send you a bill describing the tax and stating the amount you owe in tax, interest, and penalties. Check the bill. If it is incorrect, you have the right to have it adjusted.

- You may be entitled to payment arrangements (installment payments) based on your financial condition.

- Liens placed on your property to secure the amount of tax due must be released no later than 30 days after finding that you have paid the entire tax and certain charges, the assessment has become legally unenforceable, or the IRS has accepted a bond to cover the tax and certain charges.

- If the IRS knowingly or negligently fails to release a lien under the circumstances described above, and you suffer economic damages because of their failure, you can recover your actual economic damages and certain costs.

- You have the right to appeal an IRS filing of a Notice of Federal Tax Lien if you believe they filed the lien in error.

- You generally have the right to 30 days notice before the IRS levies on any property. They cannot place a levy on your property on a day on which you are required to attend a collection interview.

- Property that is exempt from levy. If the IRS seizes your property, you have the legal right to keep:

  Necessary clothing and schoolbooks

  A limited amount of personal belongings, furniture, and business or professional books and tools

  Unemployment and job training benefits, workers' compensation, welfare, certain disability payments, and certain pension benefits

  The income you need to pay court-ordered child support

  Mail

  An amount of weekly income equal to your standard deduction and allowable personal exemptions, divided by 52

  Your main home, except in certain situations

- If your bank account is levied after June 30, 1989, the bank will hold your account up to the amount of the levy for 21 days. This allows you to resolve your tax bill before the bank turns over the funds to the IRS.

- If the IRS seizes your property, you have the right to request that it be sold within 60 days after your request.

- You have the right to refuse a collection officer (to seize your property) access to your private premises, such as your home or the non public areas of your business, if the employee does not have court authorization to be there.

- If the IRS believes you were responsible for seeing that a corporation paid them income and social security taxes withheld from its employees, and the taxes were not paid, they may look to you to pay an amount based on the unpaid taxes. You may appeal if you feel you don't owe this.

The Collection Process.   To stop the process at any state, you should pay the tax in full. If you cannot pay the tax in full, contact the IRS right away to discuss possible ways to pay the tax.

Refund of Overpaid Tax.   Once you have paid all your tax, you have the right to file a claim for a refund if you think the tax is incorrect. You will receive interest on any income tax refund delayed more than 45 days after the *later* of either the date you filed your return or the date your return was due.

Cancellation of Penalties.   You have the right to show that certain penalties (but not interest) be cancelled (abated) if you can show reasonable cause for the failure (wrong advice on the toll-free telephone system or incorrect written advice) that led to the penalty.

Special Help to Resolve Your Problems.   If you have a tax problem that you cannot clear up through the normal channels, write to the Problem Resolution Officer in the district or Service Center with which you have the problem.

Protection of Your Rights.   The employees of the IRS will explain and protect your rights as a taxpayer at all times. If this is not the case, discuss the problem with the employee's supervisor.

Taxpayer Assistance Numbers.   1-800-424-1040.

APPENDIX 15-3
IRS Tax Publications

You can order any of the publications listed at no cost. These publications represent the most frequently requested forms. A full list can be found in Publication 910.

General Guides

1	Your Rights as a Taxpayer
225	Farmer's Tax Guide
334	Tax Guide for Small Business
553	Highlights of 1992 Tax Changes
595	Tax Guide for Commercial Fishermen
910	Guide to Free Tax Services

Specialized Publications

3	Tax Information for Military Personnel
4	Student's Guide to Federal Income Tax
15	Employer's Tax Guide (Circular E)
54	Tax Guide for U.S. Citizens and Resident Aliens Abroad
378	Fuel Tax Credits and Refunds
448	Federal Estate and Gift Taxes
463	Travel, Entertainment, and Gift Expenses
501	Exemptions, Standard Deduction, and Filing Information
502	Medical and Dental Expenses
503	Child and Dependent Care Expenses
504	Tax Information for Divorced or Separated Individuals
505	Tax Withholding and Estimated Tax
508	Educational Expenses
510	Excise Taxes for 1992
513	Tax Information for Visitors to the U.S.
514	Foreign Tax Credit for Individuals

Spanish Language Publications

1S   Derechos del Contribuyente

179   Guía Contributiva Federal para Patronos Puertorriqueños (Circular PR)

556S   Revisión de las Declaraciones de Impuesto, Derecho de Apelación y Reclamaciones de Reembolsos

579S   Cómo Preparar la Declaración de Impuesto Federal

586S   Proceso de Cobro (Deudas del Impuesto Sobre Ingreso)

850   English-Spanish Glossary of Words and Phrases Used in Publications Issued by the IRS

16

Creative Estate- and Trust-Planning

*Even if you have never had a will
drawn up in your life, you have a
will. It's been drawn up for you by
the state in which you live.*

FREEDOM FOCUS

- *How do you go about estate-planning, the orderly process of ensuring that your affairs are managed—during your lifetime and after death—according to your wishes, and in the most organized and least expensive manner?*

- *What do you do if you don't have a will?*

- *How do you establish domicile, designate a personal representative, select the professionals to work with, and review your will?*

- *What are some estate- and trust-planning techniques?*

- *What are the legal ways of avoiding federal estate taxes?*

- *Gifting programs and charitable giving—where do they fit into your planning, how do you do it with the most tax advantage, and when do you do it?*

241

If you're like a lot of people, you've got a thousand reasons why you don't have to think about wills, estate-, and trust-planning: They're complicated. They're depressing (because they remind you that you're mortal and aren't going to be around forever). They only matter if you are among the very wealthy. Wrong, wrong, and wrong again!

Through careful estate- and trust-planning, you are taking charge of the things you can control. Proper estate- and trust-planning techniques are *not* boring, unless you get glassy-eyed when someone starts telling you about perfectly legal ways to keep the federal government's hand from dipping too deeply into your pockets for the monies you have built up for your family's use. Wills, estate-, and trust-planning are positive tools that provide you with the ability to provide for your heirs and special interests while you're alive and still very much in control of your own and your family's financial destiny. And that's *not* depressing.

Sound estate- and trust-planning can be a truly satisfying, creative activity that will pay off for the people you care about. The spectrum of plans available to you is not restrictive in the least; your estate and trust programs can and should be tailored to meet your specific needs, limited only by the extent of your knowledge and the amount of creative thought you bring to bear upon the project.

It is especially important to realize that estate- and trust-planning is not the concern of just the very rich. None of us should be cavalier about missteps that wind up costing us—and our heirs—money. At the very least, you should have a valid, up-to-date will.

The Importance of a Will

The assets that you, through your hard work, have been able to accumulate over the years should go, first and foremost, to the heirs you select, not to the heirs selected by the state in which you live or the federal government. And the distribution of your estate to your heirs must be made carefully, in a way that will take into consideration their strengths, their weaknesses, their stages of life. Suppose that you and your spouse were to die suddenly and a significant portion of your estate were to go to your teenager, whose most pressing concern to date has been how to obtain the money to buy a new Corvette. Do you think this teenager would be able to make wise use of any wealth you might leave at this point in his or her life? Do you think that part of your job as a responsible, caring parent might be to make proper provision in your will so that your child might be protected against his or her own self for a period of time and then—after maturity has had an opportunity to set in—be permitted to come into the full inheritance?

Obviously, unless you have a will, special circumstances such as this cannot be taken into consideration after you die. But here is some disturbing news: *Even if you have never had a will drawn up in your life, you have a will. It's been drawn up for you by your state government. And chances are that it doesn't say anything even vaguely approximating what you'd like it to say.*

The vast majority of adult Americans do not have current valid wills. If you are in this number, call an attorney before this day is over and make an appointment. If you do have a will, review it (with your attorney if necessary) to make sure it is up to date and takes account of your family's current needs.

Furthermore, you should be sure you understand what your will says. Your attorney can provide you with a brief summary, in "plain English," of your will. Never hesitate to ask for services of this type, and never hesitate to ask an attorney or any other professional questions that you are afraid will sound stupid. Remember, the only stupid question is the one not asked. You have a right to ask all the professionals working with you to share their knowledge in terms that you can understand.

Don't be misled into thinking that wills and estate-planning can be put off until middle or old age. The younger you and your family are, the more important it is to put your estate in order. Under the laws of many states, should you die without a will (intestate), your estate would be split between your spouse and your children. The children's shares could then be tied up in a court-supervised guardianship, draining important dollars away in administrative costs while adding an unnecessary complication to the life of your spouse.

If you are single, many states will give your assets to your parents, whether they need them or not. This arrangement may draw federal taxes twice, once at your death and then again at your parents'. It would be less expensive and more sensible to leave a simple will, creating, for example, an educational trust for some favorite nephews, nieces, or godchildren.

How Do I Draw Up a Will?

If you do not presently have a valid will, you should consider some basic information as you go about the process. It doesn't have to be a complicated process—there are many publications and even computer software programs available to you on how to draw up a will—but you must be very cautious in using them without the benefit of professional guidance.

First, can there be a question of domicile (state considered your permanent home)? Unlike a residence, which simply requires a physical presence, a domicile requires an individual's intent to make the residence a permanent home for legal purposes. Whether it becomes an issue in estate settlement proceedings is best considered on an individual basis. However, the chances are that individuals who own significant amounts of property in more than one state run the risk of incurring death taxes on it from more than one state. Without a clear designation, each of the states you recurrently frequent as an extended guest and/or resident may render its own interpretation of domicile and subsequent jurisdiction. A similar ruling could be rendered by a state which you *formerly* called home. A case in point, In Re Dorrance, was a determination of whether New Jersey or Pennsylvania was the domicile of Dr. Dorrance, an heir to Campbell Foods. Both states claimed that Dr. Dorrance was domiciled within them and each assessed a full inheritance tax (over $33 million total in 1936). After lengthy court battles in both the state and federal courts, and after five appeals to the United States Supreme Court, both states were permitted to impose their full inheritance taxes. Although the Dorrance case is over 50 years old, cases involving multiple domiciles for estate tax purposes remain common today. Simply moving from one state to another may not automatically remove you (for estate tax purposes) from your previous state of domicile. A conflict in domicile designation could cause disputes or difficulties in handling your will; the disposition of property in the absence of a will; the rights of heirs; state inheritance; income and estate taxes; and the right of a child or spouse to property. There are a number of actions you can take to demonstrate the validity of your domicile and a legal professional will be able to direct you.

Today, given the increased mobility of our population, it's both probable and possible that greater numbers of individuals may be determined to be domiciled in more than one jurisdiction. Because of the overall complexity of the domicile issue, as well as the critical importance it may play in your estate-planning program, consider involving a legal professional in any related discussions or deliberations.

Do you need to designate a personal representative (called an Executor or Executrix in many states)—the person(s) or corporation who administers an estate after court appointment? The selection of a personal representative usually is the designation of a specific person—often a family member or friend. However, the role of a personal representative may also be filled by a corporate entity such as a bank or trust company. The individual(s) or corporation you select as a personal representative must have the available time and possess the capabilities to handle the more than 60 tasks commonly associated with estate settlement. The consequences of a disruption (for whatever reason) may involve a loss of continuity, additional costs to the estate, and missed settlement opportunities. Placing the responsibilities of estate settlement in the hands of a spouse, child, or friend may be well-meaning, but it's not without its potential pitfalls. Careful thought and evaluation should be given to the selection and all of its ramifications before making your decision.

A very important consideration in drawing up a will is its validity. Requirements vary from state to state regarding witness and recording requirements, so again, it's to your advantage to consult with a legal professional in the matter of assuring that you have a valid will.

I Already Have a Will

Great! But when was the last time you reviewed your will? Your will, regardless of when it was drafted, undoubtedly contains some of your most serious considerations. Based on a variety of personal and economic preferences and factors, you opted to have your estate distributed in a disciplined, designated fashion.

But, today you may not feel the same way about the allocations you made. Maybe circumstances have changed and you wish to make a different distribution of your assets.

Then, too, there is the possibility that your assets have changed. Certain assets, once targeted for distribution as part of your estate, may have been sold or significantly appreciated or depreciated in value, leaving the possibility of an adjustment to be made. Additionally, the death of one of your will's designated beneficiaries may also warrant a redirection of certain assets, thus necessitating a change in your will.

While a will is frequently thought to be linked to death, many experts view it as a document for the living. Its application, after all, is most often intended to help those you leave behind. Whether it is intended to benefit a spouse, son or daughter, other family members or friends, or a foundation, charity, or a combination of all of these, the chances are you want to be able to provide support to the designated beneficiaries. By being sure that your will is up to date, you'll make certain that your wishes are carried out—your way.

The Professionals

Consultation with a financial expert about your estate will benefit you right now by giving you the opportunity to review how efficiently you are handling your affairs, to consider what would happen to you should a close family member or business partner die, and to explore alternatives that could make the management of your finances easier. Good estate-planning can also lead to current tax savings should you be in a position to make charitable contributions or should you wish to take advantage of income-splitting techniques to provide a source of funds for a family member or to accelerate your savings for a child's college tuition. (See Appendix 16-1, Important Questions to Ask Yourself Before Seeing the Estate-Planning Professional.)

The purpose of estate-planning is to ensure that your property—bonds, stocks, real estate, cash, certificate of deposit holdings—is passed to your chosen heirs and that your estate receives the most favorable tax treatment available. Some of the property you have—antiques and heirlooms handed down through the generations or art objects—may have great sentimental value, but even greater hidden values. The fact is, without proper estate-planning you may end up giving your personal property to people you have never met, but you've supported all your life, the federal government! You may need little more than a two-page will or you may need complex trust arrangements to accomplish your wishes. *Estate planning can have lifetime benefits also by assuring proper management and distribution of your assets during a period of incapacity.* This chapter introduces a basic vocabulary (Appendix 16-2) and some background information so you can start thinking about your estate while you are making appointments with your financial adviser and lawyer. Remember, however, that your estate plan must be custom-tailored because no one else has the same spouse and collection of children and/or aged parents and other relatives, the same property, the same business interests, and so forth, that you possess.

Use great care in selecting your expert advisers. Look for someone with considerable experience in estate planning. Many states permit specialization in estate planning by lawyers and require these specialists to participate in continuing education. Take the time to find such a specialist (or a financial planner with a specialist on board) and to shop for a bank or trust company with the reputation of offering reliable services.

Facts about Estate Taxes

Many people are unaware of the sweeping changes in estate taxation that occurred with the 1976 Tax Reform Act and the Economic Recovery Tax Act of 1982. These laws now provide for a total exemption from gift and estate taxes for most property transferred to a spouse (the unlimited marital deduction) who is a citizen of the United States, and provide for a unified credit which is the equivalent of exempting the first $600,000 of gifts and estate value from taxation. They also changed many of the rules governing estates and gifts.

Previously, estate and gift taxes were handled separately, with an estate tax exemption of $60,000 and a lifetime gift tax exemption of $30,000. The gift tax then was 25 percent less in all brackets than the estate tax. The new law abolished this distinction and both exemptions. Now all taxable gifts are added to the value of the estate and applied against a unified tax credit. That credit is now $192,800, which has the effect of exempting the first $600,000 from estate taxes.

To see how this works, look at Table 16-1 and follow it through a simple example of a taxable estate of $750,000. The tax comes to $248,300, but we can subtract the $192,800 credit automatically and send off a check for $55,500.

The term "taxable estate" is the one that you need to understand. The taxable estate includes assets which may be income tax exempt such as municipal bonds and the *full amount* of insurance proceeds on policies which you own which are received by your beneficiaries upon death. Also, estate taxes may be imposed on assets that are not probated under your will such as assets in revocable trusts, jointly held with rights of survivorship, life insurance, annuities, pension or IRA benefits, bank account trusts or ITF accounts, etc. The size of taxable estate depends not on your current net worth, but on how you plan to reduce that net worth to a minimum taxable estate. Estate taxes are progressive, just like income taxes, so you need to analyze how available deductions and exclusions would work for your purposes and whether gifts and certain trusts would be helpful. Should members of your family also have sizable estates and interlocking interests through property, business, or trusts, you should do at least part of your planning together.

Since 1976 the gift and estate tax system has been "unified." In general, the first $10,000 of gifts made to each individual per year (other than a spouse) is exempt from the gift tax. If gifts to an individual (other than your spouse) exceed $10,000, the excess reduces your $600,000 unified credit exemption equivalent. Once the unified credit exemption equivalent is exhausted, lifetime gifts bear taxes at rates starting at 37%. Gifts are reported on IRS Form 709 or 709-A which is due April 15th of the year after the gifts are made. Upon death the estate tax picks up where the gift tax left off. Thus, any of the $600,000 unified credit exemption equivalent that you did not use for lifetime gifts becomes available to your estate, and if you have used up your $600,000 unified credit exemption equivalent, estate taxes will pick up at the brackets where the gift taxes left off during lifetime. Estate taxes are due and payable nine months after a death with the filing of IRS Form 706.

Table 16-1. Federal Estate and Gift Tax Unified Rate Schedule

If the amount is:		Tentative tax is:		
From ($)	To ($)	Tax ($) +	Percentage	On excess over ($)
-0-	10,000	-0-	18	-0-
10,000	20,000	1,800	20	10,000
20,000	40,000	3,800	22	20,000
40,000	60,000	8,200	24	40,000
60,000	80,000	13,000	26	60,000
80,000	100,000	18,200	28	80,000
100,000	150,000	23,800	30	100,000
150,000	250,000	38,800	32	150,000
250,000	500,000	70,800	34	250,000
500,000	750,000	155,800	37	500,000
750,000	1,000,000	248,300	39	750,000
1,000,000	1,250,000	345,800	41	1,000,000
1,250,000	1,500,000	448,300	43	1,250,000
1,500,000	2,000,000	555,800	45	1,500,000
2,000,000	2,500,000	780,000	49	2,000,000
2,500,000	3,000,000	1,025,800	53	2,500,000
3,000,000		1,290,800	55	3,000,000

NOTE: For U.S. citizens and residents, estate and gift tax rates are combined in a single-rate schedule effective for estates of descendents and for gifts made after December 31, 1976. Lifetime transfers and transfers made after that time are cumulative for estate purposes. The estate tax liability for any calendar quarter or year is determined by applying the uniform rate schedule to cumulative lifetime taxable transfers and subtracting the tax payable for prior taxable years.

Caution: Special rates, credits, and rules apply to nonresident aliens and to residents of the United States who are not citizens.

Starting in 1987, the unified credit for estate and gift taxes is $192,800, which is equivalent to exempting $600,000 from tax.

In 1993 and later years, the top rate will drop to 50 percent on transfers in excess of $2,500,000.

Gift tax: The gift tax can be calculated by the following five steps:

1. Calculate the sum of all taxable gifts during the donor's lifetime, including those made prior to January 1, 1977.

2. Determine the tax on the amount calculated in step 1 using the unified rate structure.

3. Calculate the sum of all gifts made by the donor during lifetime but excluding gifts made during the taxable period with respect to which the gift tax is being determined.

4. Determine the tax on the amount calculated in step 3 using the unified rate structure. If taxable gifts are between $10 million and $21,040,000, increase the tax by 5 per-

Table 16-1. Federal Estate and Gift Tax Unified Rate Schedule (*Continued*)

cent of the excess over $10 million. If the taxable amount is more than $21,040,000, the tax is a flat 55 percent.

5. Subtract the tax calculated in step 4 from the tax calculated in step 2. The resulting amount is the gift tax, which may then be offset by the unified credit.

Estate tax: The estate tax is determined by the following four steps:

1. Add to the taxable estate all taxable gifts made by the donor (other than gifts which are includable in the gross estate after December 31, 1976).

2. Calculate the tax on the amount determined in step 1 using the unified rate schedule.

3. Calculate the amount of gift tax payable with respect to gifts made after December 31, 1976.

4. Subtract the amount determined in step 3 from the amount determined in step 2 to determine the estate tax. If the taxable estate is between $10 million and $21,040,000, increase the tax by 5 percent of the excess over $10 million. If the taxable estate is more than $21,040,000, the tax is a flat 55 percent. The estate tax may be offset by the unified credit and other credits.

Marital deduction: Unlimited amounts of property (other than certain terminable interests) can be transferred between spouses without imposition of estate or gift tax. In addition, the transfer of a life income interest in property (payable at least annually) to a spouse generally qualifies for the estate and gift tax marital deduction, if so elected. However, such property is included in the survivor's taxable estate or treated as a gift by the donee if given away before his or her death.

Four Ways of Reducing Estate Taxes

The first means by which you can reduce estate taxes also happens to be the largest automatic deduction available—the *marital deduction,* which is now unlimited. That deduction applies only if you are married and if you leave everything to your spouse. Your advisers should discuss with you the type of assets you may include in the marital deduction and the restrictions you may place on your spouse's use and disposition of them. Your spouse is also entitled to receive an unlimited amount of tax-free gifts from you over your lifetime. But don't be tempted to leave it all to your spouse. In estates over $600,000, this would forfeit the unified credit exemption ($600,000) of the first deceased spouse and cause up to $330,000 of unnecessary tax when the surviving spouse dies.

For example, Mr. and Mrs. Smith hold all of their $1.2 million estate jointly. When Mr. Smith dies, Mrs. Smith inherits the entire estate but upon her demise a check is written to the IRS for $235,000 before Mrs. Smith's estate is distributed to their children. Mrs. Smith's $600,000 unified credit exemption equivalent was not sufficient to avoid tax, and Mr.

Smith's unified credit had been forfeited by his understandable desire to leave his entire estate to his wife.

Mr. and Mrs. Jones, who also have a $1.2 million estate, planned to avoid an unnecessary bequest to the IRS. With the help of their advisers, they separated their estates and created documents designed to use both of their $600,000 exemption equivalents regardless of the order of demise. When Mr. Jones died, his estate plan directed the creation of a "credit shelter trust" into which $600,000 of the estate in his sole name was placed. Under the terms of the trust, his wife was given rights of management, rights to all of the income, and restricted rights to principal if it was needed to provide for her health or support. Upon Mrs. Jones' demise, her $600,000 estate as well as her husband's credit shelter trust passed free of federal estate taxes to their children. The result, the Jones heirs received $235,000 more than the Smith heirs. Under these circumstances, I definitely advise clients to keep up with the Joneses!

Do not be under the delusion that property you own jointly will escape taxation. Joint ownership with right of survivorship is a probate avoidance technique promoted by many do-it-yourself manuals. But you should know that, unless the only joint owners are husband and wife, the full value of the property is taxed as part of the estate of the person who dies first except if the survivor can prove he or she contributed to the purchase and did not receive the contribution as a gift from the decedent. Joint ownership can also be cumbersome during your lifetime if you wish to dispose of your property. It can make your assets attachable by the creditors of the person whom you make a joint owner, or make them subject to taxes on income and gains from the joint assets. Joint ownership with a spouse can defeat arrangements designed to use both unified credit exemptions and cause a considerable amount of unnecessary estate tax. If it fits into your financial plan, you certainly might wish to keep your house and some bank accounts in joint names with your spouse, but you should examine alternatives for other holdings.

A second way to deliver money and property to your heirs on a tax-free basis is to use the $10,000 annual gift tax exclusion. Certain direct payment of educational and medical expenses is allowed in addition to the $10,000 annual exclusion. This can be an outright gift or it can be a means of income-splitting among your dependents through the use of trusts. Under this exclusion, you may give away $10,000—$20,000 if your spouse joins in the gift—to as many persons as you please without paying a gift or estate tax. That may sound as if it is just for the very wealthy, but it's also handy for those of us who are trying to save for the children's college education.

A third method is income-splitting. Here is how it works: You place your \$10,000–\$20,000 (more if you are willing to use some of your lifetime \$600,000 exemption equivalent) in a special account or trust for a child or other person. The income earned on your gift is then taxed at that person's rate, not yours, which can be a considerable savings. This would enable your fund for college to compound far more rapidly than if you retain the money in your own account. But beware the "kiddie tax" which can cause a child under 14 to be taxed at the parents' rates.

The easiest method of doing this for your child or another minor is to set up a custodian account under the Uniform Gift to Minors Act. Just be sure that someone other than you (or any other donor) is named as custodian. Otherwise, the IRS may insist on including the account in your estate. Under the Uniform Gift act, the principal amount plus earnings become the child's property at age 21 (18 in some states).

Under the new law, there are few tax reasons to make large gifts to your heirs because of the abolition of the separate gift tax schedule and the \$30,000 lifetime exemption. One exception to this might be the gift of property that is expected to appreciate or earn income after the gift has been made. The tax would be levied against the value at the time of the gift, not the larger amount you would have if the gifted property was held until death. A second exception would apply to a wealthy individual in good health. Gift taxes paid on lifetime gifts reduce the size of the estate subject to estate taxes, if the wealthy individual survives for three years after making the gift. Under these circumstances, tremendous tax savings may be gained by "prepaying estate taxes" through lifetime gifts.

A fourth method may appeal to you should you want to give a grown child help in financing a business or a house in today's uncertain money market. You might consider making a low interest loan, being sure to take back a note. You can then forgive \$10,000 a year (\$20,000 if you are married and proper gift tax returns are filed) on the note. The balance owing at your death could be included in your estate. If you are thinking of doing this, obtain expert help in preparing the note, as the IRS gives such arrangements extra scrutiny and will require or impute interest at a rate established monthly by regulations.

Trust-Planning

Recently I attended a trust-planning meeting with some clients. At one time the husband had been a prominent businessman. But now, as a victim of Alzheimer's Disease, he is totally unable to care for himself. Did he think that he would one day need someone to take care of all his needs? I don't think so. But his wife was making sure that he would receive treatment and care at a level he deserved, and that that care would continue should she become disabled. At this point in his life, those standards of care would be decided by other individuals than himself. Did he have a choice? Yes, he did. He could have planned for such an event through a living trust.

There are many more reasons to seek the use of trusts. Should you wish to provide for the control of the funds until your child is older, you might wish to look into a trust. A trust may carry conditions and restrictions on how and when your gift is to be received. Here, again, you would use a portion of your $600,000 exemption any time your gifts to the trust exceeded the $10,000 annual exclusion. A special withdrawal right called a "Crummey Clause" is required to obtain the benefits of the annual exclusion.

Trusts may play a most important role in transferring your assets, either before or after you die. Even rather modest estates may use trusts to ensure that your money is used to meet particular needs for your heirs and to keep taxes to a minimum. Trusts also solve current management problems, whether you wish to pass along income to others or want to be relieved of some administrative responsibilities.

Trusts that go into effect while you are alive are called *living trusts* (or, in legal terms, inter vivos trusts). They can be irrevocable trusts, which are a gift upon which you may put restrictions and conditions; or revocable trusts, which you can amend or abolish at any time and which are included in your estate for tax purposes. Trusts that go into effect after you die are called *testamentary trusts.*

Trusts can help you avoid "double" taxation on your estate as it is passed from you to an intermediate heir and then to a succeeding heir. Trusts can assure that the surviving spouse receives needed income and can provide for maximum use of the $600,000 unified credit exemption equivalents. You may wish to provide income for a dependent without risking the possibility of having it willed to a shiftless relative. You can solve these problems and similar ones with a trust. Trusts can be as restrictive or as flexible as you wish; just have the tax consequences reviewed by an expert.

By way of example, let's look at two common family trust arrangements. One is a pair of trusts that split your estate upon death into a *marital deduction trust* and a *family trust.* The marital trust provides your spouse with income for life. Your spouse can also be given unlimited rights to principal or these rights may be limited to an arrangement commonly called a *QTIP trust.* The family trust can provide him or her with additional income and then be disbursed to your children at your spouse's death or at a time of your choosing. Estate taxes are paid on the family trust once at your death and once on the marital trust at your spouse's death to the extent each exceeds the $600,000 exemption. Again, caution is the word of the day. Attempts to leave your grandchildren more than $1,000,000 outright or in a generation-skipping trust can produce a generation-skipping tax at the top estate tax rates. This tax is in addition to estate taxes on your estate and the combined taxes can go as high as *80 percent.*

You can also soften the tax by use of a *generation-skipping trust.* This trust allocates income from your assets to your children while preserving the principal for your grandchildren. Estate taxes are levied against the principal of your taxable estate, but when your children die, the balance of the $1,000,000 of trust principal you set aside on your death may be excluded as each of their estates passes to your grandchildren.

A *living trust* has few, if any, tax advantages, but it can be a superior management tool for your assets, both while you are living and then for your heirs. It can provide liquidity at key times and it can keep your heirs out of probate court except for whatever assets you own that aren't included in the trust. More important, a living trust can provide for the management of your assets during a period of disability.

Just what sort of assets do you have? Do you own a business or a farm? Do you have an interest in a closely held corporation? Do you have a rare stamp collection? Any other assets that aren't liquid or that may require knowledgeable supervision? Much of the value of your estate could be lost either through a forced sale or through restrictions on management during probate.

Should any of these situations be yours, you may wish to weigh the benefits of a living trust. Under a revocable living trust, you transfer your assets into a trust for the benefit of your eventual heirs. You may continue to manage, or co-manage with a trustee, all of your property and to receive all income. You may change it or scrap it all at any time you please. Although such a trust would be fully taxed in your estate, assets in the trust would pass directly to your heirs without going through probate. Avoiding probate has three general benefits:

1. Funds and property become available more readily to your heirs.

2. Management should continue without interruption.

3. That portion of your estate has complete privacy, should this be a business or personal consideration.

Although revocable living trusts are commonly thought of as probate-avoidance devices, they are extraordinarily useful in providing for the management of your assets should you become incapacitated and unable to manage your own affairs. The revocable living trust can provide for management of your affairs during illness by persons whom you have selected, according to your personalized instructions as contained in the trust instrument, and without the requirement of court guardianship or conservatorship.

Use of a living trust permits you to turn over the management of your business to another person or trust institution so that you can assess this person's or organization's abilities and, in the case of an individual, train that person before she or he assumes control.

Living trusts funded with life insurance can provide immediate cash to protect your closely held corporation or other nonliquid asset, such as an art collection, from a forced sale to pay taxes or to feed your family. Here your trust would own the policy and be named as beneficiary. If properly structured, an irrevocable trust can provide liquidity for estate taxes without the insurance it holds being taxed in your estate. This type of trust may be worth exploring with your business partner. If you have a partner or are a sole proprietor, you should seek help in estate-planning. Without continued good management and a steady cash flow, few businesses can keep the value their owners worked diligently to create.

The most tax-favored trust is the *charitable remainder trust*. If you make a charitable contribution during your lifetime, it is deductible from your income tax. If you leave that money in your will to the charity, it is deductible from the gross value of your estate. A charitable remainder trust does both these things with the added perk of giving you an annuity or an annual percentage of the trust for life.

One good use of a charitable remainder trust would be the donation of property that has appreciated considerably. Your tax adviser can show you how to make the most of your donation as an income tax deduction. You can then have the satisfaction of making a large contribution and know you have reaped tax savings on your 1040 as well as from capital gains and estate taxes. He or she will also help you navigate the new alternative minimum tax.

You can elect to receive income from your gift in three ways. Under the first two, a *unitrust* and an *annuity trust*, the value of your gift is set aside and invested for payments to you only. A unitrust provides a yearly income based upon a percentage of the trust revalued annually. Under an annuity trust, you receive a fixed percentage of not less than 5 percent of the initial value of your gift. The third type is a *pooled income fund* containing gifts made by you and others, with the earnings being shared proportionally.

Your income from any of these is usually taxed as ordinary income, but any estate tax would be levied only against the expected value of income to a beneficiary other than your surviving spouse.

Whatever the size of your estate and regardless of your wishes, Appendix 16-1, Essential Questions to Ask Yourself Before Seeing the Estate-Planning Professional, is a valuable fill-in-the-blank questionnaire that will help you organize your thoughts *before* seeing an estate-planning professional.

APPENDIX 16-1
Essential Questions to Ask
Yourself Before Seeing the
Estate-Planning Professional

1. **What is the value of your net estate?** _____
   Include all assets, including life insurance proceeds and monies maintained within IRAs and retirement plans.

2. **Will your spouse inherit your estate with no questions asked?**
   _____
   Have you considered the question of remarriage; are there children from a previous marriage; is your spouse capable of managing the estate?

3. **Whom do you want to administer your estate?**
   _____
   In making this selection, consider what will be required of the person you select to manage and administer your estate. Also consider his or her health and age.

4. **What personal items and property do you want to leave to specific individuals?** _____
   _____
   Don't forget those items that may have a high sentimental value, but not necessarily a high economic value. Perhaps attach a list to this document.

5. **Do you want to leave anything to charity?** _____
   Don't forget that there are tax benefits to be gained in doing this. Again, list the charities and the amounts or property that you wish transferred to them.

6. **Are there personal statements that you would like to include in your will?** _____
   Many individuals like to include a statement of personal philosophy or an expression of love to their family and friends; some people include requests with respect to investments.

7. **Do you have complete financial records?** _____
   Make sure your personal representative or family know where

(Continued)

your property is located, its worth, and how to take hold of it. Also include an accounting of your debts.

8. **Do you desire to avoid the probate process?**_____
Basically you would do this for privacy and less "red tape" at death. You may also save on attorneys' and executors' fees by avoiding probate.

9. **If you should be on life-support systems, would you like such support terminated?** _____
If so, you must look into a Living Will and prepare your family to give a directive to attending physicians. These procedures vary from state to state. In some states, once an individual is hooked to life support, it may take a court order to terminate such support. Find out what the legal responsibilities are in your state.

10. **Would you want your organs to be available for research or transplantation upon your death?** _____
Make sure your family and physician are aware of your desires.

11. **If you become incapacitated, who should manage your financial affairs?** _____
If you don't appoint someone, you could have the court appoint someone for you. Consider a regular power of attorney or a durable power of attorney.

12. **Who should your estate pass to should your entire family die in a common disaster?**_____
This is a frequently ignored issue, but one worth considering.

13. **Should your children receive their inheritance outright?**

_____

14. **If so, at what age (or ages) do you wish this to take place?**

_____

15. **How do you want property left to children?**

_____
Property could be left in a common fund or in separate shares for each child. Considerations should include legal incapacity of minors, use of trusts, separate trust approach, and the common pot approach.

16. **If you set up trusts, who should be the trustee?**

_____
This person should be able to serve as an investment manager, but you should also consider appointing co-trustees and successors as well.

17. **Should the need arise, who should be the guardian of your minor children?** _____
This person or persons should be able to serve as parental substitutes, possibly one with whom the minors would reside.

APPENDIX 16-2
Estate-Planning Terms
Federal Estate Tax

Annual exclusion from gift taxes: Each person (including *each* spouse) may transfer up to $10,000 each year to as many persons as they desire without tax. If properly structured, the transfers may be made to a trust. Property transferred under the annual exclusion *does not* reduce your available exemption equivalent. The annual exclusion is the basis of numerous income and estate tax-saving techniques. Certain medical and educational expense payments are allowed in addition to the annual exclusion.

Charitable deduction: Certain charitable transfers are not subject to gift or estate taxes. Maximizing benefits from charitable gifts is frequently overlooked by individuals who are making regular charitable gifts or are leaving a portion of their estate to charity, but are unaware of the wide variety of planning alternatives in this area. For example, properly planned giving can save income tax, permit sale of assets without capital gains taxes, increase investment yield, and allow substantial assets to pass to family without gift or estate taxes.

Exemption equivalent of the unified credit: The law has a system of credits against the estate and gift tax which allow the transfer of $600,000 of assets to a nonspouse without tax. Every person (including *both* spouses) have the exemption equivalent. It may be used for lifetime gifts with the balance being applied to transfers after death. The use of both spouses' exemption equivalents is not automatic, and the failure to properly plan in this area can cost the ultimate heirs in excess of $235,000 in federal estate tax. For example, the use of a simple will leaving everything to the survivor or excessive use of joint property in estates larger than $600,000 will result in unnecessary tax.

Federal estate and gift tax: A unified tax on your gratuitous transfer of property while alive (gift) or after death (estate). The tax is imposed on all classes of property and many types of transfers. For example, municipal bonds and the proceeds of insurance owned by a decedent are estate taxed even if they are not income taxed. Jointly held property or property in a revocable living trust is taxed even though it may pass outside of probate. An additional *generation skipping tax* can be imposed on transfers to grandchildren and later generations.

Generation skipping tax exemption: The law also provides a $1,000,000 per spouse exemption from the generation skipping tax. Again, only proper planning assures the use of this exemption and the avoidance of tax.

Returns: A gift tax return is made on Form 709 or 709A which is generally due April 15 of the year following the gift. An estate tax return is made on Form 706 which is due nine months after death. Returns may be required even though no tax is due.

Tax rates: No distinction is made under present law between gift and estate transfers. The tax is a cumulative single tax on all transfers. The rates for taxpaying estates range from 37 to 60 percent. The generation skipping tax is imposed at a flat 55 percent rate on taxable transfers.

Unlimited marital deductions: Most transfers of property to spouses who are U.S. citizens are no longer taxed. However, leaving everything to the survivor and then to the children may be a tax disaster as demonstrated by *exemption equivalent of the unified credit.*

State Death Taxes

Estate tax: A state tax imposed upon the total value of property transferred (like the federal estate tax). Many states have both an estate tax and an inheritance tax.

Gift tax: Many states also impose a tax on lifetime gifts.

Inheritance tax: A state tax imposed upon the transfer of all property of a resident, and the real estate and certain other property of a nonresident which is located in the state. Inheritance tax rates differ depending upon who is getting the property and in what amount.

Residency (domicile): This is one of the more difficult aspects of planning because the circumstances of each individual will differ and a "general rule" cannot be cited. Although the legal determination of your residency is a question of your intent, each state will require proof of resident or nonresident status by your actions and not your words. Each state has different laws and administrative requirements regarding residency. For example, just "becoming a Florida resident" is not enough to avoid tax in a Northern state in which you maintain a home, real estate, or other contacts. In many cases needless taxes have been paid where residency has been successfully asserted by more than one state wishing to impose a death tax or by a state in which the deceased did not consider himself or herself a resident. Remember, real estate and certain other assets of a nonresident may be taxed in the state in which they are located, as well as the state of residence.

State death tax credit: A revenue-sharing arrangement between the federal government and the states whereby up to certain limits (the available credit amount) the United States will reduce its tax by the amount paid to any states. Many states impose death taxes in excess of the available credit and thus create additional tax burden.

Court Proceedings

Administration expenses: This term refers to filing fees, appraisal costs, personal representatives or trustees fees, accountant and attorneys fees involved in the handling of a probate estate or a trust. The largest simple component is usually attorneys' fees. Frequently attorneys' fees for probate will be based upon a percentage of the gross value of assets subject to the federal estate tax (before the marital deduction, the exemption equivalent, and other deductions). Rates commonly run from 3 to 5 percent. The fairness of percentage fees is often questionable and frequently the primary motivating force in probate avoidance. Bases exist for charging reasonable estate administration fees and planning to minimize these fees. Although this is a major aspect of the estate planning process, many people neglect to discuss with their attorneys an estimate of administration expenses and methods of reducing administration expenses.

Ancillary administration: If real estate is subject to probate in a state other than where the will has initially been probated, separate probate proceedings are required. This will increase administration expenses unless planning is undertaken to avoid ancillary administration.

Guardianship (also known as conservatorship): If a person, because of a legal, physical, or mental incapacity, is unable to handle his or her affairs, the court system may be called upon to provide for the care and management of both person and property. The court will make a determination of incapacity and appoint a guardian. The incapacitated person's assets (including an interest in jointly owned assets) are then subject to court supervised management, and a court order is required to approve the purchase and sale of assets. In addition, inventories and annual accountings must be filed. Court guardianship can result in delays and thousands of dollars in legal fees.

Letter of administration (also known as letters testamentary): A court certified document which allows a personal representative to administer the estate.

Personal representative: The person(s) who administer an estate after court appointment (synonymous with executor, executrix, or administrator).

Probate: The process of court supervised administration of individually owned property after death. If a will has been written, it is referred to as a testate proceeding. If a will has not been written the intestate laws govern distribution of the estate. Formal probate may require petition for probate, proof of the will, bonding, issuance of letters of administration, notice to creditors, creditor claim proceedings, a delay in debt payment, an inventory of assets, proceedings to determine spouses' rights, accounting and court approval of real estate sales and distribution. Although assets can be distributed prior to the closing of the estate, probate cannot be concluded (if a 706 is required) until the IRS issues a "closing letter" which may take from 18–24 months after the date of death.

Property subject to probate: In general, individually held property, certain joint property (tenants in common), and property paid to the estate (e.g.; certain death benefits). Legal title to some property (*non-probate property*) causes it to pass by operation of law upon death and not through probate. For example, property held as joint tenants with rights of survivorship, certain property in the names of husband and wife (tenants by the entireties), bank accounts and automobile titles registered "or," bank account (totten) trusts, life insurance, pensions, and IRAs paid to named beneficiaries, and property passing under a trust. With limited exceptions, property not passing through probate is not governed by the will and can produce unintended results such as disinheriting heirs or unnecessary taxes. Contrary to popular belief, the size of the estate has nothing to do with the requirement for probate.

Summary administration: An abbreviated probate proceeding available, in some states, if probate property is less than an amount specified by state law.

Testamentary trust: A trust created under a will and after probate.

Estate-Planning Techniques

A word about joint property: Although the use of joint property (with rights of survivorship) can be useful in the estate plan, arbitrary use of joint property to avoid probate can produce unintended results. For example, a person who deeds a joint interest in his or her home to a child to avoid probate may find that a gift tax return is required, tax exemptions are reduced, the child must sign the deed when the property is sold, is entitled to a share of the proceeds and must pay taxes on this share, and capital gains exclusions are lost.

Constructive use of probate: Although many people are motivated to avoid probate entirely, probate can have some constructive uses. For example, the use of probate under certain circumstances can minimize family disputes, ease the disposition of personal property, handle the potential claims of creditors, and minimize income taxes. A good estate plan will provide for probate to the extent that its benefits outweigh any additional administration expenses.

Credit Shelter Trust (also known as Trust B, Bypass Trust, Non-marital Trust, Residual Trust, Family Trust): A zero tax formula under which a will or living trust will normally place the available exemption equivalent into this trust. Other credits can be used to place additional property into this trust and this is frequently overlooked in tax planning. The surviving spouse is normally (but need not be) given the income of this trust; but the survivor's ability to spend principal is restricted. If properly structured, the assets of this trust are not taxed on the second death and tremendous tax savings can be generated. Conversely, the use of this arrangement in excess of what is needed to produce tax savings will unnecessarily restrict the survivor's access to assets.

Disclaimer: A tax qualified refusal to accept property. The disclaimed property will pass to other heirs as provided in the will or trust document. If properly utilized, this technique can be used to cure defective tax formulas or allow a surviving spouse to select the amount of assets to be placed in the credit shelter trust for estate tax planning.

Funding: The transfer of assets from individual or joint names to the living trust. Although this is *required* to obtain the benefits of the trust, it is, unfortunately, frequently neglected.

Grantor or settlor: The person who creates the trust.

Living (inter vivos) Trust: Any trust created during your lifetime whether revocable (can be changed) or irrevocable (cannot be changed), as opposed to a testamentary trust which is created under a will after probate.

Living Will (also known as Mercy Will): A document which permits your family and physician to withhold life-prolonging procedures if you are diagnosed as being terminally ill. Living wills should be reviewed or rewritten periodically in accordance with the revision of your state's legislation.

Marital Trust (also known as Trust A): After the death of a spouse, the zero tax formula, under a will or living trust, will normally produce a share to be held in trust for the surviving spouse. In order to qualify for the unlimited marital deduction the surviving spouse must be entitled to all of the trust income and either have the unrestricted right to withdraw all trust property while alive or direct its distribution by will after death. Will or trust documents should provide for some type of marital trust (as opposed to outright distribution) in case the survivor is incapacitated or deceased at the time a distribution is to be made. The marital trust is taxed in the survivor's estate.

Maximum marital deduction formula: A pre-1982 standard estate tax planning formula. In almost every case a pre-1982 will or trust must be updated to avoid adverse tax or administrative expense consequences.

Power of Attorney: A document allowing another person to sign on your behalf in general or for a limited purpose. A power of attorney terminates upon incapacity (whether or not a court determination has been made) or death. Because most people do not secure approval of financial institutions prior to using a power of attorney, they are frequently not accepted. Although a power of attorney is not a substitute for a will or trust, it is a useful estate-planning tool. For example, the power of attorney can permit family members to assist with the funding of a revocable living trust, allow a trustee to handle *nontrust* matters such as signing income tax returns, and appoint persons responsible for your personal care.

(2) Durable Power of Attorney: A special power of attorney which survives incapacity until terminated by guardianship or death. Therefore, unlike the living trust, it does not avoid court supervised administration of assets.

Pour Over Will: A will which coordinates with a living trust to dispose of property which cannot or has not been placed in the trust. The will contains a provision distributing assets from probate to the living trust, hence the term "pour over."

Q-TIP Trust: A special type of marital trust which gives the survivor life income but restricts the survivor's ability to dispose of principal. This technique is exceptionally useful in second marriage situations or where the survivor may be chronically ill or subject to adverse influence. The tax law requires special language and elections in order to qualify.

Revocable Living Trust: A living trust which you can control completely and change at any time in any detail. Under the laws of some states you can be your own trustee. Property in the trust avoids guardianship in the event of incapacity or death and probate upon death. Although administration expenses are not eliminated, they are substantially reduced. This trust can be extremely flexible and tailored to individual needs. For example, a husband and wife may each establish a trust, or they may establish a joint (co-grantor) trust if this is more suitable to their circumstances. There are literally thousands of combinations of management and tax-planning options, and numerous ways to provide for the distributions of assets to heirs. The use of a living trust can avoid many of the problems inherent in powers of attorney or joint ownership.

Self-proving will: A will with special execution which allows it to be admitted to probate without further testimony of the witnesses.

Successor Trustee: A trustee who steps in if the current trustee cannot serve due to incapacity, death, or voluntary resignation. Unlike guardianship or probate, court approval or supervision is not required.

Zero tax formula: A formula which divides living trust or probate assets into marital and credit shelter trusts in such a manner as to fully utilize all credits against the federal estate tax, and eliminate federal estate taxes on the first death between spouses. This type of formula can save from $10,000 to over $300,000 in taxes for the heirs when compared with a formula which leaves everything to the survivor and then to the heirs. The arbitrary use of this formula can produce adverse tax results in the event of common disaster and in combined (husband and wife) estates more than $1,200,000. It may produce unnecessary administrative expense and loss of control in combined estates less than $600,000. There are numerous ways the formula can be structured to maximize tax savings and minimize administration expenses depending upon individual circumstances.

17

Real Estate, Stocks, and Hard Assets: Do They Belong in Your Personal Investment Pyramid?

Before investing in these areas, you must be sure of your risk tolerance and of your investment objectives.

FREEDOM FOCUS

- *What are the advantages of investing in real estate?*
- *Do you know how to find income-producing property?*
- *Can you be diversified in your real estate investments?*
- *How do you "play the market"?*
- *What role does the broker play in your stock market investing?*
- *What is a "hard" or "exotic" investment?*
- *What are the major problems you face when investing in hard assets?*

In this chapter we are going to look at several investment areas. You can generally expect these investments to comprise only a percentage of your total investment plan. In many cases they won't even be a part of your plan at all. But let's take a broad look at the areas of real estate, the stock market, and hard assets.

Real Estate

Real estate is more than just an investment; it's part of the American Dream. We all desire a spot to call our own—whether it's a tiny bungalow in the suburbs or a 40-acre spread in the country. Coupled with that desire is a pride in ownership that seems to me to be unique to this country.

Fortunately, almost anyone, armed with the proper financial-planning tools, can experience the pride of owning a home or a piece of income-producing property. Let's look at some good reasons for investing in real estate.

Real estate has been proven to be a significant inflation fighter over the long term. In fact, the real estate market actually thrives on inflation. There are two basic reasons why the value of a piece of developed real estate goes up with inflation. First, as the costs of building new homes (wages, materials, subcontractors' fees) escalate with inflation, the value of existing homes goes up simply because the cost of replacing those homes has increased. The other reason is based upon supply and demand. When higher costs make it more difficult to erect new housing, the prices of older homes get a boost. The influx of foreign money into this country, which has increased dramatically over the past decade, has helped to keep prices high.

At this writing the real estate market is experiencing a "slump." In other words, market prices are down. Historically, though, I would perceive this as a temporary situation. Remember, real estate investing should not be looked at as a short-term proposition. Rather, it is a long-term investment and history has proven that prices go down but come back up as the rate of inflation rises.

Unlike other tangible investments, real estate investments can produce income and should be designed to do so. Suppose that you rent that $60,000 house for $500 a month. In just a year's time you will have recovered 10 percent of the purchase price. Income-producing properties can be evaluated very simply using the price-to-earnings ratio—a ratio that is used in evaluating stocks (see the section entitled The Stock Market, covered in this chapter). That $60,000 home that rents for $500 a month would carry a P/E ratio of 10 ($60,000 ÷ $6000 [the annual rent] = 10). This is a very simplistic evaluation, and an investment certainly should not be based solely on this calculation.

The great thing about a real estate investment is that you can take direct action on your own to increase the P/E ratio—something you can't do with a stock. Suppose you put a fresh coat of paint on the rental home, upgrade the landscaping, or otherwise improve it. The result could very well be a hike in the rent to, say, $600 a month, which would change the P/E ratio to just over 8. (Where P/E ratios are concerned, you're aiming for the lowest possible number.)

As in other areas of investment, your success in real estate will depend, in part, on your ability to use the ever-powerful OPM—other people's money. Most real estate purchases are financed through long-term mortgage loans. That means that when you borrow money for a home and repay the loan over a period of years, you are paying back the mortgage with "cheaper dollars." If you own rental property, you can increase the supply of dollars you receive from your tenants, even as you pay back these cheaper dollars to your lending institution. In the 1980s money was plentiful from institutions for loans—sometimes it seemed that there was no end to the availability of funding. Today, that situation has reversed itself substantially. Money is much tighter today than it has been in the past.

Real estate has other advantages as well. It is subject to fluctuations just as common stocks are in the stock market. But the average person does not look at real estate daily in *The Wall Street Journal.* Unlike stocks, real estate values are not reported daily in almost every financial paper. Naturally, the price of real estate rises and falls. But as a general rule, the real estate investor is oriented to long-term investing. When people buy real estate, they are looking at it as they would a 10-year bond: They are looking at a future maturity date. But when they buy a stock, they tend to look at it daily; they become more emotionally involved, which can lead them to make a knee-jerk decision to buy or sell.

Real estate obviously cannot be considered an ideal investment for everyone. There have been major changes in the tax laws as well as the economic development. Like any other investment, it has its limitations. Probably the most commonly cited drawback is its lack of liquidity: Unlike a stock or a savings bond, the investor cannot cash in on a $100,000 house with a telephone call. That factor, however, can be as much an asset as a liability. As Franklin Delano Roosevelt once noted: "Real estate is about the safest investment in the world: It can't be lost, it can't be stolen, and it can't be carried away." However, if Mr. Roosevelt were to see how the excesses of the 1980s have come back to haunt us in the 1990s, he might rephrase his statement to say that there is no such thing as a guaranteed investment. If you remember, there was an abundance of cash available in the 1980s, and banks, flush with cash, were financing almost any project presented to them that appeared to be feasible. A massive building effort, including shopping centers and office buildings, resulted. This in turn created a glut of space in the market, which drove prices down. Landlords were forced to cut rental rates (in many cases taking losses) to attract tenants and to keep existing tenants. Businesses were not expanding, more and more space became available, and income-producing property took a beating.

When considering an investment in real estate, there are numerous tax and nontax considerations that must be carefully evaluated: investment requirement, liquidity, financing costs, depreciation, cash flows, hedge against inflation, and equity accumulation. The shrewd investor can make gains in the real estate market, but it requires skill and determination. Some investment possibilities include the following areas.

Single Family Homes

Duplex, triplex, or quadplex ownership will introduce you to the joys and frustrations of being a landlord—good practice for anyone who intends to invest in rental properties seriously. Of all real estate investments, rental homes are among the easiest to acquire with a nominal cash investment, and the most useful for tax-deferred exchanges. With a single family home, in most cases, you will be able to collect the rent yourself, keep your own books, and perhaps make repairs. This also means that you will answer those midnight maintenance calls! Depending on your time and abilities, you may be able to choose homes that need rehabilitation, renovate them, and then resell at a considerable profit, providing that you choose your property carefully.

Shopping Centers/Strip Centers

In a store block or shopping center tenants usually provide their own utilities and take care of such duties as maintenance and other expensive chores that owners of most apartment buildings must pay for themselves. Commercial tenants will also pay larger security deposits and sign longer leases than residential tenants.

"Anchor" tenants—the major retailers who consider themselves permanent residents of a shopping center—commonly sign leases with terms of 20, 30, and even 40 years, thus providing a high degree of security and cash flow predictability for the center's owners.

But this type of property also has its drawbacks. Vacancies are usually more difficult to fill than those in residential property. Small businesses, which tend to have a high mortality rate, often turn out to be short-term tenants. Even successful businesses located in small shopping centers can be driven out of business (or out of their location) if attractive new shopping malls move in nearby.

Office and Professional Buildings

Office buildings can be enticing because professionals such as doctors, lawyers, and dentists are likely to stay in the building for many years. They can afford to pay the rents and large deposits, and they often make unsolicited improvements on their offices.

But professionals bring with them some burdensome requirements. Doctors and dentists use a great deal of water and electricity, although in many cases these costs are passed through to them in their lease; and they also require more parking space. The increased parking demand may distract from another tenant moving into the building because of the lack of parking. Of course there is always the possibility that larger, newer buildings in more desirable locations can lure away professional tenants.

You must be careful to do your homework and study your area's demographics and projected growth and try to measure a projected space requirement against office space already available. Many areas are now finding that they have overbuilt and there is a major surplus of office space available. The result is empty buildings and empty pockets for investors. However, these same tough times present buying opportunities for the alert investor.

Apartment Buildings

Apartments are a relatively safe purchase for the novice investor (assuming you have done your homework). They have the advantage of generating a cash flow in the form of rental payments to the property owner. Everyone needs a place to live and the percentage of the population living in apartments is increasing steadily. This steady stream of OPM can be used to pay off your mortgage, thereby increasing the equity you have in your holdings.

Rents may increase annually—which provides a hedge against inflation for the landlord. New construction costs normally rise every year. This enhances the value of existing buildings, another advantage for the owner. But it is important that as an investor you are well aware of the tax and depreciation law changes. You could easily make a costly mistake so it is very important that you have experienced professionals such as CPAs and attorneys as members of your team.

Finding Income-Producing Property

Selecting real estate is not an easy task because many factors that can make or break a real estate deal are not evident at first glance. For example, it has often been said that the three most important rules for selecting any kind of real estate are "location, location, and location." That's still true today. No matter how attractive a piece of property is, no matter how solid its construction, if it is not in the right place, it will not command the price it deserves. Remember, though, that there are good locations and great locations. To maximize your investment dollar, search for properties that are situated where people want to go. This could be around a university, medical center, shopping and entertainment center, waterfront property, business district, etc.

How do you find that "right" place? First, pay attention to population trends. Check the latest census figures to project the rapidly growing areas of the country. Rapid growth areas of the country are generally in the sun-belt areas.

Once you have narrowed the possibilities to a specific city, the next step is to examine the real estate section of the local newspaper. Study prices and locations, and note the trends. Clip the most appealing ads and then hop in the car. The best way to size up a neighborhood is simply to drive through it. Avoid the temptation to invest in the most attractive house or apartment in a neighborhood. You may be surprised to learn that the nice, well-kept edifice you'd love to put your name on yields only about half the after-tax income of the junky-looking place across the street. Many investors have started on the path to success in real estate by buying and renovating low-cost or run-down buildings.

To decide if the neighborhood in which you want to buy will be good from an investment standpoint, use this as a beginning checklist:

- Are most residences neat, clean, and well cared for?
- Is the neighborhood quiet, with little truck and extraneous traffic?
- Is it free of any factories, sports arenas, bars, or similar nuisances?
- How convenient is shopping? Are there sufficient grocery stores, drug stores, banks, delicatessens, and other conveniences nearby?
- Is public transportation available? A nearby bus line will make your property more valuable.

- What is the reputation of the schools? Houses and apartments in neighborhoods where schools are highly regarded often go for premium prices.
- Be fully aware of any zoning restrictions.

For answers to these questions you should talk to some people who live in the neighborhood as well as to real estate agents. In addition, you should talk to representatives of the area's planning department or to the municipal clerk about such matters as zoning, water supply, and taxes.

Once you have chosen the neighborhood, carefully look over the real estate you might buy there. Have a qualified professional check the property for factors such as structural flaws, termites, seepage, asbestos insulation, lead paint, radon exposure, and so on. Consult a licensed appraiser before committing yourself to a purchase.

Buying Land

American humorist Will Rogers once said, "Invest in land—they're not making any more of it." Many investors will put stock in this logic. After all, they reason, vacant land requires no management time and the owner merely has to wait for it to increase in value. Theoretically this is true, but many landowners have lost money by adhering to this philosophy, as illustrated by the following example.

Suppose that you buy a vacant land parcel for $100,000 cash. If you are to avoid losing purchasing power on your invested dollars, the value of the land must go up at least at the rate of inflation. In addition, there will be carrying costs for property taxes and other expenses. And don't forget to consider what your $100,000 cash would have earned in a well diversified, professionally managed mutual fund that offers total liquidity and provides a hedge against inflation over a reasonable period of time.

To profit from investing in land, you must add to its value. Developers do this by subdividing and improving a land parcel. While there are many honest developers who have earned small fortunes by buying property and selling it off in smaller lots, you should be aware of abuse that does take place. Since developers often have large inventories of unsold land as well as large advertising budgets, the individual lot owner who wants to resell his or her single lot may have difficulty finding a buyer. The result is that buyers of lots in promotional land developments rarely profit.

Unless you are a seasoned professional investor in real estate or intend to put your land to some use such as farming or ranching, a land purchase can bring you unexpected problems. Suppose that promised improvements (roads, water and sewer lines, electrical lines, and so on) are slow in materializing? Or suppose that a commercial zoning that was predicted by the land salesperson is never approved, or is approved and then rezoned back to residential or farm use? Profits can be greatly diminished by such problems. And keep in mind that you may end up with a heavy amount of money in a single investment, thus no diversification.

Unlike rental property, raw land does not support you (unless, of course, you farm it). You support it, perhaps for years, by paying taxes and bearing maintenance costs. If you are not an experienced real estate speculator, you should stay away from undeveloped land—particularly since the marketplace offers you so many other more attractive opportunities.

Financing

Some of the various methods available to you to finance your real estate purchases include: creative second mortgages; wrap-around all-inclusive mortgages; lease options; contract sales; appreciation-participation mortgages (APMs); graduated payment mortgages; pledged account mortgages; variable rate mortgages; rollover or renegotiable rate mortgages; reverse-annuity mortgages; mortgage assumptions, etc.

Unfortunately we don't have the space to look at these methods individually, but you will be able to get answers from doing a little creative research and reading, as well as consulting with your financial adviser or financial institution. In addition, there are many books written by experts that deal specifically with buying and financing real estate.

Syndications: Financing
Commercial Real Estate

If commercial real estate interests you, a group investment known as a property syndication can help simplify matters. The most common arrangement is the limited partnership. In a limited partnership, the general partner, who is usually the syndication organizer, locates the property to be purchased, raises the money to buy it, manages it for a fee, and then shares in its operating profits and resale profits with the limited partners. Theoretically you have limited liability; however this is not always the case and many limited partnerships have called upon the investor to contribute more capital. When it is time to pay taxes, each limited partner reports his or her share of the partnership profits or losses.

Real estate limited partnerships are not without risks. Remember, they are extremely illiquid. The key to their success depends upon two factors: the property itself and the syndicator's past record in such ventures. Of course, before you invest in any property syndication, you should seek expert advice from an attorney or tax adviser.

Real Estate Investment Trusts (REITs)

A REIT is a way of indirectly owning real estate. Under REITs, you can acquire and hold income-producing properties of all types by buying stock in a trust that invests in real estate. A REIT may also be more liquid than direct investment in real estate since about one-third of all REITs are listed on the New York and American Stock Exchanges. A REIT is similar to a sector fund in the mutual fund business—it's investing solely in the real estate marketplace. Whenever you pick a single segment in which to invest, you run the risk of not being properly diversified. As with most investments, you will have to face some risk in a REIT, so be sure to consult a financial adviser before making your decision. And, as with all partnerships, it is strictly "Buyer beware."

The Stock Market

If you live in the United States, you have to be familiar with the name Wall Street because it is mentioned daily on virtually every television and radio station, as well as in every major newspaper. When we talk about stocks and Wall Street, what we are really talking about are the New York Stock Exchange (NYSE), the American Stock Exchange (AMEX), and the regional stock exchanges. We generally include the nationwide network of broker/dealers known as the over-the-counter (OTC) market. The OTC market is the oldest and largest securities market in the country.

Stocks offer the individual in the street an opportunity to profit from the system that has made America great; it is one of the most popular and most frequently tapped investment opportunities in the United States. Everyone knows about the market and keeps an ear open for "hot tips" (which, incidentally, are among the poorest reasons for investing in a company). In the minds of amateurs, stocks dominate the investment arena. And, in one way, this is true because there are countless ways to invest in them, from the straight purchase of common or preferred shares to put and call options, short sales, and more. There are almost as many ways to invest in the stock market as there are ways to invest.

Common stocks are bought by individuals or institutions—with the institutions investing on behalf of individuals through pensions, trusts, profit-sharing, and mutual funds. During just the past two decades, institutional investors have become the biggest buyers, holding the majority of the $3 trillion total market value for all NYSE listed stocks. The portfolio managers who handle institutional funds are true financial professionals who devote most of their waking hours to studying market conditions (usually with the help of sophisticated research staffs and computers). The moves that these people make shape the market from day to day.

"Playing the market" isn't what it used to be. And, to be sure, it's no game. As a matter of fact, I'll go so far as to say that the average individual investor has little business buying and selling stocks. There are many ways to own stocks, one of the best—in my opinion—being through mutual funds. Many people who "play the market" are victims of their own egos. With professional money managers doing the majority of buying and selling, it seems that there wouldn't be much room for the amateur. Individual investors, especially those who have little time to keep tabs on market developments, cannot hope to second guess these "big guys." Like driftwood, the small investor sometimes is taken where he or she wants to go and sometimes ends up beached. Does this mean you shouldn't get into the market at all? Of course not. It does mean that you should try to get the pros on your side in the stock selection process by finding a knowledgeable broker who understands your needs and objectives and by keeping yourself informed on trends in the market and the business world.

Stock market investments range from very high to low risks. Some stocks provide attractive dividends (generally income stocks), while others provide little or no dividend (generally growth stocks) at all but do offer long-term capital appreciation. Stocks continually rise and fall in price, and sometimes, as in October 1987, the prices fall drastically. If you find that you have a low risk tolerance, then Wall Street is not the place for you to be as an individual.

However, if you do decide to invest, there are some considerations. Where will you invest? There are many discount brokerage firms to select from. Select one firm and develop a relationship with your broker (or continue the one with your financial adviser). Trading through one firm also simplifies bookkeeping. I would advise you against signing any paper which would give your broker discretionary authority to trade without first speaking to you. As in any business, there are always unscrupulous individuals willing to take advantage of a situation. In this case "churning" comes to mind, where a broker buys and sells from your account only to create commissions, which could result in a serious dwindling down of your investment capital.

Do you have a purchasing strategy? Are you going to invest one lump sum and in one stock only? Dollar-cost averaging is a method that seems to work well here as in other investment areas. Know how much you can afford to invest, whether through dollar-cost averaging or a yearly purchase.

Be prepared to separate your emotions from your investment. This is often difficult to do when trading stocks. People tend to hold on to stock or sell it for sentimental reasons. Know that for every drop in the market there is a buying opportunity and for every rise in the market there is a selling opportunity.

If you are serious about "playing the market"—and I hope you are serious—you are going to eliminate the words "playing the market" from your vocabulary. Investing in stocks is not a game and there is no room for "players." When considering what companies to invest in, look at them for an economic factor, such as the potential to make money (isn't that what an investment is about?). If you don't already have a particular company (or companies) in mind, use resources that are right at your fingertips. Look at your children and teenagers: Where do they shop? Do you sometimes think you are supporting Gap stores just through the purchases of your teenagers? When you are shopping, do you see a lot of people continuously purchasing a particular brand of clothing? What about that company?

When you decide which companies you wish to look further at, get acquainted with them. There are many ways to do this but the first and most important way is through their literature. You can get this information free by writing to the secretary of the corporation and asking for past annual reports, quarterly statements, management speeches, and relevant information. The mailing address should be available to you at any brokerage office or in research books at the public library. Sometimes you can arrange to attend an annual meeting through a simple request.

Basics of Stocks

As you may already know, stock certificates are issued by corporations to raise operating capital in exchange for limited ownership rights. They are issued in shares, from a few hundred to millions. With each share of stock comes the right to a dividend or a share of the profits of the corporation. Stock also carries voting rights that give shareholders a voice in guiding the direction of the corporation. These rights may be exercised at the company's annual meeting of shareholders or at special interim elections. Another basic characteristic of stock ownership is its limited liability. As a stockholder, you are not liable for any damages that may be levied against the corporation (although heavy monetary damages may have a negative effect on the selling price of your stock).

One strong advantage of stock ownership is that it represents equity in the firm—"a piece of the action." As the company's fortunes improve, so do those of the stockholders, through increased share value. Always try to be an equity owner, rather than a debt owner. The reason is simple: The return on debt investments (for example, bonds) is fixed, but in equity investments, the return is theoretically unlimited. Aside from this potential for substantial price appreciation, stock owners also are eligible to receive dividends, which tend to increase as corporate earnings rise. On the negative side, there is always the potential for loss of your investment if a corporation fails, or for depletion of your capital if stock prices decline substantially.

Price/Earnings Ratio (P/E)

The P/E ratio is a Wall Street term used to appraise stocks. It describes the relationship between the price of a stock and its earnings per share. It is calculated by dividing the stock price by the earnings per share figure. For example, a stock selling at $60 with earnings of $12 per share has a price/earnings ratio of 5. Just as it says, 5 is the ratio of the stock's earnings per share to its price per share. Generally, the higher the P/E ratio, the more expensive the stock. A high P/E ratio could indicate that the stock is becoming "pricey" in value.

This P/E figure will fluctuate as the stock's price or earnings per share fluctuates due to changing investment environments, etc. While the P/E ratio gives you an indication of the company's growth, it should be considered only as a part of the total picture when evaluating stocks. Other considerations should include the investment environment at the time; the value of the stock relative to other stocks; and the value of the stock based on its own merits.

Types of Stock

Common Stocks

Common stocks are divided into two basic types: *growth* and *income*. Owners of growth stocks are hoping for selling price increases since most profit dollars are returned to the corporation to finance expansion. Income stocks turn a larger portion of their profits into dividends payable to stockholders. These stocks, which are sensitive to interest rates, can be subject to wide price swings during periods of volatile interest rates.

Preferred Stocks

Although very similar to common stocks, preferred stock receives dividend payments before common stocks, and in an amount per share that is higher. In the event of corporate liquidation, preferred stock holders are given precedence in retrieving their investments. Preferred stock is generally issued by older, more established corporations, often with less price volatility than common stocks.

Features that may be included in preferred stock offerings are cumulative provisions (which means that unpaid dividends accumulate and when a faltering company returns to profitability these are paid in full before any dividends are paid to holders of common stock); convertibility to common stock; and redemption at fixed prices. Speculating on profits to be made from these features, separately or in combination, is about the only reason for an individual to buy preferred stock. Realization of such profits depends heavily on timing and your knowledge of both the market and the company. Although preferred stock has less fluctuation than common stock, preferred stock doesn't have the upside potential of common stock.

Most people have been conditioned to prefer income stocks, with their regular dividend checks. Whether you should buy one or the other, or a combination of the two depends on your income, your investment goals, and your tax situation.

Selecting a Broker

Once you have decided to invest, you'll find that opening a brokerage account is no more difficult than opening a checking account with a bank. My advice on selecting a broker is simple: Find someone you feel sure will provide you with accurate information and well-researched advice, whether he or she is attached to a major brokerage house or a small shop. Trust is the most important ingredient in any broker-client relationship. It is the key to establishing a useful dialogue that will help the broker recommend investment alternatives within the boundaries of your risk-tolerance level. In the stock market, as in any investment area, it is important for your adviser to be fully aware of your comfort zone.

When you have paid the brokerage firm in full for the stock, you can select one of three options.

1. You can have the stock "transferred and shipped." This simply means that your name is transferred onto the stock certificate and it is mailed to the designated address. A transfer agent is involved (usually a bank) and the process takes about two weeks. You hold the certificate.

2. The stock can be "transferred and held." The stock remains in your name but is held in the brokerage firm's vault. If the stock is subsequently sold, you would have to sign a stock power allowing transfer to the new owner.

3. You can have the stock held in "street name." This means the stock is held by the broker in the broker's name for your convenience. Although there are many well respected brokerage firms in the business, I personally advise against having stock which you've purchased held in any name but yours.

Since the heyday of the Wall Street barons at the turn of the century, people have been mesmerized by the possibilities, real or imagined, of instant millions. It is a public image that has been encouraged by brokers, by corporations wanting to sell stock, and by the exchanges themselves. Hollywood has done its part, too, with glamorous characterizations of wealthy investors. But investing in the market is not for the faint-hearted. There is risk involved, so it is imperative for you to be well aware of your risk-tolerance level. You can own a balanced portfolio without having to assume all the risk. Purchase mutual funds and you will own stock from many companies and industries—all with the advantage of professional management.

Hard Assets

Hard assets include such tangibles as gold and silver, gems, rare coins, stamps, art work, antiques, baseball cards, antique cars, comic books, etc. You found these listed in the high-risk portion of my pyramid earlier in this book.

Some of the problems with hard assets include volatility, lack of liquidity, grading problems, possibilities of reproduction or of being altered, and high mark-ups. Many hard assets include the risk of robbery. Assume you buy a valuable piece of artwork as an investment and as a pleasure. While you own it, the value continues to increase. You have it displayed in your home, insured, and available for you and others to enjoy. You've owned it, you've held it, you've admired it for years. Then you die. Will your heirs be knowledgeable enough to recover its value? Most likely they'll end up selling at a loss. What of its investment value then?

Although hard assets sometimes increase in value when other investments decline, if the potential growth from them doesn't equal or exceed any potential growth from an alternative investment, the rule of thumb is to stay away.

This is a very difficult area. You must be informed and knowledgeable about the asset you are considering as an investment. Before investing, you must consider your total financial picture—what are your objectives, what is your risk tolerance level, and, again, what is your level of expertise? In Florida, just a few years ago, millions were lost by Floridians who invested in gold which turned out to be gold-painted wood shaped and stacked as gold bars. The investors even got to view the gold through the vault's port-hole window! Remember the early 1980s, when investment-grade diamonds were hot—flawless, D, one-carat stones, which went sky high. Then the sky fell. If it's too good to be true, it probably is. If you invest in art (or other hard assets), do it because you enjoy the art, not because you expect it to save you from a recession or turn you into a millionaire after a while.

If you are absolutely intrigued with the idea of owning gold, silver, or precious metals, gems, or even oil and gas, you can do so through a sector mutual fund. Unless you are knowledgeable about the hard asset, leave it to the pros.

Each of these areas could possibly have a place on your personal investment pyramid as you plan for your financial freedom. They carry the possibility of higher risks, but also the possibility of higher rewards. You can become an expert in the areas you are interested in and do it alone; you can seek the advice of professionals; or you can invest through mutual funds and have diversity and professional management built into your investment. In any case, you must be aware of your level of risk tolerance. An investment made without thorough investigation and research could cause you to take a beating in any of these areas.

18
Portfolio Optimization

Portfolio optimization is an act, process, or methodology of making your investment portfolio as fully functional or effective as possible.

FREEDOM FOCUS

- *What is portfolio optimization?*
- *What is asset allocation?*
- *What place do they have in your financial freedom?*

As defined by Webster, *optimization* is a deliberate initiative to maximize the value of something. With respect to your portfolio, that "something" is the assets you hold.

Sound complicated? It's not as difficult as it seems. One of the best ways to explain it is to compare it to baking a cake—in this instance one of my favorites, chocolate cake. To bake a chocolate cake, you start with a recipe that calls for different ingredients—some chocolate, eggs, milk, flour, sugar, etc. Chocolate, sugar, and flour are totally different ingredients. But if they are mixed according to the recipe and allowed to bake for the allotted time, you will end up with a delicious chocolate cake. If, on the other hand, your recipe calls for one teaspoon of salt and you decide to use a tablespoon instead, the person eating your cake will definitely notice the difference because you overcompensated on that particular ingredient. When you alter the measurements of any of the ingredients called for, you cannot expect to get the same results as you do when you bake the cake according to the recipe.

This is nothing more than portfolio optimization—nothing more than developing a discipline, or recipe, which is based on certain conditions. Further, this process of systematically selecting assets (optimization) must take into consideration the risk and rate of return of investments in order to achieve the most efficient trade-off between the two. This can only be done on an individual basis according to your risk tolerance and your investment objectives. An (investment) portfolio optimization program must consider these variables:

1. The forecasted rate of return for each asset class
2. The expected risk of each asset class
3. The relationship of each asset to every other asset in terms of market behavior
4. The extent to which a particular investor is willing to incur risk

Portfolio optimization begins with the simple process of identifying the concentration of an individual's assets, including both the type and investable amounts. Once this is done, the objective is to make sure that the monies committed and the investments selected will, in tandem, provide the investor with the maximum benefit for his or her financial position while taking into consideration risk tolerance.

Unlike related decisions which may fall victim to emotional prejudices (I can't sell this stock, I've had it for 15 years, or I can't sell that property, even though it is declining in value, because Aunt Jeanne left it to me) true portfolio optimization is based on facts, rather than feelings. (However, that doesn't mean that this process has to totally forgo the human element.) Any consideration of reallocation of portfolio assets begins with understanding individual goals, objectives, needs, values, and the recognition of the risk involved. Before a strategy can be developed, there must be an awareness of what is to be accomplished.

A Look at the Present

Beyond the information gathering, the initial focus of portfolio optimization lies with the identification of current holdings. (Remember

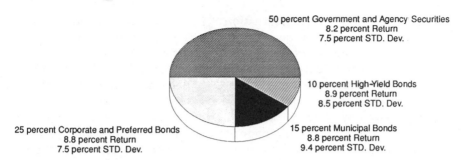

50 percent Government and Agency Securities
8.2 percent Return
7.5 percent STD. Dev.

10 percent High-Yield Bonds
8.9 percent Return
8.5 percent STD. Dev.

25 percent Corporate and Preferred Bonds
8.8 percent Return
7.5 percent STD. Dev.

15 percent Municipal Bonds
8.8 percent Return
9.4 percent STD. Dev.

Figure 18-1. Current portfolio holdings. (STD. Dev. is an abbreviation for standard deviation.)

Chapter 3, The Financial Puzzle, and the data sheet you completed? Refer to that data sheet for a look at your situation.) In the following example, Mr. and Mrs. John Doe's investments are currently allocated in:

Municipal bonds	15 percent
Corporate and preferred bonds	25 percent
High-yield bonds	10 percent
Government and agency securities	50 percent

Their expected annual return, based on this allocation, is 8.5 percent (see Figure 18-1).

The immediate picture that comes into focus from such a mix is that there really isn't much of a "mix." Rather, the portfolio is split equally between bonds (municipal, corporate, and high-yield) and fixed-rate government securities.

There is a problem here and the problem with such a limited combination is two-fold. First, while there may be four different investment vehicles, there are only two types of investments. Without the diversity of alternative holdings such as real estate, securities, precious metals, or other offerings, the portfolio has a wide window of vulnerability. At present, any change in prevailing economic/market conditions may jeopardize the portfolio's performance. Second, the similarity in the behavior of both types of investments is likely to make each of them vulnerable to the same set of conditions. While Mr. and Mrs. Doe have both brown and white eggs, all their eggs are still eggs in the same basket—resulting in no diversification.

So What Is Best?

After talking with Mr. and Mrs. Doe and reviewing their needs and objectives, we agreed on what we believe to be the optimum or best investment combination for their situation. In the Does' case, portfolio optimization stresses equity investing in professionally managed mutual funds, with an emphasis on long-term and total return.

In the planning process, the Does' definition of risk is thoroughly examined. As with many of today's critical decisions, the ensuing evaluation and analysis—looking for the right choice under the right conditions—is aided by enhanced computer technology. The result is almost unlimited in scope, allowing countless varieties of opportunities to be weighed and assessed in light of specific client considerations and constraints. Quality of selections rather than quantity is still the key to the selection process. What happened to the Does? Read on!

Asset Allocation

In order to focus on those investment selections that have the most opportunity to benefit the portfolio's performance, the process of optimization is centered around asset allocation—sometimes called modern portfolio theory. The approach bases selection on classes of assets. The objective is to select classes of assets that benefit from different financial conditions. In doing so, the value of the overall portfolio is able to prosper, even when some of its selections are exposed to less than favorable conditions. By selecting assets that behave in this fashion, the portfolio avoids radical swings in performance as financial/market conditions shift, thereby producing a safer range of returns.

The Focus

In applying this thinking to the Does' portfolio, past investment performance is used for purposes of evaluation. In so doing, the computer-aided portfolio optimization analysis draws on historical data that tracks the actual rise and fall of 14 specific investment/asset classes during the past 10 years. Included in the mutual funds that are reviewed are aggressive growth, balanced, corporate bonds, government and agency securities, growth, growth and income, high-yield bonds, international, metals, money market, and municipal bonds. Also examined for performance are small growth stocks and real estate investment trusts.

The Need for a Change

In its original state the Doe portfolio generated an annual overall return of 8.5 percent. Unfortunately, it is unlikely that this return will be sufficient to provide them with adequate cash flow and the income growth needed to stay ahead of inflation, and to sustain financial support over their lifetime.

If these objectives are to be achieved, the portfolio's investable monies will have to be realigned. Just how the monies and assets will be altered will depend upon a variety of factors, including risk tolerance and *standard deviation.* The role of standard deviation is to evaluate the *probability* of achieving the desired return. "Standard deviation indicates the volatility of a fund. It is calculated using 36-month excess returns over 3-month Treasury bills. In general, the higher the standard deviation, the greater the volatility. Approximately two thirds of the time, a fund's monthly total return will be its average monthly total plus or minus one standard deviation. Approximately 95 percent of the time, the fund's monthly total return will fall within two standard deviations of its average return. Thus, the greater the standard deviation, the greater the range of likely returns."*

As I mentioned before, risk is an acknowledged component of any investment decision. It is important that you don't lose sight of the fact that for a higher return (in most cases), more risk may have to be tolerated. The question is, "How much risk can be tolerated?" Again, that can only be decided on an individual basis taking into consideration not only the obvious present and expected future fiscal position of the investor, but also the emotional aspect.

The Optimum Combination

In following a disciplined approach in the analysis, portfolio optimization offers several suggested configurations to improve the performance of the Does' portfolio. However, each one of those configurations also carries with it a variation in targeted rate of return, risk tolerance, and standard deviation.

In considering the Does' need for cash flow (identified by them as 10 percent) while assuring sustained financial support over their lifetimes, and taking into account inflation (over the long term it's expected to average out to 3.2 percent), the targeted return is established in the range of 13–13.4 percent.

To achieve this return, the composition of the current portfolio has been altered. In its new form (see Figure 18-2), the realignment has removed all monies from investments in municipal bonds, high-yield bonds, and government and agency securities. Holdings in corporate and preferred bonds were reduced from 25 percent to 2.5 percent. In

*Morningstar, Inc.

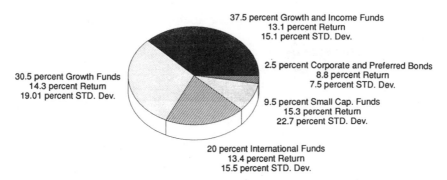

Figure 18-2. Revised portfolio holdings. (STD. Dev. is an abbreviation for standard deviation.)

the new allocation, 9.5 percent of the monies were put in small cap. funds; 20 percent in international funds; 37.5 percent in growth and income funds, and 30.5 percent in growth funds. (For an explanation of these funds refer to the Chapter 10, The Magic of Mutual Funds.)

Such a mix is designed to appeal to the Does' sensitivity to risk through greater diversity in the portfolio, while at the same time allowing for a broader-based opportunity to benefit from changing economic/market conditions. Additionally, the obvious objective of increasing the portfolio's potential return to the desired 13–13.4 percent range is also realized.

Through optimization and diversification, the Does have been able to realign and stabilize an investment strategy that now offers them a solid opportunity for success. At the same time, they've been able to do it without expending additional resources, or going beyond their own defined willingness for risk-taking.

Our world is constantly changing: the Berlin Wall came down, the Persian Gulf War was fought, interest rates go up and down. These changes ultimately affect what's going on in your investment portfolio. To cope with these changes, it is important to take a disciplined approach to your investing—to maximize your returns. When you are able to do this, then you are in control of your quest for financial freedom.

This is not the end of portfolio management. (We've only scratched the surface.) It, like countless other investment considerations, needs to be reviewed on a regular basis. Such action allows strategies to take into account changes in personal perspectives, as well as economic/market conditions.

19

The Final Touch

*In order to move toward any goal,
you have to have a plan, and you
have to begin acting on that plan
immediately.*

FREEDOM FOCUS
- *What are the six steps that lead to your financial freedom?*
- *What is your personal T-square?*
- *How do you stay abreast of economic conditions?*
- *What is your most valuable investment?*

Early in this book, we talked about the three kinds of people in this world: those who make things happen, those who watch things happen, and those who scratch their heads and wonder what happened. By now you have made a commitment to yourself that, as far as your financial future is concerned, you are going to become a member of the first group. You are going to make things happen. You will no longer sit on the sidelines and watch other people play the game. You will take an active role in charting your own financial destiny.

It is important to realize, though, that when you embark upon this course, you will feel lonely, especially at first. The road that you are setting out on is a very lonely road; only the most successful people in our society travel that road. And you are a bona fide member of their ranks, even though you might not think that you fit this description at this point in your life. You are one of the upward bound, self-directed few because you have resolved to tap your potential to achieve financial independence. Did you know that most of us use only about 10 percent of our brain power? The other 90 percent is completely virgin territory, a part of the brain that we never use for anything! Wow! I'm not suggesting that you or I or anyone could suddenly start using all of our mental potential, but can you image what you could accomplish if you could just increase it by, say, 2 percent? Can you imagine how much easier it would be for you to break through the barriers and to move forward at a steady pace, if only you will believe that you can do it and then act on that belief?

The biggest problem most people face is that they limit themselves. They put a cap on their abilities by telling themselves, either consciously or subconsciously, that they can achieve only so much, that they can rise only so high, that they can experience only so much success. They put themselves in a different league from the men and women who do really well in life—the self-made millionaires and heads of large corporations. They believe these people have different and greater gifts than they do. But they are wrong! We all have basically the same mental tools to work with; some of us simply have not put those tools to their best use yet. But anyone who wants to, can. By sticking with me through the previous chapters, you have already shown yourself to be a person who intends to develop these tools to their maximum potential.

Making decisions—and by so doing being flexible enough to accept and recognize change—may be the key to achieving your financial freedom. In all the past experiences I have had in dealing with very wealthy people, I have found that they put their pants on the same way you and I do every morning. They experience the same basic problems you and I do—planning for retirement, medical needs, college for their kids, or special care for elderly parents. But they make decisions—decisions to establish goals and to take the necessary steps to reach those goals. By now you've reached a point that you must start making decisions—no more procrastinating—and you are bound to make more right decisions than wrong ones. Even more if you are using qualified professional guidance—OPB.

Intentions and actions, though, are two separate things. In order to begin to move toward any goal, you have to have a plan, and you have to begin acting upon that plan as soon as you have devised it—not tomorrow, not next week, not after you've had a short vacation or after you've paid off your car. Now! If you take this word and make it yours, it can be the most valuable word in the English language to you. Now! If it's worth doing at all, it's worth getting started on now. Don't fall back into that old trap of procrastination! Have you ever thought about going on a diet and found yourself repeating this statement so many times it has become meaningless: "Starting on Monday, I'm going to begin my diet." Then . . . "Next week for sure." Diets only work when you have a change of attitude. Your financial fitness is just as important as your physical fitness, perhaps even more so because your family's destiny hinges on it as much as your own does. Now is the time to begin a lifelong program that will take you and your family into a better tomorrow. Let's look at a step-by-step blueprint for that program.

Step One: Finding Out
Where You Are

When a doctor assesses your physical health, he or she begins with a health history. You are asked probing questions about conditions that may run in your family, whether you smoke, whether you drink, if you get regular exercise, and so forth. This to find out where you stand, health-wise, right now. Similarly, as you begin your program to achieve better financial health, the first step is to evaluate your present financial condition. To help you make this assessment, use the lengthy data sheet that appears as Appendix 3-1. You may find, as you begin to fill in the blanks, that at this point in your life you do not have much information to enter on this sheet. Don't be discouraged if this is the case. Think of the data sheet as the blueprint of an idea that you will gradually convert into a reality. You will select the parts that you think should be in your financial game plan, and you will begin working to obtain them. Right now, for example, you may not have a single entry to put on the page that shows stock holdings, but if you decide that stocks figure in your game plan you will begin to acquire them, and soon.

Some absolutely essential forms that were presented in Chapter 3 include an Inventory of Assets, Outstanding Obligations, Family Household Expenses, and Household Income. By completing these you create a balance sheet, an expense sheet, and an income summary. If you have not yet filled them out, you should do so immediately. These are diagnostic tools that will allow you to determine where your money is going. You will no doubt find that many of your dollars are siphoned off into unproductive areas each month. Once you track on paper the precise paths your dollars are taking, both into and out of your life, you will be able to make some important decisions about the kind of changes you and your family can voluntarily put into effect in order to get your financial plans on target.

The rule of thumb to observe from the very outset is this: The first bill collector you pay is yourself. You are entitled to at least 10 percent of the net amount of every paycheck you bring home, and nothing should keep you from regularly collecting this debt to yourself. By keeping 10 percent or more of your earnings, you will build capital that can and should be used to launch your investment program. Remember the tax-deferred variable annuity described in Chapter 11? And how much you might collect in 35 years if you could afford to invest just $50 a week and realize a total annual return of 15 percent, tax-deferred? (That figure was nearly $3.3 million, in case you need reminding.) This is the kind of program that almost anyone can afford to begin right now, providing that the regular payment of the debt you owe yourself becomes a priority item in your budget. That 10 percent you "save" should not be saved at all, rather invested. Invest in increasing assets as opposed to decreasing assets. What do I mean? It's very simple, if you buy a Sony stereo system you have bought a decreasing asset—once purchased, it loses value in terms of dollars. However, if, instead, you buy stock in Sony, then you have bought an increasing asset—an asset that should grow in value. Then you liquidate portions of the increasing asset to purchase the decreasing asset!

Your next task is to determine how much you are paying in taxes and to try to find legal means of cutting that bill down. You must learn to use your 1040 form as a tool that will tell you where your tax dollars are going. You must understand that form and spend time studying it. And be inquisitive of the person who is preparing your tax return—why is this, what is that, can this be a deduction, etc.—so you begin to understand your taxes in the sense of what leads to tax savings, deferrals, or deductions, and what doesn't. Your tax planning for the year should start on January 1 of the taxable year, and members of your family—especially your spouse if you have one—should take part in that planning. If you have children, one of your objectives should be to help them develop an understanding of financial matters, in the hopes that they will mature into men and women who can automatically take charge of their own affairs. Remember again, we've done a great job at teaching our children how to make money, but a terrible job at teaching them how to manage their money. One reason so many adults fail to manage their money successfully, despite their earnest desire to do so, is that the financial arena is completely unfamiliar territory to them. You can give your children a priceless legacy by helping them to penetrate the mysteries of money at an early age. You'd be surprised at just how much a young person can understand, especially if the information is presented in a way that engages his or her interest. Let your teenager sit down with you and help fill out the family's 1040 form. Take your son or daughter to a stock brokerage office and explain what the ticker tape is all about. Let the whole family "play the market" with Monopoly money and see who comes out ahead. Do your children shop at Gap stores? After one of their trips, pick up one of the Gap annual reports and go over it with them. Have them look up their stock in the business section of your local paper.

But let's get back to your tax planning. Once you have studied the tax regulations—not only by reading the instruction booklet that comes with your 1040 form, but also by doing outside reading—you should be able to decide upon some strategic moves. Can you completely shelter some of your income from taxes? Can you at least put off the payment of some taxes under allowable provisions and let the dollars that would ordinarily go straight to Uncle Sam work for you instead, compounding returns? Are you in the right retirement program? Is the money that you have available for investment purposes right now spread across the pyramid in a way that will bring you optimum tax benefits? Can you reposition any of your investment dollars from a currently taxable to a tax-deferred or tax-free status?

This assessment of the state of your financial health may hold some surprises for you. In taking your own psycho-economic pulse, so to speak, you will find out just how concerned you have really been to date about where your money is going and just how wise you have been about remedying current problems and planning for the future.

Step Two: Determining Your Objectives

Offhand you may say that you know what your financial objectives are. Like everyone else, you want something called "financial independence." But what does that term mean to you personally? As you answer this question, you will begin to spell out your objectives. Remember that there are two types of objectives: short-term and long-term. A trip to Europe could be one of your short-term objectives, for example. Or perhaps a new car, or a boat. Long-term objectives might include a financially comfortable retirement, educational funds for your children, perhaps a second home for you in a warmer climate.

Becoming disciplined in the way you handle your money doesn't mean taking a vow never to spend any of it on the things you enjoy. The difference lies in the way you approach this expense. The ineffective money manager acts on impulse and emotions, perhaps getting deeply into debt to gratify a whim of the moment; the effective money manager, after adequate thought and consultation with family members and appropriate advisers, decides to incur an expense and then develops ways to generate funds for that purpose.

You should write your objectives down and review them periodically with the whole family. They should be flexible enough to allow you to alter their specifications or perhaps to discard them completely based on the then current circumstances of what is going on in your life.

Step Three: Evaluating Yourself on a T-Square

A T-square is a simple tool that you can use to identify two sets of facts that you must know about yourself: your weaknesses and your strengths. This is a way of evaluating YOB—Your Own Brain—so you can determine what kind of help you'll need to get from OPB—Other People's Brains. A sample T-square appears as Figure 19-1. Be as honest as possible in filling out the weaknesses. Remember, the sole purpose of this tool is to give you insight into the areas in which you need help.

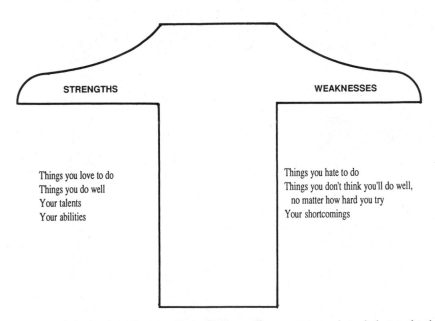

STRENGTHS — WEAKNESSES

Things you love to do
Things you do well
Your talents
Your abilities

Things you hate to do
Things you don't think you'll do well,
no matter how hard you try
Your shortcomings

Figure 19-1. Personal T-square. Remember, your T-square is a simple tool, designed to help you identify your areas of strengths and weaknesses. Try to be as objective as possible when filling out your T-square.

If you are married, your spouse should fill out a T-square too, and if you have children over 10 or 12, let them do some self-evaluating. (Incidentally, this T-square has many useful applications. You could, for instance, ask your teenagers to fill one out to determine for themselves if they are responsible enough to drive the family car.)

Evaluate your married children's marriages on a T-square when you are considering writing them into a living trust or will. And, by all means, bring the T-square analysis into play as you examine various investment alternatives. You could develop a positive numbering system for the "strengths" side and negative numbering system for the "weaknesses" side. Then, depending upon your comfort zone, you could set one number as the "buy" indicator on the positive side and another as the "don't buy" indicator on the negative side.

Filling out a T-square is another step in your self-administered psycho-economic analysis because it identifies the areas in which you need to seek outside help. The cardinal rule is this: Don't try to build on your weaknesses. This only leads to frustration. Build on your strengths and let other people help you in the areas in which you are weak. As an example, I do not perform open heart surgery on weekends; I don't do root canals or build office buildings either. But what I do is surround myself with OPB, people who have strengths in my areas of weaknesses.

Step Four: Selecting Your Advisers

Now you may decide that you want the assistance of some expert advisers. We explored the subject of financial advisers earlier (Chapter 4), so we need not go over that list here. What is important to remember is this: (1) don't be afraid to ask questions, and (2) shop around until you find advisers with whom you have a true rapport and who are willing to act as team players.

Remember that the financial adviser who quarterbacks your team can come from one of several disciplines. Your adviser may be a member of the financial planning professions per se, or a life insurance agent, or stock broker with the training and ability to see the "big picture." Once you make contact with your financial professional, initiate a continuing dialogue with him or her. Explain your strengths and weaknesses. (I'd think long and hard before retaining any adviser who claimed to be an all-around expert on everything.) Show your financial professional your list of objectives and ask for help in either paring down that list or expanding it. A good adviser will be able to offer constructive criticism of your objectives and may suggest some important goals that you had not thought of. Another very important characteristic for any of your advisers to have is empathy with you. They should be able to understand your objectives and work within that framework.

Step Five: Preparing a Written Financial Plan

Once your objectives have been defined, you must devise a means to attain them. You should have a written financial plan that will prescribe what steps to take at what times in the future if you are to realize your objectives. Visualize for one moment that we're going on a cruise and we ask the captain where we are going. The captain tells us our destination. We then ask how long it will take to reach our destination and the captain says anywhere from two to eight days. Then we ask about the Gulf Stream and the prevailing weather conditions and the captain says "Who cares?" What do we do? We pick up our bags and leave because we expect that captain to have a plan of action. Remember, if you don't know where you are going, any road will take you there. Planning is essential to your financial journey.

The key concepts here are that your plan should be written (this brings it from the abstract to the concrete) by either you or your chief financial adviser, and that it should outline action that is to be taken within a specific time frame.

Like your objectives, your financial plan should be flexible. A written plan does not have to be a rigid one. A rigid plan will not work. New ideas can be added as they occur to you and advisers.

Something that you should add to your daily routine is time for reading about events and products in the financial arena. We've become a very health and fitness conscious society. What we have to work at now is becoming fiscally fit—which includes being aware of and in tune with what's taking place in our economic environment. Publications that you will find informative and interesting include *Money, Time, Newsweek, U.S. News & World Report,* and, of course, *The Wall Street Journal.* You can make your own list of favorites. And you can combine the two—fiscal and physical fitness. Listen to tapes of subjects that interest you or that you want to learn more about while you are jogging, on the treadmill, or exercising.

As you are aware by now, I believe in the power of a positive attitude. There are a number of books, most recorded on cassette tape, available for your listening. One which I read and reread is *Think and Grow Rich* (by Napolean Hill, published by Hawthorn Books Inc.) I find it as meaningful today as the day it was written. But there are many, many worthwhile titles to choose from.

Sometimes you can give your daily study time over to a project rather than general reading. If you are thinking about joining a real estate limited partnership, for example, you might want to devote several days to a careful reading and rereading of material about it. Read with a pen in your hand and circle things you do not understand. Then take your questions to your financial adviser. Ask for solid, specific answers. That is what the adviser is there for—you and your questions.

Step Six: Learning How to Monitor Your Program

At least once every three months, you should look over your financial program thoroughly. Set aside these periods on your calender right now and then let nothing interfere with your commitment to use them for reviewing your program. During these reviews, evaluate your financial plan in terms of the "big picture." How are the various components performing? Are they living up to expectations? Are they moving you toward your objectives? Is it time to make some changes or should you leave the program alone?

If you are computer-friendly, you can do this with even greater ease with computers and software programs. There are a number of programs available to choose from. However you review, just make sure you review your program regularly because our world is not static. Just as your automobile needs tune-ups, and it doesn't mean that the auto is bad, your financial plan needs review for possible tune-ups.

A Few Final Thoughts

When you start your financial program, you're going to feel like a neophyte jogger who's just hit the street in brand new running shoes. This new exercise (mental, in your case) may make you very uncomfortable for awhile. Sometimes you're going to wonder why you ever broke out of your comfortable lifestyle and got started on this crazy new thing. You might take some kidding from other people (the "You don't do that" crowd), and you will probably want to throw in the towel more than once.

All I can tell you is to hang in there. Be the long-distance runner. This is a worthwhile endeavor—possibly the most worthwhile and promising endeavor you have ever initiated. You are working toward a goal that is important, not only to you, but to your family. The highs will start to come if you stick with it. But you'd also better be prepared to face some pretty low-down lows when things don't go your way. At times like that, remember: You can't be right all the time. No one ever is. Just try to be right most of the time and have enough staying power to hang tough when you need to. Do you remember Ted Williams? He was a batter for the Boston Red Sox in the mid-1940s and the last of the .400 hitters (for the whole season). But he didn't bat 1000. What about the other times he got up to bat and struck out or walked? He would get upset and throw bats. But the important thing is that he continued to get up to home plate and take his swings. Over the long haul he compiled an outstanding record as a hitter. The average person is afraid to step up to the plate, afraid to swing because they might miss. Don't settle for being average! The combination that will get you to your goal is:

Money + Time + Sheltering + Good Rates of Return

I hope this book has been helpful to you, and I hope it will continue to be of value as you set your game plan into motion. I said before that you should maintain an open, two-way dialogue with all of your advisers, and, if I may, I would like to include myself.

As I close this book, I want, above all, to leave you with a total belief in yourself. You are a unique individual, with special talents and abilities. The chances are good that you don't even know about some of these talents and abilities yet, or, if you do know about them, you don't realize the full extent to which you possess them.

Remember that we are all game players on the "field" of life and it is not an even playing field. But don't let that psyche you out—remember the documented stories about those people who started out with little or nothing and went on to become great success stories. The American Dream is still alive. You don't have to be wealthy to become wealthy—it's not what you make, but what you do with the money you make that counts.

You are your own most valuable investment; you are your own greatest resource. Believe this philosophy and live it to the fullest. The things that we want and need begin to come within our reach when we discover our remarkable ability to redefine ourselves, to stretch beyond what we thought were our limits, and to show through our lives what becomes possible for those who say "I can."

Glossary

Actuary: A professional insurance statistician who calculates risk, premiums, defined benefit plans, and related matters.

Adviser: The organization employed by a mutual fund to give professional advice on the fund's investments and asset management practices. (See also *investment adviser.*)

Aggressive growth fund: A mutual fund with an investment objective of substantial capital gains and little income. One aggressive growth fund describes itself as a "speculative mutual fund seeking capital appreciation."

Alternative minimum tax: An additional tax to ensure that taxpayers approaching $100,000 of taxable income pay at least a minimum tax.

American Depository Receipt (ADR): A negotiable security evidencing ownership of blocks of a foreign security held on deposit in a foreign branch of an American bank. Often used as the method of trading gold-mining stocks.

American Institute of CPAs (AICPA): A professional organization of CPAs.

Annual renewable term (ART): A form of life insurance with an annually increasing premium which provides protection for a limited period of time. Some policies are available until age 100. Policies are usually guaranteed renewable without evidence of insurability.

Annuitant: The person on whose life annuity payments are based.

Annuity: A retirement (or other) vehicle between client (annuitant) and an insurance company in which, for a lump sum payment, the insurance company provides for the payment of a specific sum of money to the annuitant either in a lump payment or in periodic payments. It provides the annuitant with a guaranteed income either immediately or at retirement. Annuities usually pay until death (or for a specific period of time) and provide protection against the possibility of outliving your financial resources.

Annuity trust: See *charitable remainder trust.*

Appreciate: To grow or increase in value.

Appreciation participation mortgage (APM): A mortgage through which the lender participates in the appreciation of the property by exchanging a reduction in the mortgage interest rate for a percentage of equity in the property. The mortgagee shares in the appreciation at the time of loan payoff or sale.

Asked: The price requested by the selling party for any particular stock. When bid and asked prices are quoted, the asked price is the lowest that anyone has offered to accept for that stock at that time, while the bid is the highest that anyone has offered to pay for it. (See also *bid* and *spread.*)

Asked or offering price: (*As seen in some mutual fund newspaper listings*) The price at which a buyer may purchase stock from the investment company. The asked or offering price means the current net asset value per share plus sales charge, if any.

Asset allocation: One method of investment planning which allocates your assets to specific investment areas in order to reach your goals and objectives.

Assets: Everything owned by or due to a person or corporate entity.

Assumed benefit plan: See *target benefit plan.*

Automatic reinvestment: An option available to mutual fund shareholders in which fund dividends and capital gains distributions are automatically plowed back into the fund to buy new shares and thereby increase holdings.

Back-end load: A charge or exit fee charged by some mutual funds when you sell your mutual fund shares.

Balanced fund: Mutual funds that maintain a balance between stocks and bonds in the investment portfolio. Rationale: stocks for growth, bonds for safety.

Balance sheet: A financial report that includes assets, liabilities, net worth (or deficit), and other related information. A statement which provides information about the assets, liabilities, and owners' equity of a company as of a particular date. Usually standardized in columnar form, subtracting liabilities from assets produces a "net worth" figure.

Bearer bond: A bond that is presumed to be owned by the individual who holds it; this bond carries detachable interest coupons.

Beneficiary: The person who receives or is identified to receive benefits from trust property or who inherits under a will. Mainly used to identify the person(s) to receive insurance proceeds at the death of the insured.

Bid: The price offered by a prospective buyer for a stock. In mutual funds, the bid price is usually the liquidating or net asset value of its shares. (See also *asked* and *spread.*)

Bid or "sell" price: (*As seen in some mutual fund newspaper listings*) The price at which a mutual fund's shares are redeemed (bought back) by the fund. The bid or redemption price usually equals the current net asset value per share.

Bond: Basically, an IOU or promissory note of a corporation or other entity, usually issued in denominations of $1000. A bond represents debt and the holder of the bond (the investor) is a creditor of the entity, not a shareholder. Hundreds of different types of bonds have been issued.

Bond fund: A mutual fund that invests mainly in bonds, hoping to achieve maximum income and safety of principal.

Book value: The net worth of a company or the value of its depreciated assets. Also referred to as capital or shareholder's equity. (Important note: Book value may differ from the liquidating value because assets are estimated by depreciated rather than market value.)

Broker: One who effects transactions in securities for the accounts of others and who receives a commission for his or her services.

Broker/dealer (or dealer): A firm that buys and sells mutual fund shares and other securities to the public.

Calculated risk: A venture that includes uncertainties, alternatives to which have been carefully studied to select the highest probability of success.

Call: Exercise by an issuer of its rights to retire outstanding securities.

Callable bond: A type of bond that can be retired prematurely by the issuer for a specified payment—usually slightly above the face value.

Call option: An option to buy 100 shares of stock or market index at a specified price within a specific time frame.

Call price: The price at which a company will repurchase a callable security. Often call price exceeds par or liquidating price.

Capital: Generally, the money, property, and other assets of a business. The term is also used to apply to cash in reserve, savings, or other property of value. In financial reports, it is the total of all assets less the total of all liabilities.

Capital gain: Profit that is gained from the sale of real estate, securities, or another capital assets. *Long-term* profits are realized from the sale of securities held for more than six months. *Short-term* profits are realized from the sale of securities held six months or less.

Capital gains distributions: Payments to mutual fund shareholders of profits realized (long-term gains) on the sale of securities in the fund's portfolio. These amounts are usually distributed to shareholders annually.

Capital growth: An increase in market value of a mutual fund's securities, as reflected in the net asset value of fund shares. This is a specific long-term objective of many investors and investment companies (mutual funds).

Cash flow: Dividends, interest payments, realized profits, and any other return from an investment.

Cash value insurance: Permanent insurance which provides for a tax-deferred build up of cash values over the life of the contract. This cash value element, combined with level or limited premium increases, means that the death benefit will be available for the "whole of life." Types of cash value insurance are: whole life, ordinary life, interest sensitive whole life, and universal life.

Certificates of deposit: Generally short-term, interest-bearing negotiable certificates issued by commercial banks or savings and loan associations against funds deposited in the issuing institution. (*Euro-CDs* are issued by foreign branches of U.S. banks or U.S. branches of foreign banks.)

Certified Financial Planner (CFP): A designation granted by the International Board for Standards and Practices for the College for Financial Planning to individuals who successfully complete a rigorous six-course curriculum.

Charitable remainder annuity trust: A trust designed to pay its income beneficiary (or beneficiaries) a specific sum that is not less than 5 percent of the initial fair market value of all property placed in the trust.

Charitable remainder trust: A trust that donates the principal to a charity at termination of the trust period.

Charitable remainder unitrust: A trust designed to pay the income beneficiary (or beneficiaries) a fixed percentage that is not less than 5 percent of the net fair market value of its assets (as valued annually).

Charitable trust: A trust created in an effort to give one or more gifts to a charitable organization.

Chartered Life Underwriter (CLU): A designation granted by the American College of Life Underwriters to individuals who pass 10 comprehensive examinations in insurance, economics, estate planning, etc.

Closed-end investment company: Closed-end companies issue a limited number of shares and do not redeem them (buy them back). Instead, closed-end shares are traded in the securities markets, with supply and demand determining the price.

Closed-end mutual fund: A fund that offers a fixed number of shares that are traded on exchanges like stocks and bonds.

Collateralized mortgage obligation (CMO): Mortgage backed security that separates mortgage pools into short-, medium-, and long-term portions. Depending on individual needs, an investor can select a CMO of an appropriate duration.

College for Financial Planning: An organization that offers professional training curricula leading to the CFP designation (Certified Financial Planner). The courses required include risk management, investments, tax planning, retirement, and estate planning, among others.

Comfort zone: As used in this book, it is that area of comfort that you feel regarding the safety of your investments.

Commercial paper: Short-term, unsecured promissory notes issued by corporations to finance short-term credit needs. Commercial paper is usually sold on a discount basis and has a maturity at the time of issuance not exceeding nine months.

Commodities: Staple products that are basic to many industries and are usually traded in bulk form. Examples include corn, copper, pork, and lumber. Frequently when investors "buy commodities" they are really signing a contract to buy or sell a quantity of the product at some future date, called a commodity future contract.

Common stock: Certificates representing financial shares of ownership interest in a corporation with no set rate of return. Ownership of common stock provides for corporate voting rights and a share in the future profit (or loss) of the corporation.

Compound interest: Interest computed on principal plus interest accrued during a previous period(s).

Contingent deferred sales charge (CDSC): A fee imposed when shares are redeemed (bought back by the fund) during the first few years of share ownership.

Contractual plan: A program for the accumulation of mutual fund shares in which the investor agrees to invest a fixed amount on a regular basis for a specified number of years. A substantial portion of the sales charge applicable to the total investment is usually deducted from early payments.

Convertible term insurance: An option offered with some term insurance policies that allows the insured to convert the term policy to a whole life policy at some future date. Most policies have a premium credit offered, during a certain period of years, against the first year whole life premium.

Corporate income statement: A company's statement of profit and loss (showing revenue, costs, taxes, and profit). One of the three major reports included in corporate financial statements.

Creative financing: Unique and innovative ways of financing a major investment purchase by reducing cash outlay and increasing leverage. Usually in the world of real estate, it would include arrangements like second mortgages, wrap-around mortgages, and appreciation participation mortgages.

Current yield: The relation of the annual interest received to the price of the bond, expressed as a percentage.

Custodian: Any person or organization holding the assets of another. Also used to refer to an adult who agrees to take responsibility for a minor who purchases securities, or to a bank that serves as a depository for the assets of a mutual fund.

Debt instruments: A written promise to repay a debt, such as bond, certificate of deposit, bill, note, etc.

Decedent: Term for a person considered legally dead.

Decreasing term: A type of pure protection life insurance (term) in which the premiums remain the same and face value of coverage decreases over the life of the policy.

Deferred compensation plan (nonqualified): A retirement strategy that defers some present employment compensation until a future date (either when you retire or leave employment). Advantages include tax-deferred investment income and substantive lack of government red tape.

Defined benefit plan: A special form of retirement plan that allows an employer to buy the amount of retirement benefits that will be received based on years of employment and past compensation.

Defined contribution plan: A special form of retirement plan that requires an employer to contribute a fixed amount to the plan each year. The ultimate benefit to the retiree, however, is not defined as above.

Depreciate: Lose value due to wear, tear, or obsolescence, usually charged against income as a business expense.

Disclosure statement: A written release, as required by the SEC, by companies of all information (materials and facts)—good or bad—that might affect an investor's decision.

Discretionary funds: Money left after expenses for essentials. Usually refers to money spent on leisure, travel, and savings.

Distributions: Dividends paid from net investment income and payments made from realized capital gains. (See also *capital gains distributions*.)

Diversification: The spreading of investments among numerous vehicles and over a distribution of risk levels. Rationale: weakness or loss in one area will reduce the adverse affect on the entire portfolio. Also known as "spreading the risks."

Dividends: Payments by a corporation to its shareholders proportionate to corporate earnings.

Dollar-cost averaging: Investing equal amounts of money at regular intervals regardless of whether securities markets are moving up or down. This practice reduces average share costs to the investor who acquires more shares in periods of lower securities prices and fewer shares in periods of higher prices. Unlike a contractual plan, dollar-cost averaging is voluntary.

Dow Jones Industrial Average (DJIA): A composite index of 30 large industrial stock prices.

Dual-purpose fund: A type of investment company introduced to the United States from England in early 1967, which has two separate classes of shares and is designed to serve the needs of two distinct types of investors: (1) those interested only in income and (2) those interested solely in possible capital growth.

Earnings per common share: Net income after all charges, including preferred dividend requirements, divided by the number of common shares outstanding. Net income does not include profits from the sale of securities.

Earnings per preferred share: Net income after all charges, including any prior preferred dividend requirements, divided by the number of preferred shares outstanding.

Endowment life insurance: In effect, a forced savings account with a life insurance company, with a death benefit as a secondary feature.

Usually purchased to ensure a future payback to met an anticipated obligation, such as children's education.

Equity: The residue of value for the owner of an asset remaining after deducting prior claims. The equity of a corporation may be divided into common shares alone or may include preferred shares as well. In calculating the equity of a common stock, preferred stock as well as debt must be deducted from total assets.

Equity security: Technically, the term refers to all securities other than debt, but is used sometimes to denote common stocks alone or preferred stocks of a quality rendering them subject to market fluctuations similar to those of common stocks.

Estate: All of a person's property; generally refers to that left by a deceased person.

Estate planning: A system of planning that ensures your estate will be passed to your chosen heirs with limited red tape and the most favorable tax treatment.

Estate tax: A tax assessed on the fair market value of all assets less liabilities held by a person at death.

Eurodollar: U.S. currency held in banks outside the United States, generally in Europe, and commonly used for settling international transactions. Some securities are issued in Eurodollars, that is, with a promise to pay interest in dollars deposited in foreign bank accounts.

Exchange privilege: Enables mutual fund shareholders to transfer their investment from one fund to another within the same fund family as shareholder needs or objectives change. Usually funds let investors use the exchange privilege several times a year for a low or no fee per exchange.

Executor, executrix: See *personal representative.*

Expense ratio: The proportion that annual expenses bear to average net assets for the year.

Expenses: Includes all costs of operation.

Face-amount certificate, installment type: A security representing an obligation on the part of its issuer to pay a stated amount at a fixed date in the future, in consideration of payment of periodic installments of a stated amount.

Face-amount certificate, fully paid: A security representing a similar obligation as above, the consideration for which is the payment of a single lump sum.

Fair value: Under the Investment Company Act, value determined in good faith by the board of directors for those securities and assets for which there is no market quotation readily available.

Family of funds: All of the funds within a system of mutual funds, managed by the same company, that provides the option of switching investments from one type of fund to another, either for free or for a small administrative fee.

Family trust: A type of trust that provides income to a spouse and, upon the spouse's death, is automatically disbursed to children.

Fiduciary: A person who is vested with legal rights and powers to be exercised for the benefit of another person.

Financial adviser: Any person who, for compensation, provides advice to a client regarding strategies and actions to achieve financial goals based on an analysis of the personal and financial condition, resources, and capabilities of the client.

First in, first out (FIFO): One of several bookkeeping techniques used to assign value to inventory. The method assumes that older inventory is used before newer, thereby keeping books consonant with current prices by valuing inventory only on recently purchased goods.

Fixed annuity: An insurance contract guaranteeing that the annuitant receives a specified number of dollars each month, even if the insured outlives his or her life expectancy.

Fixed-income security: A preferred stock or debt security with a stated percentage or dollar income return.

Fixed interest: An interest rate that does not vary and is guaranteed (can be good or bad!) for the duration of the investment term.

Floor interest: The lowest interest rate allowed. Usually used in single premium deferred annuities where a floor interest rate (most often 1 percentage point below the guarantee) is established to allow the investor to bail out if interest rates dip appreciably.

Foundation investments: In the investment pyramid, those vehicles that have guaranteed returns that are usually lower- rather than higher-risk investments, but provide safety of principal.

401(k) plan: A plan that permits employers to make tax-deductible contributions on behalf of their employees. It includes a salary deferral feature for employees. The 401(k) works well for the larger firm where the majority of employees wish to defer a portion of their salaries and for businesses wishing to contribute on a matching basis.

403(b) plan: A retirement plan for people employed by a tax-exempt organization or public school. Whether you are employed part- or full-time, the employer may make a contribution (usually through withheld salary or forfeited raise, if so requested) of approximately 16 percent of your salary to a selected group of investment vehicles. The same tax-deferral benefit of other retirement plans apply.

Fraud (tax): Willful intent by a taxpayer to evade the assessment of a tax. IRS bears the burden of proof.

Fully managed fund: Ambiguous term sometimes used to describe a fund for which there are no restrictions on the types of securities that may be held or on the extent of cash and equivalent that may be held. Strictly speaking, however, the term can be applied to most investment companies.

General obligation: A municipal bond backed by the general taxing power of its issuer.

General partner: The individual (or individuals) who has unlimited liability in a partnership. Usually distinguished from a limited partner in an investment program, the general partner secures the proper investments and has the responsibility of managing them on a profitable basis.

Gift tax: A tax levied on the transfer of property as a gift. Paid by the giver or donor.

Gold bullion: Bars of gold that can be purchased on world markets with little markup. Problems include minimum purchases, delivery, storage, and lack of liquidity.

Government agency issues: Debt securities issued by government-sponsored enterprises, federal agencies, and international institutions. Such securities are not direct obligations of the Treasury but involve government sponsorship or guarantees.

Government bond: An IOU of the U.S. Treasury considered to be the safest security in the investment world.

Graduated payment mortgages: A creative financing technique in which the earlier mortgage payments are lower than they would be with ordinary mortgage financing. Payments gradually increase at a predetermined rate. Successful for first-time young home buyers, who usually sell the home before the payments become unbearable.

Growth fund: A mutual fund with an investment objective of capital growth and capital gains. Usually, a common stock fund seeking long-term capital growth and future income rather than current income.

Growth investments: The center portion of the investment pyramid between the foundation and speculative investments. Middle-of-the-road risk investments. Usually includes mutual funds, managed equities, real estate, and stocks among others.

Growth stock: One of the two types of common stock that has shown better-than-average growth in earnings and is expected to continue to do so through discoveries of additional resources, development of new products, or expanding markets. (See also *income stock.*)

Hard assets: Investments that are tangible as opposed to paper or intangible. Include metals, gems, art, stamps, collectibles, etc.

Hedge: To offset. Also, a security that has offsetting qualities. Thus, one attempts to hedge against inflation by the purchase of securities whose values should respond to inflationary developments. Securities having these qualities are inflation hedges.

Housing authority bond: A municipal bond issued by a local public housing authority.

HR-10: See *Keogh.*

Immediate variable annuity: An annuity contract that provides for annuity payments commencing immediately rather than at some future date.

Incentive compensation: A fee paid to an investment company adviser that is based, wholly or in part, on management performance in relation to specified market indexes.

Income, gross: Total amount of dividends, interest, and so forth (but not capital gains) received from a company's investments before deduction of any expenses.

Income, net: Balance of gross income after payment of expenses, fixed charges, and taxes. Also referred to as net investment income.

Income coverage: The extent to which net income from portfolio investments (after deduction of any prior interest or preferred dividend requirements) covers the requirements of a specific senior obligation, whether bank loans, debentures, or preferred stock; in computing the coverage for bank loans or debentures, interest actually paid is added back to net income. The coverage figure may be expressed in dollars, as a percentage, or as a ratio.

Income dividends: Payments to a mutual fund shareholder of dividends and interest earned on the fund's portfolio of securities after deducting operating expenses.

Income fund: A mutual fund (or investment company) with the primary investment objective of current income. Many bond funds are considered income funds.

Income stock: One of the two types of common stock that seeks current income rather than selling price increases or capital growth. (See also *growth stock.*)

Incubator fund: A colloquial term used to describe an investment company that operates as a private fund before first offering its shares to the public.

Individual retirement account (IRA): A tax-deferred retirement program for certain individuals with earned income, established under the Employee Retirement Income Security Act of 1974.

Inflation: A persistent upward movement in the general price level of goods and services, which results in a decline in the purchasing power of money. Usually caused by an undue expansion in paper money and credit.

Insured redemption value plan: An insurance program designed to protect investors against loss in long-term mutual fund investments.

International Association of Financial Planning (IAFP): The professional trade organization of the financial planner, which also provides training in areas of estate planning, federal taxation and tax sheltering, investment and planning techniques, among others.

Investment adviser: Refers to any one of a number of individuals or corporations rendering investment advice to individuals or businesses. (See also *registered investment adviser.*)

Investment assets: Total resources at market value less current liabilities. Normally used only in connection with companies having long-term debt and/or preferred shares outstanding. (See also *net assets.*)

Investment company: A corporation, trust, or partnership which invests pooled funds of shareholders in securities appropriate to the fund's objective. Among the benefits of investment companies are professional management and diversification. Mutual funds (open-end investment companies) are the most popular type of investment company.

Investment Company Act of 1940: A federal statute enacted by Congress in 1940 for the registration and regulation of investment companies.

Investment Company Amendments Act of 1970: First comprehensive amendment of the 1940 Act in three decades. The Act establishes new standards for management fees, mutual fund sales commissions, and the periodic payment of contractual plan sales commissions.

Investment management company: Organization employed to advise the directors or trustees of an investment company in selecting and supervising the assets of the investment company.

Investment objective: Refers to the goals you are seeking to attain through your investment plan. Also refers to the goal—such as long-term capital growth, current income, growth and income, etc.—which an investor or a mutual fund pursues. Each fund's objective is stated in its prospectus.

Investment pyramid: A Jim Barry formula for identifying the mix of investments in individual portfolios. The average percentages include 10–20 percent each in the low-risk/foundation investments and the high-risk/speculative investments. The remaining 60–80 percent should be in moderate-risk/growth investments.

Irrevocable trust: A trust that cannot be changed or terminated by the one who created it without the agreement of the beneficiary. It is usually done for tax benefits received.

Issuer: With reference to investment company securities, the company itself.

Joint and two-thirds survivor annuity: An annuity under which joint annuitants receive payments during a joint lifetime. After the demise of one of the annuitants, the other receives two-thirds of the annuity payment amount in effect during the joint lifetime.

Junior securities: Common stocks and other issues whose claims to assets and earnings are contingent on the satisfaction of the claims of prior obligations.

Keogh plan: A tax-saving retirement program for self-employed persons and their employees.

Land contract: A form of creative finance used in real estate wherein the seller retains legal title to the property until the buyer makes an agreed-upon number of payments to the seller. Usually the buyer has all the benefits of tax deductions and the seller pays the existing mortgage. The technique is usually used when there is a legally enforceable "due on sale" clause in the mortgage.

Lease option: A creative real estate financing technique wherein the buyer, for a consideration, leases a home with the option to buy later when interest rates may be lower. In most cases the monthly payments and the consideration are applied to the purchase price.

Legal list: A list, published by an authorized branch of a state government, specifically enumerating or giving standards for those securities that are proper investments for trust funds.

Letter of intent: A pledge to purchase a sufficient amount of open-end investment company shares within a limited period (usually 13 months) to qualify for the reduced selling charge that would apply to a comparable lump-sum purchase.

Letter of intent privilege: In front-end load mutual fund purchases, a discount is allowed for large investors who intend to purchase amounts that qualify for the discount. When the large amounts are not purchased immediately, the fund requests a letter of intent to do so and allows the discounted load to be charged.

Level term: A form of pure protection insurance (term) in which the face value and the premiums remain level for the life of the policy.

Leverage: The use of someone else's money in an attempt to increase your rate of return on investments.

Liabilities: The negative side of a balance sheet including monies owed, debt, and pecuniary obligations.

Life annuity: Monthly payments made for the life of the annuitant regardless of how long he or she lives. An annuity that carries no death benefit. Usually, when the annuitant dies, all benefits end, even if there is a surviving spouse.

Limited partner: In a limited partnership, the investor whose liabilities are limited only to the extent of the investment capital contributed. See *general partner.*

Limited payment life: A type of whole life (cash value) insurance that insures you for life but requires premiums to be paid for a limited number of years. Sometimes named for the periods (20-year paid-up at 65), the premiums are higher than if paid for the entire term of the policy.

Limited tax bond: A bond secured by a tax that has a limited rate and amount.

Limit order: An advance order, given to a stockholder, indicating a maximum price at which you will buy a stock and a minimum price at which you will sell.

Liquid: Easily convertible into cash or exchangeable for other values.

Liquidity: The quality of assets that can easily and quickly be converted to cash without a significant loss. For example, stocks are considered to be more "liquid" than real estate.

Listed: Traded on the New York Stock Exchange or other major exchange.

Living Revocable Trust: A trust instrument made effective during the lifetime of the creator; in contrast to a testamentary trust, which is created under a will. Refer to local state laws as they affect you.

Load/no load: Mutual fund front-end or back-end sales charges and administrative fees are called loads. Funds that do not impose front-end or back-end fees are called no-load funds. (See also *selling charge.*)

London Interbank Offered Rate (LIBOR): The rate that the most credit-worthy international banks dealing in Eurodollars charge each other for large loans. The LIBOR rate is usually the base for other large Eurodollar loans.

Long-term funds: An industry designation for all funds other than short-term funds (money market and short-term municipal bond). The two broad categories of long-term funds are equity (stock) and bond and income funds.

Management company: Term used loosely to cover organizations that directly or through subsidiaries provide management and/or distribution facilities for mutual funds and that may also derive revenues from such other financial services as investment counseling and life insurance. (See also *investment management company.*)

Management fee: The amount paid by mutual funds to their investment advisers for supervision of their portfolios. The fee frequently includes various other services and is usually a fixed or reducing percentage of average assets at market value. For information on fees, refer to the prospectus of the fund.

Management investment company: A broad term covering all mutual funds and closed-end investment companies that change their portfolio holdings from time to time. The exceptions are a few funds that have fixed listings of holdings and contractual plans; these are defined by the Investment Company Act as "unit investment trusts."

Management record: A statistical measure, expressed as an index, of what an investment company management has accomplished with the funds at its disposal.

Margin: The amount representing the customer's investment or equity in an investment account. Investment leverage. For example, for each dollar you invest, the broker lends you a specified sum with which you may increase the investment value. The value of the investment is collateral for the loan and the margin agreement allows the broker to liquidate all or part of the investment if the ratio between the amount you invested and the amount you borrowed is not maintained.

Marital deduction: The largest single deduction in estate taxes. Only allowed between married couples. Maximum allowed marital deduction is the full estate if passed directly to surviving spouse.

Market order: An advance order to your broker to buy or sell stock at the best or agreed-upon price.

Market price: Usually the last reported price at which the security actually changed hands.

Maturity: The date on which the bond principal or stated value becomes due and payable in full to the bondholder.

Money managers: See *portfolio managers*.

Money market fund: A mutual fund whose investments are primarily, or exclusively, in short-term debt securities, designed to maximize current income with liquidity and capital preservation.

Money purchase pension plan: A defined contribution pension plan in which the employer *must* contribute a certain percentage of each employee's salary each year, regardless of the company's profit.

Mortgage bond: A bond backed by a lien on a specific property.

Multiple-capital-structure company: Company having more than one class of securities outstanding.

Municipal bond: The bonds of governmental units such as states, cities, local taxing authorities, and other agencies. Unlike corporate bonds, municipals pay interest that is exempt for U.S., and sometimes state and local, income tax.

Municipal bond fund: Unit investment trust or open-end company whose shares represent diversified holdings of tax-exempt securities, the income from which is exempt from federal taxes.

Municipal notes: The shortest-term municipal obligations, generally maturing in five years or less.

Mutual fund: An investment company that pools money from shareholders and invests in a variety of securities, including stocks, bonds, and money market securities. An open-end mutual fund stands ready to buy back (redeem) its shares at their current net asset value. The value of the shares depends on the market value of the fund's portfolio securities at the time. Most funds offer new shares continuously.

NASDAQ (National Association of Securities Dealers Automated Quotations): A computerized quotation system for securities traded over-the-counter.

National Association of Securities Dealers (NASD): A self-regulatory organization of brokers and dealers in the over-the-counter securities market that administers rules of fair practice and rules to prevent fraudulent acts, for the protection of the investing public.

Net assets: By common usage, total resources at market value less current liabilities, but strictly accurate only for single-capital-structure companies.

Net asset value (NAV) per share: The market worth of one share of a mutual fund's total assets—securities, cash, and any accrued earnings—after deducting liabilities, divided by the number of shares outstanding.

Net investment income: See *income (net)*.

New issue: Bonds or stocks offered to the public for the first time.

No-load fund: A mutual fund selling its shares at net asset value without the addition of sales charges.

Nondiversified investment company: A company whose portfolio may be less fully diversified than is required by the Investment Company Act for qualification as a diversified investment company.

Nonqualified plans: Retirement plans which do not meet the requirements of IRS Code to receive favorable tax treatment.

Nontaxable dividend: In connection with investment companies, a term applied to a reduction-of-tax-basis dividend or to a dividend paid by a tax-exempt bond fund.

Note: A short-term bond issued by corporations, generally maturing in seven years or less.

Numismatics: The study of collecting, or investment, in coins. Usually referring to rare coin collections.

Objective: The goal of an investor or investment company. May be possible growth of capital and income, current, relative stability of capital, or some combination of these aims.

Odd lot: Less than a round lot, which is usually 100 shares. On securities exchanges, buying and selling costs may be somewhat higher on odd lots than on round lots. Not applicable to open-end investment companies.

Offering price: See *asked price*.

Open account: An account in which a shareholder, by virtue of his or her initial investment in the fund, automatically has reinvestment privileges and the right to make additional purchases without a formal accumulation plan.

Open-end investment company: An investment company whose shares are redeemable at any time at approximate net asset value. In most cases, new shares are offered for sale continuously.

OPB: Other people's brains.

OPM: Other people's money. See also *leverage*.

Optional distribution: A payment from realized capital gains and/or investment income that an investment company shareholder may elect to take either in additional shares or in cash.

Ordinary life insurance: Cash value life insurance with a "savings" provision.

Over-the-counter market: The market for securities transactions conducted through a communications network connecting dealers in stocks and bonds.

Over-the-counter securities: Unlisted securities not traded on a major exchange.

Paid-up life insurance: See *limited payment life*.

Par value: The amount fixed by the issuer of a security as the capital represented by that security. A corporation that issues a $10 par stock and receives $15 for each share allocates only $10 to capital and the remainder to unearned surplus.

Payroll deduction plan: An arrangement some employers offer whereby employees may accumulate shares in a mutual fund, company stock, or other types of investments. Employees authorize their employer to deduct a specified amount from their salary at stated times and transfer the proceeds to the fund.

Pension plan: A retirement program based on a definite formula that provides fixed benefits to be paid to employees for their lifetime upon the attainment of a stated retirement age.

Pension portability: The ability of an employee, covered under a pension or profit-sharing plan, to move his or her interest in such a plan from one employer to an individual retirement account.

Pension rollover: The opportunity to take distributions from a qualified pension or profit-sharing plan, and within 60 days of the distribution, reinvest them in an individual retirement account.

Performance: Same as management record.

Performance compensation: See *incentive compensation*.

Performance fund: A term generally applied to open-end investment companies that appear to emphasize short-term results and that have usually had rapid turnover of portfolio holdings. May also refer to funds with outstanding records of capital growth, regardless of policies by which results were achieved.

Pledged account mortgage: A variation of the graduated payment mortgage, this creative technique uses a portion of the buyer's down payment to fund a pledged savings account. Money is drawn from the account to supplement monthly payments during the early years of the loan. Net effect: lower initial payments. Disadvantage: down payments must usually be large.

Point: In bond prices, a point is worth $10, because bond prices are quoted as percentages of $1000 maturity value.

Portfolio: The securities owned by an investment company; as it refers to an individual, the securities, property, trusts, insurances, etc. that comprise his or her total financial plan.

Portfolio managers: Specialists employed by mutual fund companies to invest the pool of money in accordance with the fund's investment objectives.

Portfolio optimization: A process of systematically selecting assets so that the combined portfolio represents the most efficient trade-off between rate of return and risk. In structuring the optimum portfolio, the following must be taken into consideration: (1) the forecasted rate of return for each asset class; (2) the expected risk of each asset class; (3) the relationship between each asset and every other asset in terms of market behavior; and (4) the extent to which a particular investor is willing to incur risk.

Portfolio turnover: The dollar value of purchases and sales of portfolio securities, excluding transactions in U.S. government obligations and commercial paper. (See also *turnover ratio.*)

Preferred stock: An equity security (generally carrying a fixed dividend) whose claim to earnings and assets must be paid before common stock is entitled to share.

Premium, common stock: The percentage above asset value at which the stock sells.

Premium, convertible preferred stock: The percentage above conversion value at which the stock sells.

Premium waiver feature: Usually referred to as waiver of premium. An optional feature of some insurance policies which waives the continued payment of premiums if you are disabled.

Price-to-earnings ratio (P/E): A ratio that indicates the value of a company's stock (rather than its strength). Achieved by dividing the stock price by its earnings per share. The P/E ratio usually appears in the last column of newspaper stock listings.

Probate: The judicial process, which varies from state to state, used to establish the validity of a will and carry out its terms. Also used to refer to the judicial proceedings needed to settle an estate.

Profit and loss statement (P&L): See *corporate income statement.*

Profit-sharing retirement plan: A retirement program to which a percentage of the gross profits (but not limited to gross profits) of a corporation (or of the earnings of a self-employed person under a Keogh plan) is contributed each year; the eventual benefits are not pre-determined as in the case of a pension plan.

Pro forma: Latin, meaning "according to form." In financial planning, usually used to refer to an analysis done by a professional regarding the prediction of tax or other financial obligations.

Property and casualty insurance: Insurance coverage to provide for the replacement of or compensation for property lost, stolen, damaged, or destroyed.

Prospectus: The official booklet that describes a mutual fund or the shares of a new security issue and which must be supplied to each purchaser under the Securities Act of 1933. (A prospectus applies to mutual funds and to closed-end companies only when new capital is raised.) The prospectus contains information as required by the U.S. Securities and Exchange Commission on such subjects as the fund's investment objectives and policies, services, investment restrictions, officers and directors, how shares are bought and redeemed, fund fees and other charges, and the fund's financial statements. A more detailed document, known as "Part B" of the prospectus or the "Statement of Additional Information," is available at no charge upon request.

Put option: An option to sell a specified number of shares of a particular stock at a specified price within a set period of time. Options are purchased by the investor.

Qualified annuity: An annuity that meets IRS requirements for inclusion in group pension plans, Keogh retirement plans, and IRAs.

Qualified plans: Retirement plans which receive favorable tax treatment under the provisions of the IRS Code.

Real estate investment trust (REIT): An equity trust that can hold real estate properties of all types and offers shares that are publicly traded. Note: this is a modification of a limited partnership that *does not* require net worth or income minimums for the investor.

Red Book: The "bible" of coin collection, nicknamed the red book, is actually called *A Guide Book of United States Coins*. It sets down standards for estimating coin condition by comparing with others of the same type and year. The standards were developed by the American Numismatics Association.

Redemption price: The amount per share that mutual fund shareholders receive when they liquidate (cash in) their shares. The value of the shares depends on the market value of the fund's portfolio securities at the time. (See also *bid price*.)

Registered investment adviser: A person who provides advice to the public concerning the purchase or sale of securities, required, by the Securities and Exchange Commission and the Investment Advisers Act, to be registered with the SEC as an adviser. Some, but not all states, require registration by investment advisers.

Reinvestment privilege: A service provided by most mutual funds for the automatic reinvestment of shareholder dividends and capital gains distributions into additional shares.

Return on common equity: A measure of a corporation's financial strength, the calculation of the corporate income available for distribution to the owners of common stock. To figure, divide the book value of the company by net profits per share.

Reverse annuity mortgage: A method of providing income (usually used by persons on fixed income who own outright a substantial portion if not all of their private residence) through the borrowing of money against equity in their home.

Right of accumulation: A mutual fund load discount provided by some companies that allows you to accumulate the amount needed to obtain the discount.

Rollover: A method of avoiding the substantial tax bite of a lump sum retirement plan payment, allowing you to roll it over into an IRA or similar vehicle to continue its deferred tax status.

Rule of 72: A simple financial formula for calculating the amount of time it takes an investment to double at any rate of return. Divide the rate of return into 72.

Sales charge: An amount charged by brokers or other members of a sales force to purchase shares in many mutual funds. Typically, the charge ranges from 1 to 8.5 (the maximum) percent of the initial investment depending on the amount of investment. The charge is added to the net asset value per share when determining the offering price. *Note:* Some funds sold by brokers and other sales personnel no longer charge the initial or front-end load or sales charge; instead they charge an annual 12b-1 fee, which may range up to 1.25 percent. In many cases, such funds also have a declining contingent deferred sales charge or "back-end load"—i.e., a charge imposed when shares are redeemed—on shares that are sold during the first few years of ownership. Funds that are sold directly to investors charge small commissions, or none at all. The latter are referred to as "no-load" funds.

Second mortgage: A creative real estate financing technique in which the buyer maintains the original mortgage and "takes back" a second mortgage on the difference between the down payment and the existing first mortgage.

Securities and Exchange Commission (SEC): The primary U.S. federal agency that regulates investment companies. Established by Congress to assist in the protection of investors, it is the government agency that administers the various laws that govern the sale and trading of securities.

Selling short: Selling stock not owned. A risky technique of borrowing stock from the broker in anticipation of a drop in stock value that will bring rewards. Instead of looking for market winners, the short seller looks for and bets on losers.

Short-term funds: An industry designation for funds that invest primarily in securities with maturities of less than one year. They include money market funds and short-term municipal bond funds. Due to the special nature of these funds and the huge, continuous inflows and outflows of money they experience, they are rarely viewed in terms of sales figures, as long-term funds are. Tracking changes in total assets is usually the preferred method of following trends in short-term funds.

Simplified employee pension (SEP): A hybrid IRA pension plan to which your employer can contribute up to 15 percent of your compensation but not more than $30,000. The plan eliminates substantial paperwork for the employer, hence its name.

Single premium deferred annuity (SPDA): An annuity that is funded with a lump sum payment (single premium) and purchased before the anticipated date of retirement (deferred). Values accumulate tax deferred.

Single premium variable life (SPVL): A form of whole life insurance where the death benefit and cash values reflect the performance of an underlying portfolio of equity investments, such as stocks and bonds. It is purchased with a one time premium payment.

Single premium whole life (SPWL): Cash value insurance purchased with a one time premium payment.

Single-state funds: These funds, which may be short-term or long-term state municipal bond funds, invest in the tax-exempt securities issued by governmental organizations of a single state. Investors in these funds who reside in that state normally receive earnings free from both federal and state taxes.

Specialty fund: A mutual fund with an investment objective that is highly speculative. A gold-mining mutual fund is one example of a specialty fund.

Speculate: To invest with a high amount of risk with the objective of substantial gain. Usually used when referring to investors who seek increase of capital rather than dividend income

Speculative investments: Vehicles at the apex of the investment pyramid. Risk-laden investments that could provide substantial gain or loss. Examples include art, rare coins, commodities, etc.

Split funding pension program: A method of channeling some pension assets into the purchase of term and whole life insurance policies. Since life insurance may be issued as part of a retirement plan without physical examinations, employees in poor health stand to benefit.

Spread: The difference between the bid and asked price for securities.

Stock certificate: A certificate, issued in shares, that verifies stock ownership and entitles the owner to dividends and participation in company profit.

Stock purchase plan: A corporate plan that allows employees to buy stock without a broker (avoiding a commission). Most plans also include an automatic dividend reinvestment plan, allowing additional purchase of shares directly from the company.

Straight life annuity: An annuity that carries a guarantee of payments to the annuitant for life. All payments stop at death, whether or not the annuitant is survived.

Straight life insurance: See *ordinary life insurance.*

Syndication: In real estate, when two or more individuals pool funds to purchase and manage one or more income-producing properties. A limited partnership is a form of syndication.

Tangibles: See *hard assets.*

Target benefit plan: A form of retirement plan that combines the advantages of a defined benefit plan and a money purchase plan (requiring the employer to contribute a certain amount without regard to corporate profit).

Tax avoidance: Legal methods of avoiding tax payments through various methods including deferral and shelter.

Tax deductible: Expenses that are able to reduce the amount of taxable income. Examples include medical expenses, charitable deductions, and interest paid.

Tax deferral: A method of planning tax that defers the payment of taxes on income until a future time. Rationale: future tax brackets will be lower and the payment of the tax will be made with inflated dollars.

Tax-exempt money market funds: Another name for short-term municipal bond funds, so called because they invest in money market securities issued by states and municipalities to finance public projects, as well as in other tax-exempt securities with short remaining maturities. Earnings from these funds are exempt from federal taxation.

Tax incentive: Corporate or venture vehicles that include major tax deferring or sheltering characteristics.

Term insurance: As opposed to cash value insurance, death protection that is pure and does not include "savings" programs as part of the policy. Usually issued for a certain period of time, hence, "term."

Time sharing: A financing technique in the field of real estate that allows the use of property on a time-shared basis while building equity for all of the owners. Two types: right-to-use (membership right) and interval ownership (purchase of a particular week or weeks each year).

Total return: A statistical measure of performance reflecting the result of acceptance of capital gains in shares, plus the result of reinvestment of income dividends.

Transfer agent: The organization employed by a mutual fund to prepare and maintain records relating to the accounts of its shareholders. Some funds serve as their own transfer agent.

Treasury bills (T-bills): U.S. government paper investments with no stated interest rate. Short-term investment, reaching maturity in 90 days and sold at a discount with competitive bidding.

Trust: A legal arrangement within which a person contracts for the management and control of certain assets for self or other benefit.

Trustee: One who holds the legal title to property for the benefit of another.

12b-1 fee: Fee charged by some funds. Its name is taken after the 1980 SEC rule that permits them the fee. Such fees pay for distribution costs such as advertising or for commissions paid to brokers. The fund's prospectus details 12b-1 charges, if applicable.

Underwriter: The organization that acts as the distributor of a mutual fund's shares to broker/dealers and investors.

Unit investment trust: An investment company that purchases a fixed portfolio of income-producing securities. Units in the trust are sold to investors by brokers.

Unit refund life annuity: A type of annuity that pays on a periodic basis during your lifetime and provides your beneficiary with a lump sum payment based on the dollar amount of your remaining annuity units.

Unitrust: See *annuity trust.*

Variable annuity: An investment contract sold to an investor by an insurance company. Capital is accumulated, often through investment in a mutual fund, and converted to an income stream at a future date, perhaps retirement. Income payments vary with the value of the account. It has the (possible) benefits of high return by allowing the annuitant to vary the annuity's investment portfolio as the market demands or suggests. One of the best investments available for retirement, although not without some risk.

Variable rate mortgage: A financing technique in real estate that allows the interest charged on the mortgage to fluctuate with the rise and fall of market interest rates.

Vested benefits: Those benefits of a retirement, pension, or profit-sharing plan that belong to the employee outright. Vesting normally takes place gradually until, after a specified period, the employee is totally vested and is entitled to 100 percent of the retirement account.

Whole life insurance: See *ordinary life insurance.*

Will: A document wherein an individual provides for the distribution of property or wealth after death. State law determines distribution if no will is provided.

Withdrawal plan: A program in which shareholders receive payments from their mutual fund investments at regular intervals. Typically, these payments are drawn from the fund's dividends and capital gains distributions, if any, and from principal, as needed. Many mutual funds offer these plans.

Wrap-around mortgage: A creative real estate financing technique that is akin to the second mortgage but includes both the original and the second mortgage in a single package, "wrapping" a new mortgage around the other two.

Yield: Income received from investments, usually expressed as a percentage of market price; also referred to as return.

Yield to maturity: Rate of return on a debt security held to maturity; both interest payments and capital gain or loss are taken into account.

Zero coupon security: A security that makes no periodic interest payments but instead is sold at a deep discount from its face value. Because zero-coupon bondholders do not receive interest payments, these bonds are the most volatile of all fixed-income securities since all of the return is in capital appreciation and there are no interest payments to stabilize the price.

Index

*Index note: An *f.* after a page number refers to a figure; a *t.* to a table.

About the Author

James A. Barry, Jr., CFP, Admitted to the Registry of Financial Planning Practitioners, is CEO of the Barry Financial
Group, a Florida-based financial planning and asset
management firm. Prior to this, he was senior vice president of the Putnum Group, a money management firm.
A certified financial planner with clients from around the
globe, Mr. Barry hosts a weekly one-hour TV show called
Talk About Money and is a nationally sought-after
speaker who has been quoted in many national publications. He also served as an adjunct faculty member at the
College of Financial Planning in Denver, Colorado.